Douglas Horton and the Ecumenical Impulse in American Religion

HARVARD THEOLOGICAL STUDIES

50

CAMBRIDGE, MASSACHUSETTS

Douglas Horton and the Ecumenical Impulse in American Religion

THEODORE LOUIS TROST

DISTRIBUTED BY
HARVARD UNIVERSITY PRESS

FOR

HARVARD THEOLOGICAL STUDIES
HARVARD DIVINITY SCHOOL

Douglas Horton and the Ecumenical Impulse in American Religion
Harvard Theological Studies 50

Produced at the Harvard Theological Studies office
Managing Editor: Margaret Studier
Copy editors: Cathy Armer and Gene McGarry
Typesetter: Margo McLoughlin
Proofreader and indexer: Gene McGarry
Cover design: Eric Edstam
Cover art: Portrait of Dean Douglas Horton by William Franklin Draper, 1959, courtesy of the Harvard University Portrait Collection, Harvard Divinity School. © President and Fellows of Harvard College
Photo credit: Katya Kallsen
Series Editors: François Bovon, Francis Schüssler Fiorenza, and Peter B. Machinist

Library of Congress Cataloging-in-Publication Data
Trost, Theodore Louis, 1954-
    Douglas Horton and the ecumenical impulse in American Religion/Theodore Louis Trost.
        p. cm. -- (Harvard theological studies ; no. 50)
    Includes bibliographical references and index.
    ISBN 0-674-00965-7 (pbk. : alk. paper)
        1. Horton, Douglas, 1891-1968. 2. United Church of Christ--United States--Clergy--Biography. 3. Ecumenists--United States--Biography. I. Title. II. Series.

BX9886.Z8 H678 2002
285.8'34'092--dc21
[B]   2002032738

For Browne Barr

Minister, Teacher, and Friend

Douglas Horton, "dean of the ecumenical observers," in conversation with Pope Paul VI during the Second Vatican Council.

Photo courtesy of the Horton Family.
Photography by Fotographia Felici, Rome, Italy

Contents

Preface

A mong my earliest childhood memories I recall an unusual portrait
that graced a corner wall of the parsonage on College Avenue in
Lancaster, Pennsylvania: a black and white lithograph of Philip Schaff,
signed by the subject. My father had written his doctoral dissertation
at the New College of Edinburgh University in Scotland about Schaff's
early career in America. I knew that Schaff had a particular "ecumenical" interest, or, as I understood the term then, an interest in bringing
churches together. Saint Peter's Church, where my father served as
pastor, had once belonged to the Evangelical and Reformed Church. I
understood this to mean that I was part Lutheran and part Presbyterian.
Besides Schaff, two heroes of the Evangelical and Reformed tradition
were Luther and Zwingli. Each of these saints was pictured on his own
stained glass window in the sanctuary of Saint Peter's Church.

Early on, perhaps around the time my brother and I started to participate in worship as acolytes, I became aware of the Evangelical and Reformed Church's union with the Congregational Christian denomination, and of our new name: the "United Church of Christ." The first
president of this new denomination was James Wagner. He visited our
home occasionally, in part because it had been his home several years
earlier, when he himself was the pastor of Saint Peter's. Dr. Wagner also
visited Lancaster because of the important seminary that was located
two blocks down the street. Lancaster Theological Seminary was the
descendant of the Mercersburg Seminary, where Philip Schaff had taught
before and during the Civil War. When I was in the fourth grade, the
seminary added a new library and named it after Schaff. At the time, the
seminary's president was Robert Moss. He was also a member of Saint
Peter's Church. In the late 1960s Dr. Moss became the third president of
the United Church of Christ.

For as long as I can remember, I recognized the differences between Protestants and Catholics. I knew that our Catholic neighbors ate fish on Fridays, went to the Sacred Heart parochial school, and wore medallions with images of saints on them. Then something happened. My father became very interested in Pope John XXIII and the Second Vatican Council. I remember the first time he took me into a Catholic church. The service was in Latin with a few phrases in English. The foreign language frightened me for some reason. My father told us that all churches would "return to Rome" someday. He repeated that theme throughout his life, which is why it has stayed with me.

After college and a decade-long career as a flight attendant for Pan American World Airways, I pursued a seminary education which involved, among other things, an internship in the town of Essen, West Germany. I served in a parish that belonged to the *Evangelische Kirche der Union*, a union of Reformed and Lutheran churches established throughout the region of Prussia in 1817 by kingly fiat. During that *Vikariat* year, I was called upon often to discuss the history of the United Church of Christ and the nature of its ecumenical partnership with the *Evangelische Kirche*. Certainly there were aspects of my presentations that were lost because of my imprecise formulations in the German language. But what baffled my German audiences most, I believe, was the nature of American denominationalism. Certain peculiarities about the United Church of Christ also confused them, such as the lack of a commonly accepted confession or creed, the general rejection of prescribed forms of worship, and the principle of local autonomy in the congregation. I had always taken these aspects of church life for granted, but they began to appear foreign to me when I was in Germany.

I returned to the States with a new interest in American religious history. Thanks to help from my maternal grandparents, I was able to undertake further graduate study. At Harvard University, I found myself in the home of New England Congregationalism. I decided to investigate the other side of my denomination through one of its major figures. I was especially interested in the period leading up to the merger between the Evangelical and Reformed Church and the Congregational Christian Churches. I knew a little about Douglas Horton's leadership in the union effort. As I studied his career, I also became fascinated by the phenomenal growth of the Harvard Divinity School during Horton's tenure as its dean. I was surprised that little Horton lore lingered at the

Divinity School after his relatively recent deanship. Unlike those of his prominent predecessors and successors, Douglas Horton's portrait did not grace the walls of the noble Braun Room, that place of honor where the Divinity School regularly conducts national and international seminars and where the American Religious History Colloquium has met fortnightly for over twenty-five years. Horton's demotion was best symbolized by the relegation of his portrait to the basement of the Divinity School library—or so it seemed to me when I began this study. Later I learned that Horton had secured the funds to build that basement, along with the subbasement and the upper floor of the library addition. He also helped plan for the construction of two additional floors which could not be built immediately owing to the slight recession that began in 1957. Those floors were finally added to the library in 2001. Perhaps Horton has been appropriately honored after all.

There are many points of intersection between my own life and the life of Douglas Horton. Mainly, I have inhabited the institutions he shaped without really recognizing the fact. In the end, this study has been, for me, an exercise in recognition.

Acknowledgements

I am grateful for the companions and scholars who have supported me during the writing of this book. In particular, Courtney Bickel, Marie Griffith, and Catherine Roach have been true friends since the beginning of our studies together in the fall of 1989. Catherine, who became my wife on 14 October 1995, restored my soul during some exceptionally bleak phases of the writing process. David Gewanter, Joy Young, Raymond E. Krome, and Robert Marquand also shared their hearts and homes with me during the years in Cambridge. In Tuscaloosa I have received generous guidance from my colleagues in the Religious Studies Department and the New College—especially from Reiko Ohnuma, Marysia Galbraith, Kurtis Schaeffer, Patrick Green, and William Doty.

Frederick Bachman, Robert McAfee Brown, John Dillenberger, and John Von Rohr offered early encouragement to undertake this study of Douglas Horton's career. Once the project was underway I received guidance, important documents, and good stories from all the members of Horton's immediate family, especially Alice and Norris Tibbetts, and Joan and Alan Horton. The music of Douglas Horton's grandson, Steve Tibbetts, was a source of inspiration throughout the writing process. At different times during the writing of this work I have benefited from conversations with David Bains, Browne Barr, Joseph Bassett, Walter Brueggemann, Marvin Chaney, Chris Coble, Polly Coote, Robert Coote, Harvey Cox, Maria Erling, Robert Goeser, David D. Hall, Allen Happe, David Lamberth, Michael McNally, Gail Miller, Richard R. Niebuhr, Arthur Rouner Jr., Stephen Shoemaker, Lawrence Sullivan, Frederick Trost, Robert Trost, Mary Waetjen, Herman Waetjen, Andrew Walsh, George Williams, Conrad Wright, Barbara Brown Zikmund, and the many members of the American Religious History Colloquium. I am especially indebted to William R. Hutchison, Gabriel Fackre, and Robert Kiely.

I am grateful for the invitation from Richard Christensen and the members of the United Church of Christ Historical Council to deliver the Annual Lecture in 1999 on Horton's ecumenism. The conversation that followed from that engagement helped me to reconsider Horton's early career. Cynthia Eller read the entire manuscript and guided me into the rewriting process—a process that could go on forever, but one that has reached a conclusion with this book. I am thankful to Peter Machinist and Francis Schüssler Fiorenza for choosing to publish this book in the Harvard Theological Studies series, and to François Bovon for his encouragement at an important moment. For diligence, patience, and for taking care of all these words I thank Cathy Armer, Gene McGarry, Margo McLoughlin, and especially Margaret Studier.

I would like to express my appreciation to the following librarians for the use of their facilities and for their help in securing the documents that provide the foundation upon which this book has been constructed: Ms. Kay Schellhase of the Evangelical and Reformed Archives at the Lancaster Theological Seminary in Lancaster, Pennsylvania; Dr. Hal Worthley of the Congregational Library in Boston; Mr. Brian Sullivan of the Harvard University Archives; and Mr. Timothy Driscoll of the Harvard Divinity School Library. The Lilly Endowment provided generous support during three years of my graduate program. I also received a dissertation fellowship from the Louisville Institute for the Study of American Religion during the academic year 1996–1997. I want to thank Dr. James Lewis for his interest in this project and the members of the Institute's January 1997 seminar for their thoughtful counsel. Finally, during the summers of 2000 and 2001, I was the happy recipient of a Research Advisory Council Grant from the College of Arts and Sciences at the University of Alabama. That financial assistance and the encouragement it symbolizes enabled me to complete this investigation of Douglas Horton's life and work.

Browne Barr, who gave me his personal autographed copy of Horton's 1962 book *The United Church of Christ*, has been an inspiration to members of my family across generations. This book is dedicated to him.

Abbreviations

Materials from the following collections were consulted in the preparation of this book. For detailed references to the location of materials within each collection, consult the author's thesis, "The Ecumenical Impulse in Twentieth-Century American Protestantism: A Study of Douglas Horton's Illustrative Career (circa 1912–1968)" (Ph.D. diss., Harvard University, 1998).

Boston, Mass.: Congregational Library
- BDH   Douglas Horton Papers, 1915–1942
- BGC   General Council Records, 1865–1961
- BLC   The Lisle Collection

Cambridge, Mass.: Harvard University Archives
- CDH   Douglas Horton Papers
- CFM   Minutes of the Divinity School Faculty Meetings
- CFS   Harvard Divinity School Faculty Search Records
- CGO   General Office Files (1932–1978), Harvard Divinity School Dean's Office
- CHU   Harvard University Archives
- CSM   Samuel Miller Correspondence (1959–1968), Harvard Divinity School Dean's Office
- CWS   General Correspondence for Willard L. Sperry (1922–1952), Harvard Divinity School Dean's Office

Lancaster, Pa.: Evangelical and Reformed Church Archives
- LLG   Louis Goebel File

Randolph, N.H.: Horton Family Collection
- RHF   Papers collected by the Horton family

The "Larson Crucifix," designed by Leslie Larson as a gift for Paul Tillich
and placed by Douglas Horton in the Andover Chapel of Harvard Divinity School in 1956
thereby instigating a brief doctrinal and semiotic controversy.

Photo courtesy of R.S.V.P./Robert Sheehan Versatile Photography

The Context of Douglas Horton's Ecumenical Career

E schatology has been defined as "an orientation toward the reality of a new moral order in the future which determines conduct and activity in the present."[1] There are two eschatological trajectories in the Bible. Following one of these, the world ends in division. According to the gospel of Matthew, the wheat is separated from the tares (13:30); the righteous are saved, and the unrighteous are damned (13:41). Following the other trajectory, the world ends in unity. All people and all nations are drawn together into one worshipful community; the wolf dwells with the lamb, "and a little child shall lead them," in the words of Isaiah (11:6).

History, from a theological point of view, might be called the movement through time toward the eschaton. Accordingly, the history of the Christian Church is marked by the same trajectories—or "drives," as one scholar calls them—that the Bible anticipates: "one toward sectarianism and division, the other toward catholicity and unity."[2]

The "ecumenical impulse" in this study refers to the drive toward unity and catholicity that became a self-conscious, worldwide move-

---

[1]Herman C. Waetjen, *A Reordering of Power: A Socio-Political Reading of Mark's Gospel* (Minneapolis: Fortress, 1989) xix.

[2]Paul A. Crow Jr., "The Ecumenical Movement," in *The Encyclopedia of the American Religious Experience* (ed. Charles H. Lippy and Peter W. Williams; 3 vols.; New York: Scribners, 1988) 2:979.

ment during the twentieth century. In particular, this book follows the career of Douglas Horton (1891–1968), a key but overlooked leader among American ecumenists. My argument for positioning Horton at the forefront of this story is threefold. First, the "ecumenical impulse" was the unifying characteristic of Horton's multifaceted career as minister, translator, denominational executive, divinity school dean, and official observer at the Second Vatican Council, to name several of his many roles. Second, for Horton, and for many leaders like him, the impulse toward church union was anchored not so much in ecclesiology or church doctrine as in a sense of responsibility for a world torn asunder by war during the first half of the twentieth century. Finally, Horton's role was pivotal. His priorities shaped the ongoing ecumenical movement: he played a particularly crucial part in establishing and redefining important institutions such as the United Church of Christ, the Harvard Divinity School, and the World Council of Churches—not to mention his contributions in fostering closer ties between Protestants and Roman Catholics.

Precursors to the Twentieth-Century Ecumenical Movement

In the mid-nineteenth century, opposition to Roman Catholicism, among other concerns, drew American Protestants together into various cooperative enterprises. The Evangelical Alliance, because of its international reach and diverse approaches to cooperation, was among the most important of these organizations. Through its dominant leaders, the American branch of the Alliance introduced important themes that occupied ecumenists during the following century. These themes include the relationship between Protestants and Catholics, the call for church union, and the proclamation of the Social Gospel.

Established in 1846 in London, the Evangelical Alliance was an international confederation of individual Christians who were dedicated to the promotion of religious liberty and Christian unity throughout the world and to the resistance of infidelity and "Papism." Membership in the Alliance was open to all who could affirm a common core of evangelical beliefs that included the divine inspiration, authority, and sufficiency of the Holy Scriptures; the right and duty of private judgment in the interpretation of the Holy Scriptures; and the doctrines of the Trinity, the utter depravity of human nature, and justification by faith alone.[3] Most important, members of the Alliance also affirmed "the glorious truth, that the Church of the living God . . . is one church, never having lost, and being incapable of losing, its essential unity."[4] The precise meaning of "essential unity" was contested throughout the half-century or so of the Alliance's effective existence. For most members, the affirmation of common beliefs was a sufficient demonstration of unity. For one early leader, however, the mere alliance of individual Christians was not enough. Samuel S. Schmucker (1799–1873), president of the Lutheran Seminary at Gettysburg, played a key role in the founding of the Evangelical Alliance. He was the spokesman for the committee that proposed the organizing principles and composed the organizational formula for the Alliance at its inaugural meeting in London. Schmucker brought to this task a prior commitment to uniting numerous American churches under the banner of "consensus Protestantism." Already in 1838, for instance, Schmucker had issued his first "Fraternal Appeal to the American Churches," calling the churches to form one "Apostolic Protestant Church." According to Schmucker's plan, all churches would subscribe to a "United Confession," surrender their "party names," and become branches of a unified church. The Schmucker-composed "United Confession" wove together strands extracted from various Reformation-era creeds. In the "Apostolic Protestant Church" for which Schmucker planned, congregations would still retain their particular forms of worship, doctrine, and polity, but there would be an intensification of cooperation among churches, mutual recognition of ministries, and intercommunion.[5]

Schmucker presupposed a general theological consensus across denominational lines, especially in view of the revival emphasis that had taken hold of American Protantism during the Second Great Awaken-

---

[3]"Constitution and Officers of the Evangelical Alliance for the United States," in *Evangelical Alliance of the United States of America, Document Number One* (New York: Carter and Brothers, 1867) 7.

[4]Rev. Ralph Wardlaw, cited in Philip D. Jordan, *The Evangelical Alliance for the United States of America, 1847–1900: Ecumenism, Identity and the Religion of the Republic* (New York: Mellen, 1982) 37.

[5]This account of Samuel S. Schmucker is indebted to the following sources: Sydney E. Ahlstrom, *A Religious History of the American People* (New Haven: Yale University Press, 1972) 520–21; *A History of the Ecumenical Movement, 1517–1948* (ed. Ruth Rouse and Stephen Charles Neill; 2nd ed.; Philadelphia: Westminster, 1967) 244–45;

ing (circa 1810–1840). But his hopes to advance the cause of the "Apostolic Protestant Church" through the Evangelical Alliance were thwarted when a dispute over the issue of slavery effectively excluded Americans from membership in the international organization. His subsequent efforts to establish an independent American branch of the Evangelical Alliance failed, again because of differences among the American denominations concerning slavery.

Schmucker continued to develop his own ideas about church confederation in the years before and after the Civil War. One of the last publications of his life was a revised "Fraternal Appeal" (1874) to the Protestant churches of the world. Schmucker's new appeal called for unity to stem the tide of sectarianism, which fostered jealousies and resulted in "the immense waste of the resources of the churches, both pecuniary and intellectual." He also sought to protect a Protestant way of life, "especially in view of the constant secret machinations of the papal leaders, and progressive aggression [sic] of their compact and well-organized legions in this country, toward gaining control of our government and of the education of the rising generation."[6]

Schmucker's anti–Roman Catholicism was a typical rallying cry for Protestant leaders in the nineteenth century. The Roman Catholic Church seemed undemocratic to some Americans, in part because of the religious authority symbolized in the papacy. The doctrine of papal infallibility, promulgated after the First Vatican Council of 1870, confirmed for many Protestants the suspicion that Roman Catholics had no freedom in matters of faith; rather, according to this point of view, Catholics believed what they were told to believe and did what the church's hierarchy told them to do. In addition to suspicions regarding the loyalty of Catholics, many Protestants feared the increasing presence of Catholicism on the American religious landscape. Vast immigration of Catholics during the nineteenth century made the Roman Catholic Church the largest denomination in America by mid-century. As Schmucker's

---

Jordan, *Evangelical Alliance*, 34–35; and Crow, "Ecumenical Movement," 982. The account of Schmucker's "Fraternal Appeal" is from Abdel Ross Wentz, *The Lutheran Church in American History* (Philadelphia: United Lutheran, 1923) 133.

[6]Samuel S. Schmucker, "Fraternal Appeal to the Friends of the Evangelical Alliance and of Christian Union in General," in *History, Essays, Orations, and Other Documents of the Sixth General Conference of the Evangelical Alliance* (ed. Philip Schaff and Irenaeus Prime; New York: Harper, 1874) 742.

rhetoric suggests, this influx of Catholics was perceived as a threat to Protestantism's "quasi-establishment" control of the nation's educational and governmental institutions. At the same time, the increasing Roman Catholic presence likely decreased the prestige and influence of Protestant leaders, particularly in the nation's growing cities.[7]

The anti–Catholicism of Alliance members was not universal, however. Philip Schaff, who is often casually coupled with Schmucker as an early, lonely prophet of the ecumenical movement, differed sharply with Schmucker over both the relationship between Protestants and Catholics and the role of creeds and confessions in the Protestant tradition.

Philip Schaff (1819–1893) arrived in the United States in 1843 from Berlin and began his teaching career as professor of church history and biblical theology at the seminary of the German Reformed Church in Mercersburg, Pennsylvania. Schaff had traversed several confessional boundaries during his advance toward America: he had been baptized in the Swiss Reformed Church, confirmed in the Lutheran Church, and ordained in the Church of the Prussian Union (a consolidation of Calvinist and Lutheran churches throughout the Prussian state). Almost from the beginning of his tenure at Mercersburg, Schaff worked to forge closer ties among the Reformed, Lutheran, United, and Moravian churches in the state of Pennsylvania — and nationally — through his publication *Der Deutsche Kirchenfreund*.[8]

Schaff initially opposed the Alliance. He objected in particular to the stance that seemed to be taken for granted by Schmucker and his colleagues, namely, that Roman Catholics represented a serious threat to Christian unity. In 1853, Schaff described the Evangelical Alliance as a "total failure" because of its stated anti-Catholicism. He argued that the Alliance limited its understanding of the Christian Church to a particular kind of Protestantism — a reduction that Schaff characterized as "an enormous stupidity."[9] The idea that Roman Catholicism had somehow left the confines of Christian community was a heretical notion to Schaff. Indeed, he maintained from his earliest days in America and throughout his life that "Protestantism cannot be consummated without Catholi-

[7]Ahlstrom, *Religious History*, 556–66.

[8]Schaff edited *Der Deutsche Kirchenfreund* from 1848 until 1853, when he was succeeded by William Julius Mann.

[9]Cited in *Philip Schaff: Historian and Ambassador of the Universal Church* (ed. Klaus Penzel; Macon, Ga.: Mercer, 1991) xlix.

cism."[10] Any efforts that looked toward Christian unity, therefore, had to take Roman Catholicism into consideration.

A trip to Europe in 1854 convinced Schaff that the American emphasis on anti-Catholicism had skewed his understanding of the Evangelical Alliance's true nature and purpose. During the next few years, as the American branch of the Alliance floundered and then fell apart over the issue of slavery, Schaff maintained contact with the world organization through the leaders he had met during his European tour. Once the Civil War had ended, Schaff—now relocated to New York City—initiated plans for a new American branch of the Evangelical Alliance. Although he was unable to keep anti-Catholic oratory completely out of the resuscitated American Alliance,[11] Schaff did insist that it was "no negative anti-popery society" and that its primary objective was "to promote Christian unity for its own sake."[12]

A second tension that arose during the period from 1867 to 1879, when Schaff exerted most of his influence, concerned the quality of the Christian unity the Evangelical Alliance sought to promote. In an early disagreement over Schmucker's "United Confession," Schaff had expressed his distrust of efforts to fabricate a creed by a process of ahistorical juxtaposition in order to arrive at a consensus form of Protestantism. "What a full mistake it is," he wrote in 1846,

---

[10]Philip Schaff, *The Principle of Protestantism* (Chambersburg: 1845; reprinted as Lancaster Series on the Mercersburg Theology 1 [ed. Bard Thompson and George H. Bricker; Philadelphia: United Church Press, 1964]) 216. See also Schaff's final statement on this matter, "The Reunion of Christendom" (1893), in *The Dawn of Religious Pluralism* (ed. Richard Hughes Seager; LaSalle, Ill.: Open Court, 1993) 93–128.

[11]Consider, for example, this remark by the Rev. Dr. H. D. Ganse, in 1870, in anticipation of both the Vatican Council (1870) and the meeting of the World Evangelical Alliance (scheduled for the summer of 1870, but later postponed until 1872): "We are proposing an Oecumenical Council. . . . Contrast the power of a Protestant Council in such a diverse community [as New York] with that of the approaching council at Rome. That comes together at the bidding of one man, in that old Italian city, amidst the monuments of dead paganism, and under the rule and ritual of an iron hierarchy, to acquiesce in certain foregone conclusions, which shall then be imposed by bull and rescript on passive consciences the world over." Unlike the Vatican Council, according to Ganse, the Protestant gathering would be a model of democratic process. See *Conference of the Evangelical Alliance at the Reformed Dutch Church* (New York: Baker and Goodwin, 1870) 15.

[12]"The Report of the Rev. Dr. Philip Schaff," in *Conference of the Evangelical Alliance at the Reformed Dutch Church*, 32.

to project a symbol before the body is born that shall take it for its confession! It is as though one should think to speak before he has a mouth, or to walk before he has feet! [A creed is] a formal representation on the part of the church, of a *common living faith already at hand.* . . . A church is not to be fabricated in the study, by simply extracting and putting together in an outward way, some propositions of apparently like sound, out of different symbolical books. It comes not by the pious wish and operation of a human individual as such. God alone can produce a union, by the objective course of history itself.[13]

For Schaff, creeds were historical treasures of the Church catholic. They posed no essential barrier to Christian unity. Instead, they preserved crucial theological insights that ought not to be wrecked, but rather reckoned with, in the movement toward the reunion of Christendom. Schaff's watchwords on the matter were stated in the introduction to his important collection *The Creeds of Christendom*: "Honest and earnest controversy, conducted in a Christian and catholic spirit, promotes true and lasting union. Polemics looks to Irenics — the aim of war is peace."[14]

Schmucker, on the other hand, believed that Protestant union was a relatively simple and wholly uncontroversial matter. In his final "Fraternal Appeal," Schmucker offered a "Provisional Sketch of a Plan for a General Protestant Union." Schmucker's new plan called for slight modifications in the Alliance's organizational structure to make it an official confederation of Protestant denominations. "By this simple arrangement," Schmucker suggested, "a fraternal, voluntary, organic union will be accomplished between all the confederate denominations, closer than

[13]Philip Schaff, "What Is Church History? A Vindication of the Idea of Historical Development" (Philadelphia: Lippincott, 1846) 125–26; repr. in *Reformed and Catholic: Selected Historical and Theological Writings of Philip Schaff* (ed. Charles Yrigoyen Jr. and George M. Bricker; Pittsburgh: Pickwick, 1979) 141–42. Italics in original. Significantly, Schaff continued (with words that might be applied to Schmucker, Schaff himself, Josiah Strong, and perhaps Horton): "history . . . does indeed concentrate, and as it were corporealize [*sic*] itself, in single towering personalities; but in doing so, forms these also as organs for its service, and thrusts them forward in it as by a divine force, instead of allowing itself to be fashioned according to their pleasure, or even to be anticipated by them in any way."

[14]Philip Schaff, introduction to *The Creeds of Christendom* (ed. Philip Schaff; 3 vols.; repr., Grand Rapids: Baker, 1983) 1:v.

the organic union of the churches in the apostolic age."[15] The "Appeal" appeared in the papers of the Evangelical Alliance's sixth General Conference (1873). In his role as coeditor of the ensuing volume, Schaff included a preface to Schmucker's article that once again signaled his differences with Schmucker:

> This is a proper subject for discussion at a Conference, and possibly for future action, though not by the Alliance as now constituted. The Alliance aims simply at a voluntary union of individual Christians of different churches, without interfering with their denominational relations or assuming any power of ecclesiastical legislation.[16]

For Schaff, the idea of organic union had its basis in the life of Christ. Therefore, the Protestant denominations were already "organically" united to each other because of Christ's presence in them—both through Christ's promise to be with his Church until the end of the age, and through the sacraments that the Church administered. Thus, Schaff was less concerned about uniting churches across confessional boundaries and more concerned about acquiring confessional clarity—as a gift to the whole Church—within confessional families. As such, Schaff actively supported the reunion of the Old and New School Presbyterians, for example, and worked for a common confession and general cooperation among the churches of the World Alliance of Reformed Churches.[17] But the Evangelical Alliance, in Schaff's opinion, had a different mission. It served to manifest the international dimension of the kingdom of God: a community of persons already united in the Spirit through faith in Christ. In later years, the American branch of the Evan-

---

[15]Schmucker, "Fraternal Appeal to the Friends of the Evangelical Alliance" (1874), 742–44.

[16]Philip Schaff, preface to Schmucker's "Fraternal Appeal" (1874), 742.

[17]Stephen R. Graham has noted that Schaff underwent a change from equating American denominationalism with sectarianism (when Schaff first arrived in the United States) to appreciating the special gifts that denominations and voluntary societies offered to the larger Church. Because of their positive contributions to Christianity in general, Schaff expected denominations to endure until "the second advent." See Stephen R. Graham, *Cosmos in the Chaos: Philip Schaff's Interpretation of Nineteenth Century American Religion* (Grand Rapids: Eerdmans, 1995) 38.

gelical Alliance would reject Schaff's internationalist—and somewhat mystical—version of the kingdom of God in favor of an activist, Social Gospel manifestation.

This activist, Social Gospel orientation was strongly signaled in 1885, when Josiah Strong published his famous book *Our Country: Its Possible Future and Its Present Crisis*. Strong, who was serving as pastor of the Central Congregational Church in Cincinnati at the time, drew attention to the social problems in American cities—crime, poverty, drunkenness—and called upon the churches to address them. *Our Country* announced: "It is fully in the hands of the Christians in the United States, during the next ten or fifteen years, to hasten or retard the coming of Christ's kingdom in the world by hundreds, and perhaps thousands of years."[18] In particular, Strong believed that the process of "amalgamation" into the inherently Anglo-Saxon culture of America had been hindered by massive immigration during the last quarter of the nineteenth century. The need that faced the Protestant churches was twofold: to develop programs to combat the squalor of the cities and to bring the message of "spiritual Christianity"—i.e., evangelical Protestantism—to the unchurched masses, including Jews and Roman Catholics.[19]

Strong's book appeared at a propitious moment in the life of the American branch of the Evangelical Alliance. A new generation of leaders, under the direction of William Dodge Jr., was assuming responsibility for the organization through its executive committee. These new and younger leaders felt that the age demanded a different focus for the Alliance. They rejected a proposal advanced by Schaff to foster closer ties with international elements of the World Alliance; instead, the new leaders were determined to address the acute domestic crisis. Specifically (and perhaps with portions of *Our Country* in mind), they identified the following problems: immigration as a threat to Protestant religion and culture; the increasing influx and influence of Roman Catholics and Mormons (both of whom, presumably, were controlled by their religious leaders and were, therefore, a threat to democracy); illiteracy; and intemperance. A cooperative effort among Alliance branches throughout

---

[18]Josiah Strong, *Our Country: Its Possible Future and Its Present Crisis* (New York: American Home Missionary Society, 1885; repr., ed. Jurgen Herbst; Cambridge: Harvard University Press, 1963) 256.

[19]Ibid., 202–3.

the country was needed to combat the "common perils of the land."[20] New times also called for a new kind of leadership. Along with the changes in the American Alliance's emphasis, therefore, the new executive committee called for the establishment of the position of secretary general to coordinate mission activities. The job was offered to Josiah Strong and he accepted.

Strong articulated a plan of evangelization, conversion, and "Americanization" for the Alliance. Building on the executive committee's emphases at the time, he announced: "The gospel is the great remedy for the evils which afflict us. Wise legislation and education can do much to mitigate them, but cannot eradicate them. Sin is the root evil of society. God's remedy for sin, therefore, is the radical remedy for these evils."[21] Strong intended to combat sin by evangelizing the whole human being: not only would he convert the soul, he would also change the environment in which the sinner had been languishing. Along this line of reasoning, the American branch of the international Evangelical Alliance offered the necessary organizational structure for a cooperative war on sin. Furthermore, the uniting of the various denominations for the purpose of saving America with the salt of Christianity would be the first step toward bringing Christian civilization to the world. The urgency of the situation required the cooperating churches to set theological issues aside in the great call to action. "We are bound to have a new theology," Strong noted, "but let that come later. If the movement on behalf of applied Christianity becomes identified with a strange theology (whether true or false) it will postpone the acceptance of her social mission, by the church, for an entire generation."[22]

The American branch of the Evangelical Alliance used its successive national conferences to enlist church leaders in its new social works. Besides featuring addresses from national figures such as Strong and Washington Gladden, the conferences were also occasions for develop-

[20]Jordan, *Evangelical Alliance*, 155.

[21]Quoted in ibid., 159–60. Although Strong focused particularly on the national problem, the international dimensions of his concern were obvious to many people. John R. Mott, for example, was inspired by Strong to help form the Student Volunteer Movement. This organization adopted the Strong-like slogan "The evangelization of the world in this generation." See Winthrop S. Hudson, *Religion in America* (4th ed.; New York: Macmillan, 1987) 299.

[22]Jordan, *Evangelical Alliance*, 165. Eventually the "new" theology was provided by Walter Rauschenbusch.

ing and deploying the techniques of what they referred to as "applied Christianity." After the Washington, D.C., conference in 1887, two other major conferences were held during the Strong era, one in Boston in 1889 and another in Chicago in 1893. But by Strong's design, the "real work" of the Evangelical Alliance shifted away from the national leadership to the "grass roots." Churchmen and churchwomen of all denominations were encouraged to join together and work for the redemption of their own communities. The key ingredient in the local movement was the house-to-house visitation system. Women in particular (because strangers were more likely to open their doors to them) would visit homes in a specific neighborhood on a monthly basis to determine the precise needs of the community. The churches would then address these needs and open up the unchurched and irreligious to the influence of the gospel.[23]

Although testimonies at the national conferences reported the success of the visitation system, by 1895 Strong had become disillusioned with the inability of local churches to take decisive action in social mission work. He therefore proposed that the branches of the Alliance cooperate with any group that was at work for the common well-being, including those that professed no religious conviction whatsoever. Strong's final program as secretary general of the Evangelical Alliance was to organize campaigns throughout Pennsylvania in an effort to affect social legislation in the state.

But Strong had moved too far too fast for the leaders of the American branch of the Evangelical Alliance. To state his position in favorable terms, a powerful doctrine of divine immanence had led him to identify God's redeeming work with a variety of groups that maintained no relationship whatsoever with the Protestant churches. But the theologically more conservative governing board interpreted Strong's position differently; they felt that, for their secretary general, salvation had lost its transcendent dimension and had come to have an exclusively social meaning. Hence, in the board's opinion, Strong had led the organization far from the evangelical basis that had held its members together for united efforts. And so, in 1898, after the chasm between Strong's position and that of the Alliance's executive committee became clear to both parties, Strong resigned his office.

[23]Ibid., 170.

The American branch of the Evangelical Alliance faded after Strong's departure. Yet, the Social Gospel impulse that Strong had developed in the Alliance survived, and ten years later was redirected into the Federal Council of Churches of Christ in America. Established in 1908, the Federal Council differed from the Evangelical Alliance in that it was made up of member churches, not individuals alone. The churches of the Federal Council adopted a "Social Creed of the Churches" and cooperated together through the Council on a wide range of social projects including the economic conditions of workers, family life, urban problems, and the pursuit of social justice. The purpose of their activities was — as with the Alliance — to bring the kingdom of God into being on earth.[24] Undergirding this missionary zeal was an important shift in eschatological thinking. Rather than wait for the return of Christ's reign through catastrophe or a more benign form of divine intervention, "social" Christians argued that Christ was already present, was immanent, in the processes of history. The ideal Christian society to come, therefore, developed out of the actions for social justice and righteousness in the present.[25]

An Overview of Douglas Horton's Ecumenical Career

Douglas Horton's ecumenical sensibilities were formed in the Social Gospel environment at the turn of the twentieth century by individuals like Josiah Strong, including Strong's Congregational colleague, Washington Gladden, and Baptist theologian Walter Rauschenbusch. As a youth in Brooklyn, Horton inherited a sense of responsibility for American culture through the institutions of family and church. His parents were prominent members of the Brooklyn Congregational Club, an organization devoted to the promotion of the general welfare through cooperation among the churches. Moreover, his minister, S. Parkes Cadman, was a leader in the Federal Council of Churches. Through travel during his college years, and especially through the missionary emphases that were central to Hartford Seminary's purpose during the

---

[24]Donald K. Gorrell, "Social Gospel Movement," in *Dictionary of the Ecumenical Movement* (ed. Nicholas Lossky, et al.; Grand Rapids: Eerdmans, 1991) 928.

[25]See Walter Rauschenbusch, *A Theology for the Social Gospel* (New York: 1917; repr., Nashville: Abingdon, 1978) 224–27.

years he studied there, Horton's sense of Christian social responsibility acquired an international dimension.

Then the Great War (1914–1918) struck. Horton and other proto-ecumenists struggled to come to terms with the world's fragmentation in the aftermath of that calamity. Some religious thinkers—European dialectic theologians such as Karl Barth and Emil Brunner, and American neoorthodox theologians such as Reinhold and H. Richard Niebuhr—abandoned much of the liberal theology that had given rise to the Social Gospel in the late nineteenth century. Barth, in particular, emphasized the irreconcilable division between Christ and culture, the division between God's transcendence and human schemes to reform society in Christ's name.[26]

Horton was the first American to translate a work by Barth, but he never became "neo-orthodox," as did many of his peers. Horton's sermons after the war and even after his translation of Barth's *The Word of God and the Word of Man* (1928) retained strong liberal and Social Gospel elements. Gradually, however, Horton's pleas for transforming society came to focus particularly on the transformation of the churches. In *The Social Sources of Denominationalism* (1929), H. Richard Niebuhr described the multitude of denominations in nineteenth- and twentieth-century America as "emblems . . . of that divisiveness which the church's gospel condemns" and representatives of "the moral failure of Christianity."[27] Horton accepted Niebuhr's critique. As the years moved from economic depression at home toward another world war, Horton came to feel that the churches could only address the brokenness of the world by offering a visible, living sign of Christian unity. His Social Gospel concern to bring about the kingdom of God became focused on the effort to unite Protestantism.

At a time when the word "ecumenical" began to be applied to numerous movements for intra-Protestant cooperation and study—such as the Life and Work movement and the Faith and Order movement—Horton belonged to a segment of the broader movement that went beyond coop-

[26]Whether Barth's insistence upon the radical "otherness" of God led, inevitably, to social and political quietism (as Reinhold Niebuhr maintained) is a matter beyond the scope of this book. But *The Word of God and the Word of Man*, at least, did not shy away from social concerns; Barth was an active socialist when he wrote the book.

[27]H. Richard Niebuhr, *The Social Sources of Denominationalism* (New York: Holt, 1929) 25.

erative, or "federal" union. His first effort to articulate the possibility of "organic union" was *The Basic Formula for Church Union* (1938). Written by Congregational and Episcopal church leaders and edited by Horton, the *Basic Formula* offered a blueprint for uniting churches with vastly different polities and styles of worship.[28]

Horton committed the rest of his life to putting the theory of church union into practice. His great accomplishment in this area was the formation of the United Church of Christ. The story of the merger—or "union," as most of its proponents preferred to call it publicly[29]—is a tale of protracted conflict within the Congregational Christian Churches, as the denomination wrestled itself into relationship with the Niebuhrs' denomination, the Evangelical and Reformed Church. The uniqueness of the United Church of Christ merger was not obvious at the time. It took place in 1957, after efforts in the 1940s by E. Stanley Jones to establish a federal union of churches called "The United Church of America" and before Eugene Carson Blake's attempt to form an organic union of churches called the "Consultation on Church Union." Both efforts, grand in scope and publicity, were ultimately unsuccessful in bringing about the unions these leaders proposed. After 1960 a number of denominations in the same confessional family united: for example, several Methodist groups in 1968 and two Presbyterian denominations in 1983. But the United Church of Christ remains to this day the first and the last major union of American denominations from differing confessional families.

At Harvard Divinity School, Horton's ecumenical concerns and priorities helped to rejuvenate a nearly moribund institution. As dean, Horton added a Greek Orthodox professor as well as a Roman Catholic professor to the faculty and negotiated the establishment of the Center

[28]Douglas Horton, ed., *The Basic Formula for Church Union* (Chicago, Ill.: Chicago Theology Seminary, 1938).

[29]The primary argument for using the word "union" was metaphorical. The phrase "organic union" suggested bodies: the Church as the body of Christ on the one hand, and two (or more) church bodies joined together in marriage on the other. The word "merger" suggested the world of commerce. It represented the way corporations did business. Although efforts were maintained to restrict the use of the word "merger" in official denominational publications, these efforts were only minimally successful. Meanwhile, in the private correspondences that were the source for much of this particular account, the words "union" and "merger" were used interchangeably. I have retained that practice in this discussion.

for the Study of World Religions, which eventually housed (and continues to house) scholars and representatives of many of the world's religions. Horton's four-year tenure at the Harvard Divinity School is notable, for during that time the school began to recognize pluralism as a positive feature to be cultivated in the overall scheme of theological training.

During the last decade of his life, after his retirement from Harvard, Horton struggled to keep the Faith and Order movement focused on church union as its primary contribution to the larger World Council of Churches. He also participated actively as a Protestant Observer at the Second Vatican Council and then campaigned widely for what he envisioned as the next great step in the ecumenical movement: the movement "toward an undivided Church," as he phrased it in the title of his last completed book.[30] In the developing relationship between Catholics and Protestants, Horton saw evidence that a new age was dawning. Ecumenism remained, for him, the key to bringing into being the eschatological kingdom of God.

---

[30]Douglas Horton, *Toward an Undivided Church* (Foreword by Richard Cardinal Cushing; New York: Association Press, 1967).

CHAPTER ONE

To the Manner Born

Douglas Horton's preparation for mission in the larger world was nurtured at home and in church. By day his father, Byron, taught the sons and daughters of senators how to keep accounts, while by night he socialized with such men as the president of the New York stock exchange. As a leader of the Brooklyn Congregational Club, Byron Horton was himself a member of the Protestant establishment — an informal network of church people who assumed a kind of moral custodianship for the nation.[1] Beyond the confines of their monthly meetings, club members agitated for temperance, prison reform, the higher education of women, improvement in race relations, and world peace, among many other causes.[2]

As a member of the Brooklyn Congregational Club and also as the Hortons' minister and family friend, S. Parkes Cadman was a role model

[1]The concept of a "Protestant Establishment" is developed in *Between the Times: The Travail of the Protestant Establishment in America, 1900–1960* (ed. William R. Hutchison; New York: Cambridge University Press, 1989) 3–16.

[2]For example, after a presentation by Mrs. Ballington Booth of the Salvation Army, the club sent a letter under the signature of Byron Horton, the club's secretary, to the governor and legislators of New York State demanding an end to unfair prison labor practices. See Minutes, Brooklyn Congregational Club, January 1897, 194, BLC. From time to time, other letters were sent to members of Congress and presidents. The club also took an active role in social reform through cooperation with groups such as the Church Extension Society and the Men and Religion Forward Movement. See Minutes, Brooklyn Congregational Club, 31 March 1902 and October 1910, BLC.

for Douglas Horton. He was the quintessential leader of the Protestant establishment: a great preacher of national reputation, a consistent advocate of church cooperation as a means of improving society, and an active participant in the growing movement of organizations that fostered both cooperation and union among churches. British by birth, Cadman was an internationalist who, according to Douglas Horton's description in a 1941 speech, "crossed and recrossed the Atlantic weaving the bonds of understanding between the nation of his birth and that of his adoption."[3] The pattern of Horton's own ministerial career can be traced back to Central Congregational Church and the Brooklyn Congregational Club in the early years of the twentieth century.

Inheriting the Protestant Establishment

Douglas Horton was born in Brooklyn, New York, on 29 July 1891. His mother, Elizabeth Swain Douglas Horton, was of Scottish extraction. Many of her relatives lived in the midlands near Lockerbie, where towns such as Ingleston and Castle Douglas served as home to some members of her extended clan. His father, Byron Horton, traced his ancestry back to Leicestershire in England through Barnabas Horton. This early colonist had settled on Long Island by 1651, died in 1680, and was buried in the old churchyard in Southold, New York. Douglas Horton grew up cherishing his colonial, English, and Scottish heritages. In later years he frequently visited his European cousins.[4]

Byron Horton was graduated from Union College in Schenectady, New York, in 1875. Union College was an institutional remnant of the "Plan of Union" of 1801, an early instance of cooperation between Congregational and Presbyterian churches. He left for New York City with excellent recommendations from his professors and found work as a teacher at the Packard Business College on 23rd Street near Lexington Avenue. By 1903 Byron had become the superintendent of the school, which was perhaps the first business school in the nation to teach women

---

[3]Douglas Horton, "Samuel Parkes Cadman: An Address Delivered in the Brooklyn Academy of Music on the Occasion of the Memorial Meeting, December 18, 1941," 5, CDH.

[4]Byron Barnes Horton, *The Ancestors and Descendants of Isaac Horton of Liberty, N.Y.* (ed. Gurney A. Jewell; Warren, Pa.: The Mohr Printery, 1946) 13–16, 130–34. See also Family History, CDH; Horton's Diary, 1913, RHF.

as well as men the secretarial and accounting skills so in demand in the burgeoning New York business community. A letter he kept in his possession for his entire life suggests that Packard offered an extensive yet practical education and was attractive to a wide range of students, including the progeny of the nation's elite. In the letter, written on U.S. Senate stationery, Senator Chauncey McAfee expressed his wishes for his son, also named Chauncey:

> I wish, now that Chauncey has begun another term, that you would specially instruct him in things that would be useful if he had charge of an estate, that is to say, in keeping bank account and check-book, in making deposits, in knowing what his balance is and if he has overdrawn, and in making investments by the purchase and sale of securities, and anything in that line you think advisable. These college-bred men are deficient in these simple business matters and have to learn them from the beginning.[5]

By all accounts, Byron Horton was a religious person. His minister, S. Parkes Cadman, described him as a man of quiet demeanor with "a most sensitive heart [and] a power of projection into another's trials and difficulties which revealed itself in his beautiful eyes." Horton had been a member of the Theological Society at Union College. In Brooklyn, he served for many years as a deacon of Central Congregational Church. Michael Fackenthal, a fellow deacon (and father of Joseph Fackenthal, who would become Douglas Horton's eventual adversary), considered Byron "the most valuable member of our Deacons Board" and "an unassuming Christian gentleman."[6] Byron Horton was also an active member of the Brooklyn Congregational Club. Nominated for membership in 1895, he became the club's secretary in the following year, thereby putting into service some of the skills he taught at the Packard School. During the course of his affiliation with the club, Byron served on all of its major committees, including a term as the chair of the executive committee. In fact, meetings of the executive committee were conducted frequently in the Horton home.

---

[5]Chauncey McAfee to Byron Horton, 24 February 1903, CDH. Alan Horton, son of Douglas, recalls that the Packard Business School "trained the [nation's] very first women secretaries" (letter to author, 8 December 2001).

[6]S. Parkes Cadman to Horton, 28 September 1926, and Michael Fackenthal to Horton, 27 September 1926, in Family History, CDH.

The Brooklyn Congregational Club was founded in 1888, coincidentally the same year that Philip Schaff established the American Society of
Church History. The purpose of the club was "to promote the welfare of
the churches and bring all the pastors of the denomination together with a
view to co-operating with one another."[7] Charter members of the club
included Josiah Strong, then president of the American division of the
Evangelical Alliance; Lyman Abbott, minister of the Plymouth Congregational Church in Brooklyn and editor of the Protestant newspaper *The
Outlook*; and A. J. F. Behrends, minister of Central Congregational Church
and the first chair of the club's executive committee. The club's first president, James Mitchell, was a member of the Clinton Avenue Congregational Church and the president of the New York stock exchange.

For the club's thirty-six years of existence, the monthly evening program followed the same basic format. After a brief period of general
conversation a meal was served, followed by dessert and coffee (the
club did not favor liquor). In contrast to the Boston Congregational
Club—the model for the Brooklyn Congregational Club—cigar smoking was forbidden after dinner owing to the fact that women were present.
(The Boston Club permitted only men to attend its meetings.) After the
meal, a featured speaker would address the group; limited discussion
followed. A musical program including quartets, choral music supplied
by members of neighborhood churches, or solo singing, rounded out the
evening. The club's constitution required that meetings end at ten o'clock,
although this rule was suspended on at least one occasion: in 1905, when
Washington Gladden, minister, social reformer, and moderator of the
National Council of the Congregational Churches, spoke on the topic
"The Heart of Democracy."[8]

Although women were admitted to the meetings of the club as guests
of their husbands, brothers, or fathers, initially they were not allowed to
join the club as members.[9] In a proposal that Byron Horton had supported
in the executive committee, women were admitted into full membership

---

[7]Minutes, Brooklyn Congregational Club, 26 March 1888, BLC. See also "A Congregational Club," *Brooklyn Daily Eagle*, n.d. (circa 3 February 1888), and "The Club
Well Underway," *Brooklyn Daily Times*, 27 March 1888; both in the Scrapbook of the
Brooklyn Congregational Club, BLC.

[8]Minutes, Brooklyn Congregational Club, 23 January 1905, BLC.

[9]Following the Boston pattern, the first meeting was attended by men only. But by
the second meeting women were invited.

on 24 January 1898. The speaker on that particular evening was Clara Barton, who discussed her efforts to nurse the sick and maimed during wartime. This was the best-attended meeting of the club in its ten-year history and it established the tradition of having the first meeting of the new year serve as "Ladies Night," when topics concerning women were discussed and women speakers addressed the club. As the accounts in the *Brooklyn Daily Times* and the *Brooklyn Daily Eagle* revealed, both Mr. and Mrs. Byron Horton attended the historic January meeting; indeed, they attended most other club events together as well.[10] In the same spirit of inclusion that brought women into active membership roles within the club, Byron Horton proposed in the following year a constitutional amendment that would allow "persons who are not connected with Congregational churches [to] become associate members of the Club."[11] This proposal, too, was passed unanimously by the membership.

The address at the very first meeting of the Brooklyn Congregational Club was given by the minister of the Hortons' own Central Congregational Church, A. J. F. Behrends. He spoke as an advocate on the topic of "Church Union." Dr. Behrends based his prediction for the future visible unity of all the major Protestant denominations on the presumption of an original unity of the Church in New Testament times. He noted that the Congregational and Episcopal churches were closest to union, but he anticipated that Unitarians and Universalists would soon join them; then the Presbyterians and Methodists—and eventually even the Baptists—would join in. Professor Truman Backus, a Baptist, recommended the virtues of cooperation over union. The Rev. Dr. R. S. Storrs, Congregational pastor of the Church of the Pilgrims, argued that the existing diversity of denominations produced "the best results" for the religious and social well-being of the community.[12] The themes of unity and diversity were sounded repeatedly throughout the club's thirty-six year history. Other topics of consistent interest included world peace, temperance, denominational identity, race relations, missionary work, the education of women, and social service. Most of these themes—church union in particular—became Douglas Horton's preoccupations in adult life.

---

[10]"Largest Meeting in the History of Club," *Brooklyn Daily Eagle*, 24 January 1898, and the announcement from the *Brooklyn Daily Times*, 25 January 1898; both in the Scrapbook of the Brooklyn Congregational Club, BLC.

[11]Minutes, Brooklyn Congregational Club, 30 January 1899, BLC.

[12]"Club Well Underway."

The club members evinced a clear interest in speakers who applied a Protestant perspective to contemporary social and political issues. In October 1898, for example, Josiah Strong spoke on the topic, "A Change in the Foreign Policy of Our Government Is Required." In November of the same year Lyman Abbott discussed "Cuba as I Hope to See It."[13] The relationship of the races in the United States was an annual topic, usually at the February meeting. In 1894 Rev. C. J. Ryder spoke about "Christian Truths in Slave Songs." Present on the occasion was a male quartet from the Tuskegee Institute in Alabama. After the men sang, Booker T. Washington gave a short review of "The Negroes' Progress in the South." Speaking to an elite, white, Northern crowd, Washington noted that although "Negroes were not as yet admitted to the same social circles as the white man . . . when they managed to put a few mortgages on white men's property the social requirement would be quickly and effectively secured."[14]

Among those who spoke to the Brooklyn Congregational Club about the missionary enterprise, two are of particular significance because of their later, important relationships with Douglas Horton. In 1904 the newly appointed president of the Hartford Theological Seminary (where Douglas Horton would, in due course, receive a theology degree), Dr. W. Douglas Mackenzie, addressed the club on the "Religious Roots of Social Progress." Mackenzie became a frequent guest of the club and spoke on numerous occasions thereafter. Another person who spoke about missions was Cleland B. McAfee, the director of world missions for the Presbyterian Church. McAfee had been contacted to speak during the 1906 season by Byron Horton, then chair of the executive committee. Thirty years later, after the death of his first wife, Carol Williams Horton, Douglas Horton would marry Cleland McAfee's daughter, Mildred.

Innumerable important church leaders from around the country and the Brooklyn neighborhood were known to the Brooklyn Congregational Club.[15] They were, in all likelihood, familiar names in the Horton house-

---

[13]Minutes, Brooklyn Congregational Club, 1898–1900, BLC.

[14]"Doctrine in Old Songs," *Brooklyn Daily Eagle*, 27 March 1894, Scrapbook of the Brooklyn Congregational Club, BLC. In 1894 the meeting on race did not take place during the month of Lincoln's birth but rather in March. Washington returned to Brooklyn several years later to give an address at Byron Horton's Packard College. See the letter from Booker T. Washington to L. H. Packard, 28 February 1899, Family History, CDH.

[15]These speakers included Mrs. Ballington Booth of the Salvation Army; John R. Mott of the YMCA and other organizations; Harry Emerson Fosdick; Nehemiah Boynton

hold. However, Douglas Horton's earliest writings do not record an awareness of these people, with one important exception: S. Parkes Cadman.

Horton maintained a small diary for about a month at the beginning of 1905, when he was fourteen years old. For the most part, he kept track of the weather and his schoolwork in courses such as Elocution and Latin; he also made notes about the many books he was reading. On 2 February, for example, he recorded: "Finished *Oliver Twist*. Read it in eight hours. Took in every word." In the diary's last entry, dated 6 February, Horton reported his resolve to study Greek for three years and German for two, reflecting an interest in languages that remained with him his entire life. The diary does not reveal a particular awareness of his parents' activities among the Protestant elite of Brooklyn (and the nation) at the Brooklyn Congregational Club. It does demonstrate, however, that Douglas attended Sunday School and church every Sunday between 15 January and 6 February. On one occasion the youth ventured an unprecedented critical assessment, recording that a "fine sermon" was delivered in church.[16] The preacher on that occasion was S. Parkes Cadman.

By 1905, S. Parkes Cadman had been the preacher at the Central Congregational Church for four years. An Anglican by baptism, Cadman prepared for the ministry at Richmond College in London, a Wesleyan Methodist school. In 1888, while still a student, he married Lillian Esther Wooding of Shropshire. The denomination had a rule against student marriages for its ministerial candidates; this fact may have affected Cadman's decision to turn from England and pursue his calling in the United States. He arrived in New York in 1890, joined the Methodist Episcopal Church, and began his ministry in a town near Fishkill-on-Hudson. After serving successively larger churches in Yonkers and New York City, Cadman was called to the Central Congregational Church in 1901. At the time it was the second-largest Congregational church in the nation.

---

of the Clinton Avenue Congregational Church; Shailer Matthews of the University of Chicago; Charles Stetzle of the Men and Religion Forward Movement; Raymond Fosdick, former undersecretary general of the League of Nations; and Sherwood Eddy of the Christian Student Movement. See Scrapbook of the Brooklyn Congregational Club, BLC.

[16]The "*fine sermon*" (emphasis in the original) was delivered on 29 January 1905. See Horton's Diary, 1905, RHF.

Douglas Horton once claimed that S. Parkes Cadman "was the greatest man in whose presence I have ever been."[17] Discussing the qualities that engendered this assessment, Horton referred to Cadman's character, energy, intellectual power, preaching skill, ecumenical spirit, and reading habits. The last of these Douglas Horton had already acquired himself by 1905, as his quick and comprehensive reading of *Oliver Twist* suggests. Cadman's letters to Horton after the deaths of his mother and father show that Cadman was an intimate friend of the Horton family. Cadman was also a frequent guest in the churches Douglas Horton served between 1915 and 1937. He preached Horton's installation sermons at both the Brookline and the Hyde Park churches. Given the intimacy of their longstanding relationship, the career of S. Parkes Cadman offers particular insight into Douglas Horton's subsequent development.

Cadman preached his first sermon at Central Congregational Church on Sunday, 3 March 1901. On 25 March he gave an informal address at the Brooklyn Congregational Club and became a member of the club that same evening. Within a year he began to serve on the club's executive committee alongside Byron Horton, who was on the reception committee at the time. The club attracted its largest number of members between 1904 and 1914, during which time Byron Horton chaired the membership committee and Cadman served as the club's president.

A notable feature of Cadman's presidency was the appearance of non-Protestant speakers at the club. In 1909, for example, Stephen Wise, the rabbi of the Free Synagogue of New York, spoke at the February meeting on "The Civic Crisis." In 1910 a panel discussed the topic "Modernism in the Roman Catholic Church." (Cadman's openness to other faiths led him to help found the National Council of Christians and Jews a number of years later.)[18]

Cadman also gave the club a sense of connection to British congregations. He and his wife spent most of their summers in England, and he

---

[17]Horton, "Samuel Parkes Cadman: An Address Delivered in the Brooklyn Academy of Music," CDH. At the top of the first page, Horton noted that he was unable to deliver the entire address, given the number of testimonials that preceded his own speech and the consequent lateness of the hour. Horton spoke briefly and extemporaneously on the occasion.

[18]Minutes, Brooklyn Congregational Club, pp. 14, 28, 122, and 130, BLC. For a brief discussion of Cadman's role in the National Council of Christians and Jews, see Samuel McCrea Cavert, *The American Churches in the Ecumenical Movement, 1900–1968* (New York: Association, 1968) 123–24.

fostered friendships with numerous Free Church and Anglican leaders whenever he was abroad. The relationships were both personal and communal. For example, Cadman composed a resolution on behalf of the Congregational Club extending condolences to the members of the City Temple Church in London after the death of their minister, Dr. Joseph Parker, in 1903. Cadman's own talks, too, generated an awareness of church life across the sea, as indicated by the title of his speech at the April 1906 meeting: "London Life and Manners."[19]

In addition to the Sunday services he conducted at Central Congregational Church during the year, Cadman took on Sunday afternoon preaching and teaching responsibilities at the neighborhood's Bedford YMCA. Early on, Cadman offered one preacher's voice among many in the often-packed auditorium at the "Y." But as time went by, Cadman assumed responsibility for arranging the entire program himself. The most popular feature of the afternoon became the question-and-answer hour, when members of the audience directed their questions about religion and contemporary living to Cadman, who would respond with Bible stories, short sermons, and moral advice.[20] These unrehearsed exchanges were transcribed and published in a newspaper column that appeared in the *New York Herald Tribune* and was syndicated across the nation. One editor praised the heart-to-heart exchanges as the Protestant equivalent of the Roman Catholic confessional. A collection of the columns was published in 1930 as a book entitled *Answers to Everyday Questions*.[21]

Cadman's Brooklyn YMCA programs were transmitted through another medium as well: radio. After turning down an offer from New York City radio station WEAF to broadcast Sunday services from Central Congregational Church, Cadman suggested that the station broadcast a portion of the Bedford YMCA service instead.[22] Thus the National Radio Pulpit began broadcasting on 3 May 1923, and Cadman's

[19]Minutes, Brooklyn Congregational Club, pp. 26 and 86, BLC.

[20]This account is drawn from Fred Hamlin, *S. Parkes Cadman: Pioneer Radio Minister* (New York: Harper and Brothers, 1939) 112–30. See also Henry Smith Leiper, *S. Parkes Cadman: Great Churchman and Christian* (Boston: Congregational Christian Historical Society, 1967).

[21]Geoffrey Parsons, introduction to *Answers to Everyday Questions*, by S. Parkes Cadman (ed. Geoffrey Parsons; New York: Abingdon, 1930) 11–12.

[22]Cadman felt it would not be "fitting" for his church to broadcast during regular church hours. See Hamlin, *S. Parkes Cadman*, 125.

program quickly became "a radio and religious institution." As the flagship station for the emerging National Broadcasting Corporation, WEAF eventually changed its call letters to WNBC. When the nationwide network came into being, Cadman became the nation's first radio preacher; his voice and message were soon recognized throughout the United States and the world. His biographer, Fred Hamlin, speculated that up until the mid-1920s more people had heard the sound of Cadman's voice than anyone else in all of human history.[23] Certainly this fame contributed to the *Christian Century*'s designation of Cadman as the best preacher in the United States, following a 1925 poll of its readers.[24]

Cadman's decision to broadcast from the YMCA rather than the Central Congregational Church is indicative of a predilection for inclusiveness that characterized his Christian outlook. The YMCA meetings attracted a much wider range of believers both confessionally and in terms of social class than did Cadman's own congregation. Meanwhile, as a worldwide organization, the YMCA both symbolized and demonstrated unified action on the part of Protestants from many different denominations. As Douglas Horton recalled years later, Cadman's Christianity left "no room for intolerance and ill will but call[ed] for positive cooperation."[25]

Cadman's belief in this principle of cooperation was longstanding. In a 1908 address before the National Council of the Congregational Churches, he recommended a wide-ranging cooperative effort in the areas of national and international missions. From Cadman's point of view, the world was being drawn closer together. The great ship *Lusitania* offered one poignant symbol of the age's progress (and a notably dubious symbol, given her subsequent history). According to Cadman, the *Lusitania* linked continent to continent in much the same way that the Christian missionary enterprise "made a bridle of the earth and sky, linking the lowliest needs to the loftiest truths." Cadman prophesied doom for those who would cling to a sectarian Congregationalist identity—a sense of being independent of other church people—in the face of the challenges that confronted contemporary Christendom:

[23]Ibid., 129. See also Dennis N. Voskuil, "Reaching Out: Mainline Protestantism and the Media," in Hutchison, ed., *Between The Times*, 82.

[24]"Peers of the American Pulpit," *Christian Century*, 8 January 1925, 54–55; Leiper, *S. Parkes Cadman*, 62.

[25]Horton, "Samuel Parkes Cadman," 5.

> If independency is a barrier to the essence of [Christian-
> ity], if superiority shuts us off from assimilation with
> popular movements and delivers us over to cliques, then
> these churches of ours will end in a record of shame and
> confusion. While we are busy in trivial things . . . the
> living God will hand over the crusade to those who have
> proven worthier and who knew the day when it did come,
> even the day of their visitation.[26]

Besides his work at the Brooklyn Congregational Club, Cadman exercised leadership in a variety of national and international organizations. Following World War I, for example, he served on the "Commission on the Relation of the YMCA to the Churches." The group, chaired by W. Douglas Mackenzie, produced the famous "Mackenzie Report," which helped foster closer ties between the YMCA and the world's Protestant churches.[27] In 1920 Cadman presented a paper to the Christian Unity Foundation of America entitled, "Can a Divided Church Meet the Challenge of the Present World Crisis?" With the recent world war in view, Cadman concluded that it could not: "The historic separatisms have ceased to charm," he said; "union would give us a working basis from which to attack the iniquities that have agreed while churchmen have wrangled."[28]

In 1924 Cadman was elected president of the Federal Council of Churches (founded in 1908 as successor to the Evangelical Alliance), an organization whose primary mission was, according to Cadman, "to find anew and apply on the widest scale available the peace and oneness of the earliest Christian discipleship."[29] After giving an address on "Methods of Co-operation and Federative Efforts" at the Stockholm Conference on Life and Work in 1925, Cadman was elected president of the American section of the Life and Work movement.[30] Two years later he

[26]Samuel Parkes Cadman, "A New Day for Missions," in *The World's Greatest Sermons* (ed. Grenville Kleiser; New York: Funk and Wagnalls, 1908) 10:210, 214.

[27]S. Wirt Wiley, *History of Y.M.C.A.–Church Relations in the United States* (New York: Association, 1944) 74–87.

[28]S. Parkes Cadman, *The Problem of Christian Unity* (ed. Frederick Lynch; New York: Macmillan, 1921) 5, 7.

[29]S. Parkes Cadman, "The Genius of the Federal Council," in *Twenty Years of Church Federation: Report of the Federal Council of Churches of Christ in America, 1924–1928* (ed. Samuel McCrea Cavert; New York: Federal Council of Churches, 1928) 17.

[30]Idem, "Methods of Co-operation and Federative Efforts," in *The Stockholm Conference 1925: The Official Report of the Universal Christian Conference on Life and Work* (ed. G. K. A. Bell; London: Oxford University Press, 1926) 668–74, 758.

delivered an address on "The Nature and Function of the Church" at the first World Conference on Faith and Order, held in Lausanne, Switzerland. For the remainder of his life Cadman was an active leader in both of these international groups, which eventually united in Amsterdam in 1948 to form the World Council of Churches. Before the word "ecumenical" was in common use, Cadman was an ecumenical pioneer. And Douglas Horton was his youthful apprentice.

Inheriting the World

Douglas Horton left home and church in 1908 to attend Princeton College. He pursued the regular four-year college course of the era, primarily classical in content, and he excelled in Latin, Greek, and Hebrew. Woodrow Wilson, the president of Princeton at the time, a son of the Presbyterian manse, and future president of the United States, had a strong sense of the moral responsibility education placed on those fortunate enough to attend college. In his famous inaugural address "Princeton in the Nation's Service," Wilson discussed Princeton's role in the development of world leaders. Education was no private affair for Wilson—not simply a relationship between students and their books; rather, private successes were meant to serve the public good. "We are here not merely to release the faculties of men for their own use," Wilson proclaimed,

> but also to quicken their social understanding, instruct their consciences, and give them the catholic vision of those who know their just relations to their fellow men. Here in America . . . social service is the high law of duty, and every American university must square its standards by that law or lack its national title.

Princeton's purpose, in other words, was first and foremost moral, and its teachings were necessarily "informed with the spirit of religion and that the religion of Christ, and with the energy of a positive faith."[31]

Horton's years at Princeton were years of social and academic growth. He was a popular student who participated in glee club, theater groups,

---

[31]Woodrow Wilson, "Princeton in the Nation's Service," in *The Public Papers of Woodrow Wilson* (6 vols.; New York: Harper and Brothers, 1924) 1:458–59.

and sports of all sorts. He inherited his parents' commitment to temperance, and unlike his near-contemporary at Princeton, F. Scott Fitzgerald, Horton was unimpressed by the "emancipation of sophomore year," that is, the liberation from societal bonds that he had witnessed among some of his classmates. Rather, Horton recalled in later years "simple disgust of a crowd in the last trolley at night back from the neighboring town soaked in alcohol to the sprawling point." He also attributed the first inklings of his own spiritual awakening, which he described in liberal Protestant (or near-Quaker) fashion as "a light . . . from inside," to a prayer group of men who gathered at the local YMCA building every night at nine during his senior year.[32]

Among Horton's numerous accomplishments at Princeton was a complete translation of the *Oedipus Rex* of Sophocles, which he dedicated to his professor William Prentice. Thus, the Greek study he had proposed for himself as a youth of fourteen years had borne fruit. Furthermore, he graduated in June 1912 as class valedictorian.[33]

Horton's first exposure to the world beyond the borders of North America came during the summer of 1910, between his sophomore and junior years. He traveled aboard the passenger ship *Kroonland* to the port of Antwerp, Belgium, with two of his Princeton professors and a group of fellow students. From Belgium the group ventured south through Germany. Most of the summer was spent climbing mountains in Switzerland under the guidance of Princeton's Professor Anderegg, who was well known to the villagers throughout the countryside. Horton loved traveling and extolled its many virtues in his letters home. The excursion through the Alps continued Horton's lifelong fascination with mountains.

By the end of the trip, Horton was ready to venture off on his own. After passing through Paris, he attempted to delay by two weeks his scheduled return to the States from London. He hoped to visit a few family members and friends, including Cadman, in England. The effort did not succeed, however, and his exploration was postponed for a year

---

[32]Douglas Horton, "Through Forty Years: A 'Spiritual Autobiography,' " *Advance*, 8 February 1934, 94. The wild exploits at Princeton of Fitzgerald's youthful hero, Amory Blaine, are depicted in *This Side of Paradise* (New York: Scribners, 1920). The fictional Blaine and the nonfictional Fitzgerald arrived at Princeton in the fall of 1913.

[33]Douglas Horton, "A Translation of *Oedipus Rex* Dedicated to William Kelley Prentice," 22 May 1912, BDH.

when he returned to England with his parents. These adventures served as a prelude to the grand tour he would undertake following his graduation from Princeton in 1912.[34]

Horton had planned to study for the ministry after he graduated from Princeton, but the previous two summers had instilled within him a wanderlust he could not easily ignore. In consultation with Cadman and Mackenzie, Horton managed to unite his desires for both study and travel into a single project. As his letters and personal diaries for the years 1912 and 1913 reveal, Horton traveled to Europe with letters of introduction from Cadman and Mackenzie. He pursued an arrangement of study at Mackenzie's alma mater, the New College of Edinburgh University, whereby a yearlong program of study would constitute a year's worth of credit toward graduation from Hartford Theological Seminary.[35] In addition, time was reserved for further theological study elsewhere in Europe after his studies in Edinburgh.

Throughout his life, Horton's résumé prominently featured a trinity of European universities; "Edinburgh, Oxford, and Tübingen" inevitably appeared, like the degrees of European academicians, after his name. Although his time at these three universities accounted for less than one full year of his life, that year was pivotal for Horton: the *annus mirabilis* of his first twenty-two years and a turning point into the next fifty-five. In each place, Horton's own denominational affiliation made him the member of a minority sect in contrast to the predominant established churches: the Church of Scotland (Presbyterian) at Edinburgh, the Church of England (Anglican) at Oxford, and the Evangelical Church of Württemberg (Lutheran) at Tübingen. But what counted for Horton in these foreign encounters—both theologically and socially—were commonalities. The task of discovering religious commonalities in his studies was intimately related to Horton's general purpose in visiting new people and places—to forge friendships.

In Scotland, according to Harold Warren, Horton's friend from Princeton and Edinburgh, "Doug had more relatives scattered around . . . than you could shake a stick at." These were the relatives on his mother's side of the family, the ones who lived in the vicinity of Castle Douglas. Horton

---

[34]This account is derived from the series of eight letters from Horton to his parents, 25 June 1910 (aboard the *Kroonland*) to 15 August 1910 (London), RHF, and from entries in his Diary, 1913, RHF.

[35]Horton to his parents, 9 October 1912, and Horton's Diary, 20 March 1913, RHF.

introduced this extended family to the many friends he was making at Edinburgh, as he brought friends to the family headquarters in Ingleston or took them on walking tours with his relatives through the moors during brief holidays. Horton was also part of a large international community at New College, the divinity school within the University. He recalled a meeting of these "non-regular students" and marveled at the variety of nations and tribes represented there: students from Japan, Hungary, Italy, Switzerland, Armenia, and Denmark mingled with those from England, Scotland, Wales, and North America. According to Warren's account, he and Horton "learned on the run" at Edinburgh because they were invited to so many parties during their stay there. "The highlight of each party was a bass solo by Douglas Horton," Warren remembered.[36]

While Horton's diary confirms Warren's depiction of an active social life, it also shows that Horton undertook an ambitious program of study at New College. He attended lectures in church history with Professor MacEwan, homiletics and apologetics with Professor Martin, Hebrew with Professor Paterson, and dogmatics with Professor H. Ross Mackintosh. In addition, Horton pursued his own curriculum, reading (in French) the gospel of Mark as well as numerous works of literature, including Victor Hugo's *Les Misérables*. At the close of the year, Horton sat for exams in dogmatics, apologetics, and Hebrew.

Horton left Edinburgh at the beginning of April and set out on a walking tour through the Lake District on his way south to Oxford. After arriving and settling into a boarding house, Horton ventured over to Mansfield College—the Congregational enclave within the university—to meet with its principal, W. B. Selbie. Selbie granted Horton permission to attend lectures at Mansfield College, and perhaps it was on this occasion that Horton and Selbie discovered their mutual affection for tennis. In any case, the two of them played tennis together many times during Horton's seven-week stay.[37]

After his two academically productive semesters at Edinburgh, Horton chose to devote much of his Oxford stay to playing tennis with an ever-

---

[36]Harold Warren, "I Knew Him When We Were in Edinburgh," in "Douglas Horton, I Knew Him When: A Book of Reminiscences" (1966), RHF; Horton's Diary, 17 January 1913, RHF. Warren assumed responsibility for the bass solos, confessing: "I whispered to each hostess that Doug was unhappy if not called upon to sing."

[37]Horton's Diary, 18 April 1913, RHF.

widening circle of friends. Beyond sports, his interests at Mansfield College included New Testament studies and Sunday chapel. One morning after a lecture, Horton asked James Moffatt, professor and translator of the New Testament, what reading he ought to be doing to prepare for the ministry. Moffatt's response was immediate and it produced a profound impression on Horton: "Forthwith [Moffatt] went with me to the library, gave me a résumé of all the books of interest to me in New Testament literature, and sketched a course of reading for me. This is a real professor!" On another occasion Moffatt told Horton that the University of Chicago was the best place in the States for a student of Greek. Moffatt also lent Horton a copy of Harnack's book, *The Sayings of Jesus*, a testament to the liberal theological sensibilities of the times.[38]

Chapel services at Mansfield College featured faculty preachers and visiting preachers from around the British Isles. One Sunday Horton heard Dr. P. T. Forsyth of London's Hackney College: "[Forsyth] gave a studied address on 'Holy Love,' bringing out the responsible side of it. Very good and very orthodox."[39] (In contrast, Horton considered his own theological viewpoint to be quite liberal.) On another Sunday, Horton's professor from Edinburgh, H. R. Mackintosh, preached "a splendid sermon."[40] But Horton saved his greatest praise for his tennis partner, Mansfield College principal Selbie, who preached at chapel during Horton's last Sunday in town. "Doc Selbie has more pep in his little bean than several of his staff have in their whole bodies," Horton exclaimed. "Pep" was the quality Horton appreciated most in a sermon; he generally limited his use of the term to his assessments of Cadman's work.[41]

During most of his stay at Oxford, Horton focused on the matter of where to study, or at least where to travel, next. He was convinced early on—possibly by Mackenzie, certainly by Professor D. S. Cairns at whose home he stayed earlier in the year during a conference in Aberdeen—that he ought to go to Germany. The trip was meant to be a preliminary venture into the German scene; Horton had hopes of returning to Germany for more sustained study the following summer.[42]

Eventually, Horton settled on a program at the University of Tübingen, where he spent three weeks. On his first day in a German

---

[38]Ibid., 30 April 1913 and 25 May 1913.
[39]Ibid., 4 May 1913.
[40]Ibid., 25 May 1913 and 5 March 1913.
[41]Ibid., 8 June 1913.
[42]Ibid., 7–8 February 1913.

lecture hall, Horton listened to an extended discourse concerning "the progress and prowess of the German nation," delivered in honor of the Kaiser's twenty-fifth year of rule. Horton noted that he understood "one word in 3,000" (not a promising statistic for the future translator), but he was impressed by the banners and by the students in their uniforms and the professors in their gowns.[43] After that first day, however, he rarely set foot in a lecture hall. Instead, he played tennis, went hiking in the surrounding mountains, and spent his evenings in conversation at the *Deutsche Studenten Christen Verein* (the German Student Christian Association—similar to the YMCA). From his colleagues at the *DSCV*, Horton learned that the Germans revered their great theologians in extraordinary ways. By his own account, Horton did not really study theology at Tübingen; rather, he read German novels when he was not otherwise engaged in hiking or some other form of sport.

When his brief stay in Tübingen came to an end, Horton remarked: "I have made good friends, even in Germany! No one shall tell me of its inhospitality again!"[44] For his homeward journey, which began in Liverpool, Horton boarded the *Lusitania*—that great symbol of the world's progress, as Cadman had characterized it in 1908. Horton's response was practical: "Say but this Lusitania is a queen!" he recorded in his diary on 13 September 1913.[45]

So Horton returned to America a "man of the world." He had studied under (and played tennis with) some of Europe's great theology professors. He had come to know something about ministerial training in Scotland, England, and Germany, and he had made friends everywhere he went. Friendship, ultimately, was the significance of the three words that he attached often to his moniker: "Edinburgh, Oxford, Tübingen." They represented, above all, boundary crossings and places where friends were made. Yet he never lost his loyalty to the neighborhood of his childhood. Indeed, on his first Sunday back in Brooklyn, he noted: "Doc Cadman gave one of the peppiest sermons I've heard the whole year. His language lasts, lasts, lasts."[46] But Cadman was now a part of a much larger neighbor-

[43]Ibid., 16 June 1913. Several years later, the Swiss theologian Karl Barth would recall with horror his professors' close alignment with the State as exemplified in similar demonstrations that took place throughout Germany during the years that led up to the Great War.

[44]Ibid., 13 July 1913.

[45]Ibid., 13 September 1913.

[46]Ibid., 21 September 1913.

hood, conceptually conceived. And soon Horton was to embark on his ministerial education proper at Hartford Theological Seminary.

Inheriting the Post-Edinburgh Conference Ethos

Hartford Theological Seminary was founded in East Windsor, Connecticut, in 1834 by a "Pastoral Union" of Connecticut Congregational ministers who deplored the fact that the Yale Divinity School—particularly in the person of Professor Nathaniel W. Taylor—had abandoned orthodox Calvinism's understanding of the nature of sin and the need for atonement. Taylor's views were challenged by Bennet Tyler, the minister of a Congregational church in Maine, who served as Hartford Seminary's first president. The Taylor-Tyler controversy is often depicted as theological hair-splitting over how far from God's goodness humanity had fallen. But from another point of view, the controversy represented a different matter of enduring significance among the Congregational churches, and one Horton would encounter much later during his tenure as minister and secretary of the general council: namely, the extent to which a particular doctrinal standard could be determinative for Congregationalist identity.

According to the East Windsor group, Congregationalism was best defined by "the creeds long accepted by the Congregational Churches of New England."[47] The ministers of the Pastoral Union spelled out the doctrinal basis of their union in the twenty-point Articles of Agreement. Each year the trustees and the faculty of the seminary reaffirmed their commitment to these Articles orally and in writing. The Articles thus ensured doctrinal conformity within the seminary and beyond, for if students wished to become ministers in any of the Connecticut churches related to the Pastoral Union, they were required to subscribe to the Articles.[48]

The Articles of Agreement served as the foundation for the seminary and maintained a confessional tradition within Congregationalism until the early twentieth century. But while Hartford's stance with regard to

---

[47]*The Constitution, Rules of Order and Catalogue of the Pastoral Union and the Charter, Constitution, and Laws of the Hartford Theological Seminary* (Hartford: Case, Lockwood, and Brainard, 1886) 3.

[48]Curtis Manning Geer, *The Hartford Theological Seminary, 1834–1934* (Hartford: Case, Lockwood, and Brainard, 1934) 33–35.

creed secured a certain Calvinist orthodoxy, it did not prevent innovation. In 1889 Hartford became the first seminary in the nation to admit women "to the regular, special and advanced courses of the seminary on the same terms as men."[49] The female presence on campus was part of the seminary's turn toward professionalism. Women were not expected (nor encouraged) to become preachers; rather, they were being prepared to enter the specialized fields of education and missions. And though yearly subscription to the Articles was still required at Hartford Seminary until 1912, the school became better known in the twentieth century for its focus on social and international missions. The person most responsible for this transformation was seminary president W. Douglas Mackenzie.

Mackenzie was born in South Africa in 1859, the son of missionary parents who devoted more than forty years of their life together to missions. Educated at Edinburgh and several universities in Germany, Mackenzie started a new church in the Edinburgh suburb of Morningside, and served there as minister from 1889 until 1895. In 1891 he attended the first meeting of the International Congregational Council as a representative from the Congregational Union of Scotland. He would attend future meetings of the Council as an American delegate, for in 1895 he assumed the chair of the systematic theology department at the Chicago Theological Seminary. His 1897 book, *Christianity and the Progress of Man as Illustrated by Modern Missions*, explored what he considered to be "the two greatest facts" at the close of the nineteenth century: first, the "unification of the human race" as one people beyond national, tribal, or racial loyalties; and second, "the establishment of the Christian religion as a working force among nearly all nations." Mackenzie went on to argue that the two facts were intimately related. Indeed, he concluded that Christianity, as "the universalistic religion," was responsible for bringing into being "the one race of mankind during the nineteenth century." Both his zeal for mission and, as his book demonstrated, his concern for thorough training of missionaries had made Mackenzie a desirable candidate for the presidency of the Hartford Theological Seminary in the early 1900s.[50]

---

[49]Ibid., 174.

[50]Ibid., 202–3; *The International Congregational Council: Authorised Record of Proceedings* (ed. R. W. Dale; London: James Clarke, 1891) 9; W. Douglas Mackenzie, preface to *Christianity and the Progress of Man As Illustrated by Modern Missions* (Chicago: Revell, 1897).

Mackenzie gave a series of forty lectures in systematic theology at Hartford during the 1902–1903 academic year. In 1904 he returned to become president of the seminary and professor of systematic theology.[51] At Hartford he wrote most of *The Final Faith*, a book that combined his earlier thoughts concerning the unifying power of the Christian message with the traditional Hartford concern for doctrine. The book explored theological categories such as revelation, Christology, and sin and salvation, in order to promote Christianity in language that would "expound Christianity afresh to this generation as the true religion of the world." Mackenzie argued that Christianity was "the absolute religion, the one final way in which God . . . is concerned with the saving and perfecting of mankind." For Mackenzie the heart of all Christian preaching and teaching contained the "missionary impulse": "the mighty desire to make known to others the gospel which [the individual] has received and . . . believes that God gave to the world." But one could not communicate mere desire or "feeling." The practical task that accompanied the impulse was to be able to articulate the Christian system and its relation to all of humanity. In the last chapter of *The Final Faith*, Mackenzie offered his own synopsis of those aspects of the Christian system—specific doctrines and compelling lore—that he deemed crucial for convincing the world of Christianity's finality.[52]

The manuscript of *The Final Faith* was completed in Scotland at the end of July 1910. Although Mackenzie habitually traveled to Europe during the summers, he was in Scotland on this particular occasion to attend the Edinburgh Conference on World Missions. This conference is remembered by historians as the start of the twentieth-century "ecumenical movement" (though the word "ecumenical" did not come into general use until at least the mid-1920s).[53] Mackenzie himself was an important leader of the conference. Through him and other members of the Hartford faculty, the Edinburgh Conference had a profound effect on the institutional development of the Hartford Theological Seminary during the time Douglas Horton studied there, and for many years thereafter as well.

[51]Among those present at his inauguration was Woodrow Wilson of Princeton. See *Services at the Inauguration of William Douglas Mackenzie* (Hartford: Hartford Seminary, 1904) 47.

[52]W. Douglas Mackenzie, *The Final Faith: A Statement of the Nature and Authority of Christianity as the Religion of the World* (New York: Macmillan, 1910) vii–viii, 222–42.

[53]For example, Rouse and Neill, *A History of the Ecumenical Movement*, 355–62.

The Edinburgh Conference was a gathering of delegates from the world's Protestant missionary societies. From the earliest phases of planning, the hope was expressed to make Edinburgh a "consultative assembly," during which the participating societies could envision and coordinate joint missionary activities. The primary emphasis of the conference was "missionary problems in relation to the non-Christian world." By choosing this focus, the conference planning committee inevitably had placed certain limitations on the gathering. First, the committee excluded missionary societies of different sects or denominations whose mission was to members of other Christian churches, such as Protestant societies that sought to convert members of the Roman Catholic Church. Second, the planning committee decided to confine the conference discussion "to the most urgent and vital problems confronting the church in prosecuting [missionary work]." Two years in advance of the conference, the committee had selected eight topics and appointed commissions of twenty persons to each topic. The commissions were given the task of studying the topic and reporting their findings at Edinburgh. These commissions were known by their Roman numerals: I, Carrying the Gospel to all the Non-Christian World; II, The Church in the Mission Field; III, Education in Relation to the Christianization of National Life; IV, The Missionary Message in Relation to Non-Christian Religions; V, The Preparation of Missionaries; VI, The Home Base of Missions; VII, Missions and Governments; and VIII, Cooperation and the Promotion of Unity. Third, the committee refrained from considering ecclesiastical or doctrinal differences among the participating societies. No expression of opinion on such matters would be sought by the conference.[54]

John R. Mott, a Methodist layman, president of the Student Volunteer Movement, and leader of the YMCA, called the Edinburgh Conference to order on 14 June 1910. The two-week conference was filled with business meetings, resolutions, and addresses. Significantly, of the thirty or so addresses delivered, two were by men who would be Horton's professors at Edinburgh in a couple of years. Professor Paterson spoke on the theme of Christian redemption; Professor MacEwan discussed "The Expansion of Christianity in the Early Centuries." The main work of the conference was in the presentation and discussion of the reports

[54]George Robson, "History of the Conference," in *World Missionary Conference, 1910: The History and Records of the Conference* (New York: Revell, 1911) 7–8.

of the eight commissions. Here W. Douglas Mackenzie played a major role, serving as chair of Commission V on the preparation of missionaries. Members of the commission included two men from the Hartford Seminary faculty who would become Horton's teachers: Edward Capen and Curtis Geer. Also on the commission besides Professor MacEwan of New College was Principal Selbie of Mansfield College (and Horton's tennis partner three years later).[55]

In its report, Commission V reviewed current methods for preparing missionaries and lamented the lack of consistent and proper missionary training. The report called for specialized missionary education to meet the needs of the new century. These needs included complete knowledge of "the missionary message" (the Bible and the "essential truths of Christianity"); an understanding of the history, institutions, and customs of the people to whom the missionary would minister; training in comparative religion so that the missionary could use the common elements of all religions to show "the ways in which Christianity meets needs which no other religion can satisfy"; and thorough preparation in foreign languages so that the Christian message might be communicated more directly.[56]

The Edinburgh Conference spawned several new groups as it came to a close. Some participants who were inspired to continue with cooperative missionary work founded the International Missionary Council. Other participants, who wanted to organize concerted Christian action in the social sphere, founded the Life and Work movement. Participants who wanted to explore the taboo subjects of doctrinal differences and ecclesiastical union founded the Faith and Order movement. Not surprisingly, Mackenzie and his fellow faculty members wanted to implement the proposals of Commission V. They went back to Hartford Seminary and began to turn proposal into practice. In later life, Horton would be involved with all of these movements growing out of Edinburgh, and like Mackenzie, he would also be a builder of institutions.

Horton disembarked from the *Lusitania* on Friday, 19 September 1913, ending his European sojourn. That Sunday, as has been noted, he

---

[55]Three of the twenty-four members of Commission V represented Hartford Seminary. This concentration of influence from one organization on a single commission was not duplicated in any of the other commissions. The chair of Commission IV was D. S. Cairns, whom Horton visited in 1913.

[56]*Report of Commission V: The Training of Teachers* (New York: Revell, 1911) 115–23. See also Edward Warren Capen, *Special Missionary Preparation* (Hartford, 1912), pamphlet.

attended Cadman's church with his family. By the following Friday, less than one week after returning to American soil, he was in Mackenzie's course on creeds and confessions.[57] Concerning his first impressions of Hartford, Horton wrote to his family: "The classes I attended this morning after chapel exercises were all good, but believe me, there's none of them can hold a candle to Dr. Mackenzie. I'm taking all the courses he offers and it's not half enough."[58]

In consultation with Professor Curtis Manning Geer, Horton devised an ambitious program for his first semester at Hartford: Old Testament theology, church history, homiletics, creeds and confessions, ethics, Hebrew, Greek, and Arabic. Horton noted that he spent an average of eighteen hours in class per week. He reassured his parents that this was not an overly ambitious schedule by pointing out that he had often carried twenty-one hours at Princeton.[59] In response to his father's inquiry about the study of Arabic, Horton commended the language for having "the finest modern literature in the world" next to English. For Horton, language study was an essential element of his theological education: "[Arabic] is good solid earth: not water, like apologetics; not fire, like philosophy; not gas, like homiletics."[60]

Outside of his studies, Douglas Horton was active on the campus and in the Hartford community. He taught Sunday school at South Congregational Church and helped organize a group at the YMCA that ministered to Hartford's immigrant Greek community. Horton was grateful for this work, for it gave him the occasion to learn, or at least to hear, modern Greek. He was also chosen as the Middler Class member of the Seminary's Missionary Committee. Because of this latter involvement, he traveled to Kansas City at the end of 1913 to attend a nationwide youth missions convention. The speakers at the opening session included John R. Mott, who had called the Edinburgh Conference to order in 1910 and whom Horton would come to know well in later life; R. F. Horton (with whom Douglas Horton would be confused on occasion by later scholars[61]), formerly of Mansfield College, a founder of the Interna-

[57]Horton's Diary, 19–26 September 1913, RHF.

[58]Horton to his family, 25 September 1913, RHF.

[59]Ibid.

[60]Ibid.

[61]In an otherwise brilliant article, Alan P. F. Sell merges Douglas Horton and R. F. Horton into "Douglas R. F. Horton." See Alan P. F. Sell, "Congregationalism," in *Dictionary of the Ecumenical Movement*, 219. The conflation is reinscribed most re-

tional Congregational Council and minister of the Lyndhurst Road Church in the Hampstead district of London; and Robert E. Speer, the man who replaced Cleland McAfee as secretary of the Board of Foreign Missions of the Presbyterian Church.[62]

During his final year at Hartford Seminary Horton had two major concerns. The first of these was to secure a ministerial position. He met with several church committees and preached a number of sermons at churches in places such as Middleboro, Massachusetts, and New Haven, Connecticut. None struck a chord for him.

While Horton's Hartford training had prepared him for ministry in the local congregation, his course work showed a strong missionary emphasis. Horton may have been considering the missionary field as a setting for his ministry. In April he visited Professor Harlan Beach of Yale Divinity School. Dr. Beach had served with Mott as a member of Commission I at the Edinburgh Conference. He was a leader of the International Congregational Council, and he was on the faculty committee for the Cairo Christian University. Beach asked Horton not to commit himself to any congregation or mission board until June, so that Horton might be available for a faculty position at the Cairo Christian University. The school was about to complete negotiations for a site, and once that was done, Beach expected that the training of the first three or four designated faculty members should commence.[63] As the months progressed, the arrangements proved unfruitful, although in later years Horton would serve on the board of directors of the American University in Cairo.

Horton's second major concern as his final semester of formal academic training drew to a close was his departure from Hartford Seminary's "Bachelors' Club." In April he announced his engagement to Carol Scudder Williams, who was also a student at Hartford. On her

cently in *Growing Toward Unity* in *The Living Theological Heritage of the United Church of Christ* (ed. Elsabeth Slaughter Hilke; Cleveland: Pilgrim, 2001) 6:547–48.

[62]Horton's Diary, October-December 1913, especially 31 December 1913, RHF. This was not the first time that Mott, Speer, and R. F. Horton had appeared on stage together. All three of them had delivered addresses at the Edinburgh Conference in 1910. The addresses of Robert E. Speer on "Christ the Leader of the Missionary Work of the Church" and R. F. Horton on "The Sufficiency of God," together with John R. Mott's "Closing Address" were published in *World Missionary Conference, 1910*, 151–55, 336–41, and 347–52, respectively.

[63]Horton to Carol Williams, n.d. (circa 15 April 1913), RHF.

mother's side, Carol was from a line of Dutch Reformed missionaries who had worked in India under the auspices of the Congregational American Board of Commissioners for Foreign Missions. In fact, Carol's mother, Frances Scudder Williams, was born in India and all of her brothers were missionaries in India. Carol's father was the owner of the J. B. Williams Company (a leading manufacturer of soap products, including the well-known "Aqua Velva") and an active member of the Connecticut Congregational Club.

In the end, Horton chose to combine his personal and professional lives. He decided to move slightly closer to Brooklyn and in close proximity to the Williams's family home in Glastonbury, Connecticut. He accepted a call to the position of assistant pastor at First Congregational Church in Middletown, Connecticut, shortly after graduating from Hartford Theological Seminary. His days of apprenticeship were coming to a close.[64]

What might in retrospect be called Douglas Horton's ecumenical manner was acquired early in life. In the Horton family home, Douglas Horton learned a generosity of spirit that was exemplified in his father's successful appeal to allow women and non-Congregationalists to participate in the Brooklyn Congregational Club. From S. Parkes Cadman, his minister and counselor, he learned to deplore narrowness in relation to denominational affiliation, for Cadman had himself been an Anglican, a Methodist, and a Congregationalist. Cadman was also a mentor for Horton in a number of other ways: as a leader in cooperative religious efforts, as a disciplined learner and teacher, and as a man of the nation and the world.

From his experiences in Europe, Horton had learned that he was at home in the world and that he could make friends with people from many nations and backgrounds. His Princeton experience reinforced his sense — inculcated by family and church — that he had a responsibility to serve in the world. And in W. Douglas Mackenzie, Horton met a man who, through the powers of will and reason, was able to transform ideas into institutional reality. Finally, in Carol Scudder Williams he found a partner whose embrace of the world was as bold and generous as his own.

[64]Horton to Carol Williams, 12 April 1915, RHF; interview with Alan Horton, 28 May 1997; Horton's Diary, 1918 (describing a visit with Mr. Williams to the Conneticut Congregational Club), RHF.

CHAPTER TWO

Ministry in and beyond the Local Congregation

Horton was graduated from Hartford Theological Seminary with prizes in Latin and theology in May 1915, not long after the British passenger ship *Lusitania* was torpedoed off the coast of Ireland by a German submarine. S. Parkes Cadman had seen the ship as a symbol of the world's progress toward greater unity, but now the *Lusitania* was transformed into a symbol of the world's deep division. Indeed, world conflict and division shaped the background of Horton's entire career: over the course of his life, Horton witnessed at close hand the Great War, the Japanese invasion of Manchuria, Gandhi's resistance to British rule in India, and the German invasion of Czechoslovakia. Meanwhile, tensions abroad were matched by an economic depression at home, one that raised the issue of social fragmentation in the churches that Horton served.

The years between his seminary graduation in 1915 and his appointment as minister and chief officer of the Congregational Christian Churches in 1938 set the tone for Horton's life, both professionally and personally. During this time, he served as pastor in three churches: First Church (Congregational) in Middletown, Connecticut; the Leyden Congregational Church in Brookline, Massachusetts; and the United Church of Hyde Park, a united Presbyterian and Congregational church in Chicago. In addition, he served briefly as a chaplain in the U.S. Navy toward the end of World War I. Within ten years of his marriage to Carol

Scudder Williams in May 1916, their family had grown to include four children. During this period of ministry in local congregations, Horton developed a national reputation as a translator and preacher. He became involved as a leader in his own denomination and represented the interests of American Congregationalism to the international community of Congregational churches. Meanwhile, his international predisposition led him to participate in key organizations of the emerging ecumenical movement.

Toward Leadership: First Church in Middletown

Horton's account of his early ministry in Middletown suggests that his main tasks included sermon preparation, visits to church members in their homes, and supervision of the Sunday school program.[1] He was influenced by First Church's close proximity to Wesleyan University through faculty members who belonged to his congregation. He also attended many cultural events that took place at Wesleyan. In January 1917, for example, Horton heard the evangelist Billy Sunday speak at the Wesleyan chapel. In his diary, Horton noted that Sunday was "a complete vaudeville artist tempered with morality."[2]

The relative calm of Horton's apprenticeship in the First Church ended after 2 April 1917. On that evening President Woodrow Wilson delivered what Horton considered "one of the great speeches of history." In it, Wilson requested that Congress declare war on Germany. Horton was so moved by the speech that, in good Princeton fashion, he wrote a personal letter to Wilson "offering [his] services to the nation in any capacity." Wilson did not respond directly to Horton's overture. But in a little over a year, the secretary of the Navy (by order of the president) appointed Horton chaplain in that branch of the armed services.[3] So the war became the central fact of Horton's first pastorate and his entire career: it marked the end of the world he had known, a world of perme-

---

[1]Horton's Diary, 1917, RHF.

[2]Ibid., 15 January 1917.

[3]Ibid., 4 April 1917 and 25 September 1918. For Wilson's speech, see Woodrow Wilson, "Speech for Declaration of War Against Germany," in *Documents of American History* (ed. Henry Steele Commager; 9th ed.; 2 vols.; Englewood Cliffs, N.J.: Prentice-Hall, 1973) 2:128–32.

able boundaries and increasing unity; it marked the beginning of a fragmented and divided world, a world that he endeavored for the rest of his
life to mend.

Following a brief period of training at the Naval Hospital in Boston,
Horton reported to the U.S.S. *Michigan*, a naval warship stationed in
the Chesapeake Bay, at the end of October 1918. The *Michigan*'s mission was to patrol the Atlantic coast in search of German submarines,
but it was only on alert for a short period of time after Horton's arrival:
on 11 November 1918, Germany signed the armistice and the war in
Europe came to an end. "Pray God it may be the last [war]," Horton
recorded in his diary.[4] By the end of the year, the U.S.S. *Michigan* prepared for a new mission: bringing American troops home from Europe.

As chaplain, Horton made two trips across the Atlantic aboard the
U.S.S. *Michigan*. During the eastward journey of the second voyage, a
series of calamities (including rough seas, a broken propeller, and leak-
ing compartments) caused the *Michigan* to be towed into the dry dock
for repairs at the port of Brest in Brittany, on the northwest coast of
France. Instead of remaining in Brittany, Horton secured a six-day leave
that would make a lasting impression on him. On the morning of 2 April
1919, he boarded a train to Paris. After a brief pause to discuss a career
option, Horton returned to the mission at hand, namely, to travel to the
battlefront and, if possible, to cross over into Germany.[5] Horton had
been discouraged from pursuing this course of action because of the
various passes one needed to acquire in advance to travel from one military sector to another. But he was determined to see something of the
war and so he ventured forth.

Leaving Paris by train, he was surprised to see how close to the French
capital the German army had advanced before it was finally stopped.
After about thirty miles he came to the devastated town of Chateau
Thierry. In a letter to his family, Horton described his impressions of
the ruin, though he admitted that he had no words for the sensations he
experienced "at the first glimpses of the desolation and destruction."

---

[4]Horton's Diary, 10–11 November 1918, HFC.

[5]At the Paris YMCA Horton met with Dr. Charles Watson, who was coordinating
missionary activities in Egypt. Watson suggested that Horton travel to Egypt the following summer and "look over the ground there" with an eye toward becoming a
missionary in the region (Horton's Diary, 1 April 1919, RHF; Horton to his family, 8
April 1919, BDH).

Land laid waste and buildings pockmarked by bullets confronted him everywhere he turned in this city, which, he noted, was about the size of his own Middletown. No glass panes were left in any of the windows, so "the inhabitants tr[ied] to shut out the cold and dampness with oiled paper, reinforced with a network of strings."

Horton ventured out to the battlefield of Belleau Wood just beyond the city. There, amid fallen trees and shell holes, he saw traces of the battle: unexploded grenades, guns, shells, many articles of clothing lying about, "and, very seldom, a few bones." He remarked in his letter home: "It is maddening to think that such carnage can be allowed in the Christian era. And such waste! Metals, land, timber, lives, everything!" Horton's sense of revulsion then turned inward:

> We . . . returned to our waiting auto with a feeling that we had done something not quite right. We should have been there before, when there was action, instead of looking over the place now when all was peace and quiet, and making remarks about it.[6]

That night, with companions he had collected along the way, Horton worked his way by car and train to Rheims. The city, he noted in a letter home, was once the size of Hartford, but "far more beautiful with its parkways and boulevards, its graceful bridges and cathedrals." Now Rheims was a vast heap of "tumbled ruins," "like nothing before . . . in history, or ever again." In the starlight, the city looked otherworldly. Horton wandered about in awe—and also in search of a place to sleep. After half an hour of rest in an American officer's hut, he journeyed onward by passenger train to Verdun and by freight train across the French-German border into Metz. His route took him through the most severely ravaged sector of France. From the porch of the freight train's caboose, Horton observed the evidence of warfare in the open wilderness that once was a forest: "rifles, machine gun parts, knapsacks, clothing of every description . . . mess kits, everything. In one of the valleys there were even unburied dead."[7]

After viewing the Hindenburg Line, the once-fortified trench that wound from north to south through the eastern edge of France, and venturing over into Germany at Metz, Horton returned to Brest by way of

---

[6]Horton to his family, 8 April 1919, 2–3.
[7]Ibid., 6–7.

Nancy and Paris. Although it was a short trip, this April journey to the wasteland of Western civilization changed Douglas Horton. The world he had known during his student days—a world of easy travel across borders and fast-made friendships—lay behind him ruined and in fragments. His dilemma was that of many men and women of his generation: to make something whole out of the brokenness; or, to use the language of Horton's contemporary T. S. Eliot: to shore fragments against the personal and collective ruin.[8]

Horton began this process of restoration in the first sermon he delivered to his Middletown congregation upon his return from the Navy. He believed that the war had exposed the inability of the churches to exert influence over the nation and over other nations of the world. What the world required now, Horton argued, was "enlightened and Christian leadership." A major focus of his sermon was on the need to attract "virile young men and women" to the churches so that they might become these new leaders. The war to save the "body" of America from "aggression and desecration" had been won. Now it was up to the churches to "save [the nation's] soul." No clear plan emerged from this early sermon as to how the churches might address the condition of the nation's soul. But Horton did speak favorably about the "tendency toward world federation" as exemplified by the League of Nations. He noted that such an organization could be an effective instrument of "the kingdom . . . if people who know and respect Christ have a dominant hearing in international affairs."[9]

Over time these first fragments of a response to the war developed into a more coherent critique of the process that led to war and an ap-

---

[8]Eliot's poem "The Waste Land" concludes: "These fragments I have shored against my ruins" (line 431). The immediate reference is to the syllable "Da," or "what the thunder said." But the reference is also to the fragments of Western and Eastern civilization that Eliot has gathered together to construct the poem. See T. S. Eliot, *The Complete Poems and Plays* (New York: Harcourt and Brace, 1971) 49–50. Although it is beyond the scope of this book, the connection between Eliot and Horton would be a fascinating subject to explore. After World War I, Eliot became interested in the problem of developing a "Christian society." He attended the Oxford Conference on Life and Work in 1937 (as did Horton) and was a member of the British committee, headquartered at Mansfield College, that prepared for the World Council of Churches. See Peter Ackroyd, *T. S. Eliot: A Life* (New York: Simon and Schuster, 1984) 242–44, 248–57.

[9]Douglas Horton, "Leadership: Demand and Supply," n.d. [circa September 1919] 3–4, CDH.

peal for a new spirit that would, according to Horton, lead to peace. In an Armistice Day sermon delivered in 1923, Horton recalled his journey five years earlier to the "death valley" beyond the town of Verdun. Somewhere among the dead was a friend from college who had gone to participate in "a war to end all wars." Horton argued that it was not really the Germans who killed his friend or all the others like him; rather, it was his friend's own ancestors: the "Senates and Congresses and peoples of the last century . . . men whose widest political conception was nationalism." An indefensible isolationism allowed the Great War to happen, Horton contended, and he warned that war would take place again unless the world's people developed "a fierce international will toward companionship."[10]

Horton subsequently converted his Armistice Day sermon into one of his first published articles. In the form of an open address to the U.S. Senate, Horton presented the religious underpinnings of his "internationalist" position:

> I assure you from the viewpoint of a churchman that there is no idea more germane to the genius of the Christian Church than that of international cooperation. It is implied in Jesus' doctrine of the Kingdom of Heaven, wherein all nations shall one day be provinces. Any political party which declares itself for national aloofness thereby takes leave of the world's best religious thought and matriculates for defeat.[11]

For Horton, the root cause of the war was poor political leadership based on a nationalistic — and therefore a dangerously limited — worldview. His solution to this problem was twofold: first, to advance the ideal of international cooperation as a means of ensuring a lasting peace; and second, to develop Christian leaders who would bring the internationalist perspective to bear in the spheres of government and business. Underlying his holistic view of the world was a doctrine of the "kingdom of heaven." Horton applied this doctrine to the relation-

---

[10]Douglas Horton, "Guide Our Feet into the Way of Peace" (sermon, 11 November 1923), CDH. See also "Says Great Lessons of War Not Learned," *Middletown Press*, 12 November 1923.

[11]Douglas Horton, "To the Gentlemen of the Senate Assembling," *The Christian Work*, 15 December 1923, 718–19.

ship among nations first and foremost. The "will toward companionship" among churches themselves — what later might be called the "ecumenical impulse" — was not yet his primary concern. In time, however, the churches would become, for Horton, the main conduits for the kingdom's advance. For now, they were the training grounds for leaders of a new internationalism.

Horton's response to the war was similar to that of many other American Protestant liberals at the time. He did not reexamine his fundamental theological convictions, as did many European pastors affected by the war. Rather, Horton felt compelled to redouble his efforts to "Christianize" society, thus demonstrating a sentiment not too distant from those expressed in the previous century by men like Josiah Strong and Washington Gladden. What the war revealed, from this liberal point of view, was that America and the world were not yet sufficiently Christian in character. Horton resolved to heal the wounds of war by drawing closer in practice to the ideals Christianity espoused.[12]

Horton's further efforts toward international companionship began the year after he returned from the war. Following a pattern established by his mentors Cadman and Mackenzie, Horton and his family spent the entire summer abroad. At Mackenzie's suggestion and under the auspices of the Congregational Union in London, Horton arranged to preach on Sundays in independent (Baptist and Congregational) churches in England and Scotland. During the week, as tourist, Horton retraced his travels of an earlier era by visiting friends in Oxford and Edinburgh; he thus maintained and extended a network of friendships that would serve as a system of support in later years.

Wherever he went during these travels through Great Britain, Horton was deeply impressed by the sense of loss that permeated the population in the aftermath of the Great War. A photograph of his graduating class at Edinburgh showed most of his fellow students clad in khaki. Practically all of them had been wounded in the war and at least one of

---

[12]Horton's postwar stance resembled closely that of William Adams Brown and Washington Gladden. See William R. Hutchison, *The Modernist Impulse in American Protestantism* (Cambridge: Harvard University Press, 1976) 229–44. Karl Barth assumed that if his teachers could embrace the Kaiser's program of military aggression so readily there must have been something fundamentally wrong with their theological perspectives; thus Barth abandoned liberal theology. See Eberhard Busch, *Karl Barth: His Life from Letters and Autobiographical Texts* (Philadelphia: Fortress, 1975) 81–92.

them had been killed. "I had known that they had all gone into the war," he wrote to his family, "but I had never pictured to myself exactly what it meant before."[13] It seemed to him that everyone he met had a friend or relative who died because of the war. He was particularly moved by the sadness that had overcome his friend W. B. Selbie, the principal of Mansfield College, on the loss of his eldest son. Contrary to his earlier regrets about missing the action on the battlefield, Horton realized the folly of the often-expressed American sentiment that "the war didn't last long enough." Horton observed that "one really doesn't know what a real thing the war was until he meets these families which were stricken by it."[14]

Horton also made a pilgrimage to the small village of Scrooby. In the seventeenth century members of Scrooby's Independent congregation left England with their minister, John Robinson, for Leyden, in Holland. Later the congregation, minus its leader, passed through Plymouth, England, en route to establishing the permanent settlement of the same name in the New World. By chance, on arriving in Scrooby, Horton met a man named John Robinson, a direct descendant of his seventeenth-century namesake. He also befriended the vicar from the neighboring village of Austerfield, who opened the church's records to Horton, showing him the faded parchment with the baptismal entry for William Bradford, the first governor of Plymouth Colony. "Tourists don't see this!" Horton wrote. He speculated that the document was "almost priceless."[15]

Horton's interest in his Pilgrim heritage coincided with events in both America and England that celebrated the tercentenary of the Pilgrims' arrival at Plymouth Rock. During the early summer of 1920 the International Congregational Council met in Boston to commemorate the anniversary and to hold its fourth international convention. W. Douglas Mackenzie served as chair of the interim committee, the group responsible for organizing the council. Other members of that committee included S. Parkes Cadman and P. T. Forsyth.

---

[13]Douglas Horton, "Narrative, 1920," 20 July, BDH. The "Narrative" is a fifty-eight-page typewritten account of the Horton family's travels during the summer of 1920.
    [14]Ibid., 9 August.
    [15]Ibid., 10 August.

The Horton family had already sailed for England by the time the convention gathered at the end of June, and so Douglas Horton did not participate in the first round of celebrations. After some readjustments to his travel plans, however, Horton did manage to participate in a second gathering of the International Congregational Council in Plymouth, England, toward the end of the summer. Congregationalists from all over the world—many of them recently returned from the convention in Boston—converged in Plymouth for a week of celebration and speeches. Horton was one of the American ministers invited to preach in the town's independent churches on Sunday, 5 September, the climax of the celebration. Cadman, his friend and minister, was the featured preacher at the open-air Congregational service that morning. Later that day, Cadman preached "to an enormous crowd" at the Wesleyan church while Horton preached at the Salisbury Road Baptist Church. Horton spent much of the time between services with Cadman, who introduced him to many of the leaders of British Congregationalism.

Horton's early contacts with the International Congregational Council gave him a broad perspective on the prospects for Congregationalism around the world. Already in the first quarter of the century, "independency" as a principle was in decline, at least in Great Britain, Australia, Canada, and India. In light of this trend, the topic of "Congregational identity" had been a consistent theme at all of the International Congregational Council gatherings since its founding in 1891. Often this theme was coupled with the theme of church union—particularly as a means for the survival of some aspects of Congregational identity. At the Boston meeting in 1920, for example, Selbie participated on the British commission that discussed "the influence of Congregationalism in promoting Christian unity and the lines upon which it should draw that influence."[16] At the gathering in Plymouth, meanwhile, Horton attended the conference on "The Call of the Present Situation to International Protestantism."[17] Individuals with whom Horton was closely acquainted, including Mackenzie, Cadman, and Selbie, were all prominent leaders in the International Congregational Council. Horton's fa-

---

[16]Truman J. Spencer, ed., *Proceedings of the Fourth International Congregational Council* (New York: National Council of the Congregational Churches of the United States, 1921) 5.

[17]Horton, "Narrative, 1920," 6 September.

miliarity with Congregationalism and its particular concerns on both sides of the Atlantic made him a likely candidate to follow in their footsteps as a leader in the Council.[18]

For the next twenty years the Horton family spent most summers in Europe: in England, on occasion, and also in Switzerland and Germany. Through this frequent contact with the continent, Horton took it upon himself to translate, as it were, his European experiences for an American audience. References to European events appeared often in his sermons. In published articles especially, Horton explored trends in current European thought. A 1921 article in the *Christian Century*, for example, recommended Sigmund Freud's psychotherapeutic method as an aid for preaching. Horton argued that the ideal preacher should function like a Freudian therapist, exposing the individual to her or his sin. Once the barrier of sin was broken down, Horton suggested, the message of Christ could be heard rightly. "The profession of the Christian ministry is the highest of callings," Horton wrote, "because it entails the infinitely delicate and awful responsibility of setting hearts free from the sin which shuts out the presence of God."[19] As the summers passed, Horton grew in this role as a mediator between cultures. His exposure to Europe continually informed his understanding of the religious scene, not only in America generally, but also within his own denomination, as well as within the particular congregations he served.

One unsuccessful translation from Europe to America concerned the liberal social and political values Horton encountered in Great Britain. During his travels in 1920, he came into contact with many church leaders and prominent laypersons, including some wealthy industrialists, from the denomination. Horton was impressed that so many of them had adopted a socialist position in relation to wealth distribution and care for the poor. "Here, for instance," Horton wrote,

> was this Mr. Moore, who is a most successful consulting
> engineer. He has made his fortune by and out of the present

[18]Indeed, Horton began his active participation in the International Congregational Council at the next gathering in Bournemouth, England, in 1930. He spoke on "The Place of Congregationalism in the Living Church: Our Distinctive Contribution" (*Proceedings of the Fifth International Congregational Council* [ed. Albert Peel; London: Camelot, 1930] 242–51).

[19]Horton, "The Freudian Theory and Preaching," *Christian Century*, 13 January 1921, 13–15.

existing capitalistic system, but he is ready to admit in no uncertain terms that this system is, as at present organized, wrong, and he sees that the ever-recurring labor problems will never be resolved until some change is made in the social order.[20]

Elsewhere in a letter to his family, Horton wrote: "I feel perfectly certain that the strength of Britain is her liberal citizen. We must not let the genus die out in America."[21]

Inspired by the generous capitalists he met in England, Horton returned to Middletown determined to address issues of social reform in his own congregation. Horton's ideas met with general acceptance, but a group within First Church took exception to their minister's efforts to "outline an economic programme to govern industrial relations and problems." This group alleged that Horton's opinions were the product of a "definite school of political-economic thought" that was "regarded with almost universal distrust and fear by men of business experience." They called on the congregation as a whole to reject any efforts to preach a "social gospel" in the church, arguing that the real issues facing the church were moral, not political.[22]

The controversy did not last long. The congregation voted to have Horton's position and that of his opponents published and distributed to all church members in an effort to "find what is the mind of Jesus in this matter."[23] Horton suffered no ill consequences as a result of the controversy, although his subsequent sermons in Middletown and later in Brookline tended to emphasize personal rather than systemic reform in response to the Christian faith. Yet, Horton's impulse to reform society did not die out after the challenge at Middletown. Rather, a subtle shift occurred, developing slowly over the course of the next fifteen to twenty years. Instead of arguing that church people ought to fix the brokenness of the society around them, Horton began to examine the broken character of the Church itself. Healing the Church's division and the divisions among churches became, for Horton, the primary task from out of which the transformation of society would follow. If the Church could

[20]Horton, "Narrative, 1920," 10 July.

[21]Ibid., 8 August.

[22]"A Resolution from the Standing Committee of the First Ecclesiastical Society, n.d. [circa January 1921]," 1–2, CDH.

[23]"A Resolution after the Annual Meeting of January 14 [1921?]," CDH.

not bring about the "kingdom of heaven," it could at least be a model of that kingdom to the rest of the world.

Translating the World: Leyden Church in Brookline

The Horton family moved to Brookline, Massachusetts, a town adjacent to Boston, in the fall of 1925. Boston, the historic home of Congregationalism in America, housed many of the denomination's great churches and institutions. The Leyden Church, too, bore the marks of this long Congregational history. It was named after the town in Holland that had served as a refuge for the members of the Scrooby congregation before they embarked on their pilgrimage to America. A replica of the pulpit from the Saint Pieterskerk in Leyden, Holland, adorned the Brookline sanctuary; it had been crafted in intricate detail to resemble the very pulpit from which John Robinson had preached in the early seventeenth century. The members of the Leyden Church maintained their historical link to Holland through contemporary contacts. The ceremony to celebrate the dedication of the John Robinson pulpit, for example, featured a representative from the University at Leyden—a living witness to the continued relationship between the Dutch and American churches.[24]

The internationalism of the Leyden Church was in harmony with Horton's continued efforts to foster communication between continents. Horton's years in Brookline saw an expansion of his reputation as an "acute observer . . . unusually equipped" to write about European trends and affairs.[25] In the aftermath of his article on the use of Freudian psychoanalytic theory and technique in ministry, Horton assumed the role of unofficial European correspondent for a variety of religious publications. His 1927 article in *Christian Century* introduced Protestant readers to "the thinking priest of Paris," the Reverend Father Sanson of Notre

---

[24]"A Record of the Interior Improvements Made in Leyden Church, 1929," CDH. The Dutchman, a Professor Herring, became a leader in the International Congregational Council during the years of Horton's greatest influence (1940 and afterwards). Cadman was also featured at the dedication.

[25]Editor's note to "Germany: What Will be the Outcome?," by Douglas Horton, *The Christian Leader*, 11 October 1930, 1286.

Dame Cathedral. The priest was attracting "huge assemblies" to Mass, and this was a newsworthy fact during the "Roaring Twenties," a time of diminished interest in church matters. What Horton particularly admired about Sanson was his unorthodox manner. Sanson expounded dogma "without reference to the fathers, in utterly rationalistic and unCatholic style." Indeed, Horton called Sanson's "an essentially Protestant mind" and expressed amazement that he had been tolerated for any length of time by the Catholic hierarchy. In a postscript to the article, Horton reported that since his writing, Father Sanson had been removed from his position by order of the pope. Horton concluded that there was no room, as yet, for a "superior mind" within the Roman communion. The struggle, Horton wrote, "was between a modern priest and the church of the middle ages, and the church of the middle ages ha[d] apparently triumphed."[26]

This article is significant in light of Horton's later ecumenical development. It reflects a prevailing Protestant distrust of Catholics, a distrust Horton did not lose until the 1960s.[27] Also noteworthy is Father Sanson's status as a European Catholic. Horton was surrounded by large Catholic communities in the Boston area, but he rarely mentioned these people in his sermons or writing. Indeed, his Brookline congregation apparently had more frequent contact with Jews than with Catholics. For Horton, Christian Boston was mainly a Protestant town, at least at his socioeconomic level; Catholics in the vicinity and in general were invisible.

A second article written by Horton in 1930 offered a survey of the postwar Germany to which the Horton family repaired frequently during their summers abroad. Horton warned that the struggle for democracy in Germany was in danger. He surveyed the ongoing grievances Germany held against the Allies in such matters as the exclusive assignment of war guilt to Germany and the extended French occupation of the Ruhr region, and determined that the German protest had merit. Although Horton thought that "the general moral and spiritual habits of

[26]Douglas Horton, "The Thinking Priest of Paris," *Christian Century*, 15 September 1927, 1072–73.

[27]Even Horton's effort to bring a Roman Catholic professor onto the faculty to the Harvard Divinity School in 1958 can be interpreted as an act of distrust; the concern was to "control" the Catholic voice through a token inclusion of it. For further discussion, see chapter 5.

[the] people" would bring Germany out of the present crisis, he noted with concern that "the greatest internal foe to German democracy," Adolph Hitler, was dangerous because of "his unwavering distrust of other nations, his hostility to all international projects . . . and [his] venomous anti-Semitism." Hitler's anti-internationalism, meanwhile, was in direct opposition to Horton's own concern for world community. Fortunately, Horton thought, Hitler was unlikely to gain command of the government any time soon. Horton suggested that people of goodwill everywhere should support the leaders of the moderate parties and thereby welcome Germany into the community of nations.[28]

The great achievement of Horton's early years as a European correspondent—and the one that brought him national recognition—was his translation of Swiss theologian Karl Barth's book *The Word of God and the Word of Man* (*Das Wort Gottes und die Theologie*).[29] Religion historian Sydney Ahlstrom maintained that Horton's translation "mark[ed] an era in American Christian thought": the turning point away from liberal theology toward neoorthodoxy under the direction of theologians such as Reinhold and Richard Niebuhr, Walter Marshall Horton (no relation), and Wilhelm Pauck.[30] Certainly Horton's popular translation (the book went through four printings by 1931) introduced English-reading America to Karl Barth's thought. But, as another scholar has noted, Horton himself was never "a full-fledged Barthian"; that is, he neither advocated nor really studied Barth's theology as it unfolded during the

---

[28]Douglas Horton, "Germany: What Will Be the Outcome?," *The Christian Leader*, 11 October 1930, 1286–89. Horton's early sense of the danger behind anti-Semitic rhetoric is noteworthy. Reinhold Niebuhr made similar observations two years later in the denominational magazine of the Evangelical Synod. See in particular Reinhold Niebuhr, "A Trip Through the Ruhr (1932)" and "Christianizing International Relations," in *Young Reinhold Niebuhr* (ed. William G. Chrystal; Saint Louis: Eden, 1977) 124–27, 199–208.

[29]Horton later explained that he changed his translation of the book's title from *The Word of God and Theology* to *The Word of God and the Word of Man* at the request of his editor at Pilgrim Press. The editor had insisted that Americans did not buy books with the word "theology" in the title. See Horton to Donald Ward, 21 November 1958, CSM.

[30]Sydney E. Ahlstrom, "Continental Influence on American Christian Thought Since World War I," *Church History* 27 (1958) 264. Before accepting a position at Yale, Ahlstrom taught briefly at Harvard University (though not at the Divinity School) during Horton's tenure as dean.

1930s and 1940s.[31] Thus, in relation to Horton's own development, the Barth translation is better understood in the context of Horton's effort to keep Christians in America apprised of developments in the European community.[32] Barth was attractive to Horton not for the intricacy of his theology, but for that theology's popularity. Barth, who taught at the university in Göttingen, was "the man who saved protestantism in Germany," according to Horton. Barth preached and lectured to overflow crowds, and he had even been designated "the greatest man since Schleiermacher" by one of Germany's prominent theologians.[33] Here was a thinker—like Freud and Father Sanson—that Americans should know about; thus, Horton translated and wrote about Barth.

In 1928, several months before his book translation appeared, Horton published an article titled "God Lets Loose Karl Barth" in *Christian Century*. "Beware," Horton wrote, quoting Emerson, "when the great God lets loose a thinker on this planet. Then all things are at risk." Horton held Barth responsible for sparking a theological conflagration throughout Europe. In the aftermath of the Great War, Horton maintained, Barth challenged all of the inherited assumptions of German liberal theology. Where liberalism had argued for the immanence of God and had even suggested that Jesus was merely an exemplary human being, Barth proclaimed God's transcendence, God's absolute otherness in relation to human beings, and especially God's sovereignty. Where liberalism put faith in human progress and the natural goodness of human beings, Barth emphasized the fallen character of sinful humanity. Where liberalism

[31]Dennis Voskuil, "From Liberalism to Neo-Orthodoxy: The History of a Theological Transition, 1925–1935" (Ph.D. diss., Harvard University, 1974) 80.

[32]One of Horton's chief detractors during the protracted merger debates of 1948–1955 was Marion Bradshaw, professor at Bangor Theological Seminary in Maine. Bradshaw perceived a threat to Congregational freedom in Horton's ecumenical stance. He traced this threat to an authoritarian strain in what he labeled Horton's "Barthianism." Following Bradshaw's argument, scholar Charles Harvey argued that the devotion to "organic union" on the part of men like Horton and George Richards was derived from Barth. But the concept of "organic union" had a long history in America prior to Barth, as the 1918 Philadelphia Conference on "organic union" attests. George Richards played a prominent role in that conference. See Charles Harvey, "Individualism and Ecumenical Thought: The Merger Controversy in Congregationalism" (Ph.D. diss., University of California, Riverside, 1968).

[33]Horton, "God Lets Loose Karl Barth," *Christian Century*, 16 February 1928, 204–6. Horton did not identify the prominent theologian in the article.

associated itself with particular social movements within the culture—such as pacifism, socialism, or the state itself—Barth deferred to the "uncertainty [*sic*] though actually felt will of God."[34]

Horton praised what he saw as Barth's Calvinistic emphasis on God's sovereignty, but his review focused on the "paradox" at the center of Barth's theology. God and humanity were thrown together (as in the English translation of Barth's title), and yet an "estranging sea" separated the two, with no way to move from humanity to God. In ethics as in worship, one sought "God's will zealously, with the foregone conclusion that God's will cannot be found." The solution was not to give up on God but rather to find refuge in the paradox: "let a man realize at once his infinite need for finding God, and the infinite futility of his search," Horton wrote, "and in the clash of those two futilities within his soul, the God of infinities will be adumbrated—but only adumbrated."[35] In his own thinking, Horton found the will of God less difficult to discern than did Barth. But Horton retained the concept of paradox for use in later ecumenical conversations.

Toward the end of the *Christian Century* article, Horton summarized the broad appeal of Barth's theology in the context of contemporary Germany:

> To the German people, stunned by the war and the consequences of defeat, their former optimism shattered and spent . . . Barth, in the phase of his dreadful insight into the futility of all searches for security must seem a veritable Jeremiah, and his teaching an evilly perfect rationalization of their indigence and perplexity. But in the phase of his harking back to the perfect sovereignty of the ruler of this world and all worlds, his words must seem an embodiment of their one hope.[36]

While the situation in the United States was very different from Germany, the reality of the Great War was something that liberal American theology could not explain away. The onset of economic depression the year after Horton's translation appeared also undercut American notions of human prosperity and inevitable social progress. In this

---

[34]Ibid., 206.
[35]Ibid.
[36]Ibid.

context, Barth's theology was perceived as a significant critique of religious liberalism specifically, and the prevailing American theological mindset in general. The appearance of Horton's translation helped to set in motion the neoorthodox movement in the United States by providing the source for a steady stream of Barth appraisals and critiques from some of the nation's most important Protestant theologians.[37]

For the most part, Horton stayed away from the Barth debates of the next decade. He did write a handful of articles explaining and criticizing Barth's theology,[38] and he initiated further international conversation by hosting Emil Brunner, another proponent of the "crisis theology," when Brunner visited Boston in 1928 on a lecture tour arranged by fellow Barth translator George Richards of Lancaster Theological Seminary and the German Reformed Church.[39]

Boston was not only an important city for Congregationalists, it was also the home of Unitarianism in America. The Unitarian churches withdrew from the orthodox Congregational fold in the early 1800s because of doctrinal differences concerning the Trinity and the deity of Christ. They also believed in the goodness of human nature and therefore did not accept the doctrines of the fall or eternal damnation. Because of these beliefs—particularly the rejection of Christ's deity—Unitarians were not permitted to join other major American denominations in the Federal Council of Churches. Yet within the Congregational fold, many people shared beliefs quite similar to those of the Unitarians. As there was a certain laxity within Congregationalism in relation to doctrine, "unitarian beliefs" were able to thrive alongside more traditional Christian ones under the broad banner of Congregationalism.

[37]Voskuil, "From Liberalism to Neo-Orthodoxy." See especially chapter 3, "Continental Influence on the Transition from Liberalism to Neo-Orthodoxy."

[38]For example, Douglas Horton, "Karl Barth and the Dreadful Necessity," *The Christian Register*, 24 January 1929, 63; idem, "The Religion of Our Age as Seen by Karl Barth and His Friends," *The Congregationalist*, 7 February 1929, 178–79; and idem, "Prophet or Professor? A Review of Karl Barth's Credo," *Christian Century*, 3 February 1937, 146–47.

[39]Horton and Richards became friends toward the end of the 1920s; in 1930 Horton delivered the sermon at Lancaster Theological Seminary's commencement exercises.

Horton was well aware of this aspect of Congregational identity when he delivered an address on "Contemporary Congregational Doctrine" at a meeting of the Unitarian, Universalist, and Congregational Associations in Lowell, Massachusetts, in 1930. Horton admitted that "Congregational doctrine" might seem like an irreducible paradox to many Congregationalists, given the expressions of individualism in the denomination and the presumed general aversion to doctrine. But Horton argued that there was indeed a Congregational orthodoxy, if orthodox were defined as "nonheretical." Heresy, for Horton, meant "choosing, taking a part for the whole, placing such emphasis on certain doctrines that other doctrines are muted." The genius of Congregationalism, Horton argued, was its openness to a variety of doctrinal options in the context of fellowship.

To the perceived concern of his audience that this openness left ample room in the denomination for fundamentalists—that is, persons who held that the Bible in its entirety presented the literal truth which must be believed and obeyed—Horton noted that excluding such persons would only "be shortening the periphery of their denominational usefulness." Horton welcomed fundamentalists in the denomination because they provided a needed corrective to a liberal religion that placed no demands at all on the will of the believer. Horton's main argument was that true "Congregational doctrine" in its broadness moved toward unity. The day was not far distant, Horton asserted, "when the Congregationalists shall come from the east and the west, and shall sit down with the Unitarians and Universalists in the Kingdom of heaven."[40]

Building on this doctrine of unity, Horton saw a resolution to the problem of international fragmentation in Congregationalism, which, he argued, was "developing according to an inherent principle of catholicity." In a speech he delivered later that year at the International Congregational Council in Bournemouth, England, Horton claimed that Congregational polity could adapt itself to any doctrinal situation; therefore, the gift of Congregationalism to the world's churches was a polity that allowed all sorts of theological differences of opinion within the universal Church. With reference to the recent gatherings of the Life and Work and Faith and Order movements and the International Missionary Conference, Horton inquired rhetorically:

[40]Douglas Horton, "Contemporary Congregational Doctrine," *The Christian Leader*, 15 February 1930, 204–5.

> What was Stockholm? A Congregational meeting. What was
> Lausanne? A Congregational meeting. What was Jerusalem?
> A Congregational meeting. They all maintained the tension
> between freedom and fellowship. Continue such meetings until
> self-consciousness emerges in Protestantism and you will have
> the beginnings of a universal church—Congregational in
> form.[41]

The great paradox of the Congregational system, Horton insisted, occurred in the tension between "freedom" and "fellowship." In its ability to maintain this tension, Horton argued, Congregationalism held the key to the future unity of the universal Church. "If other churches can make the same claim," said Horton, ". . . the Kingdom of Heaven is so much the nearer." To bring the "Kingdom of Heaven" nearer, a theme of the earlier Social Gospel movement, continued to be Horton's mission during his years in Chicago. This task would require the effort not simply of the churches but also of the universal Church.[42]

Rethinking the Church: United Church of Hyde Park in Chicago

Horton entered into conversations with the search committee from United Church of Hyde Park in Chicago during the fall of 1930. United Church was made up of members from both Presbyterian and Congregational denominations. Given Horton's inclusive vision of the Church, United's standing in two denominations appealed to him. Horton was also drawn to the challenges the church faced in the city of Chicago, the nation's fastest growing city, at a time of national depression. And, significantly, certain members of United's church council shared Horton's general church interests. Wilhelm Pauck, a member of the Chicago Divinity School faculty, was in the process of writing a book on Barth's theology when Horton's candidacy was under consideration. Another member of the council, John T. McNeill, had been involved with the discussions that led to the formation of the United Church of Canada. His book *Unitive Protestantism* was perhaps the first to use the word "ecumenical" in relation to national and international movements of cooperation among Protestant churches. According to McNeill, con-

---

[41]Horton, "The Place of Congregationalism in the Living Church," 249.
[42]Ibid.

temporary "unitive" movements were grounded in the Reformation, and "ecumenism" was far more characteristic of Protestantism than the sectarian spirit.[43] In all likelihood, Horton came to apply the term "ecumenical" to his own efforts shortly after coming to Chicago.

One factor that delayed Horton's call to United Church for a time was his expressed desire for an annual summer vacation of two months, a period of time he used "for the business of getting stocked up intellectually" at quiet resorts abroad. Horton noted that this longstanding practice of his served the church better than working at home during the "slack season." Eventually the search committee was swayed by this argument, and Horton began his work at United Church after the summer of 1931.[44]

Soon after the Horton family arrived in Chicago, United Church faced a serious financial crisis. The depression had limited the ability of church members to meet their support commitments, and by the spring of 1932 the church was saddled with a growing deficit. In a letter to the chair of United Church's board of trustees, Horton reported that the staff members of the church—the church secretary, the director of religious education, the director of music, and the sexton—had all agreed to accept a 10 percent salary reduction during this time of "general economic embarrassment." Given the sacrifices made by others, Horton proposed that his own salary be cut by 12.5 percent.[45]

Horton's salary reduction proposal was submitted in the context of ongoing conversations at United Church that focused on the nature of the economic depression. In late May 1932, members of a round table group from the church published "A Declaration," an account of "the fundamental laws against which we seem as a race to have offended and which, if we are to enjoy the orderly processes of economic evolution, we must obey." Among the fundamental laws the members had broken was a failure to recognize that "the world is essentially one economic unit, and that prosperity of the whole is dependent on the prosperity of each part." The round table members pledged to devote their energies to

[43]Wilhelm Pauck, *Karl Barth: Prophet of a New Christianity?* (New York: Harper, 1931); John T. McNeill, *Unitive Protestantism: The Ecumenical Spirit and Its Persistent Expression* (Philadelphia: John Knox, 1930).

[44]Horton to W. S. Macleod, 31 December 1930 and 9 January 1931, RHF. During Horton's pastorate, United Church established the practice of inviting a guest minister from England to assume preaching duties during the summer.

[45]Horton to Charles Rittenhouse, 29 April 1932, RHF.

the promotion of cooperation among nations. In particular, they insisted that "planning for a better world" needed to be centered in the church, the one institution that "throughout the ages has been the chief source and treasury of the belief in man and his future."[46]

These sentiments are reminiscent of the Social Gospel convictions of the pre-World War I era. A Barthian orientation might suggest that the Church should foster belief in God (as opposed to, simply, humanity) and God's future, with the transformation of society following inevitably from acts of faithful obedience. Instead, Horton's new congregation strongly sensed that society at large was the focus of the church's ministry and that the church should be first and foremost the agent of change. This liberal theology, as opposed to a more orthodox or Barthian standpoint, coupled with a Wilson-esque internationalism were characteristic of Douglas Horton's developing ecumenism.

Horton's preaching during his years in Chicago was in line with his congregation's convictions about the church's responsibility for the betterment of human society. In his sermon "The Last Refuge of a Scoundrel," for instance, Horton argued that true patriotism was rooted in a "concern for the general good . . . not in a vertigo of rivalries" that inevitably led to "the bloody holocaust of war." Echoing the social doctrine he espoused early on at Middletown, Horton said that the church had the responsibility to foster leaders committed to this general good. He noted that such people "belong[ed] to the company viewing life 'coming down from heaven' "; that is, they were partisans of the "holy city of the New Jerusalem" as described in the book of Revelation (21:2). But how could the church effectively transform the world if the church itself was in fragments? This question increasingly came to haunt Horton. His ecumenical convictions as they emerged during the later Chicago years were his answer.

Horton published two books of sermons while in Chicago. His sermon on patriotism appeared in the first of these, called *Taking A City*. The book was part of the prestigious Harpers Monthly Pulpit Series and placed Horton in company with such notable preachers as Henry Sloane Coffin, president of Union Theological Seminary in New York; Horton's mentor, W. Douglas Mackenzie; and Bishop Ivan Lee Holt, president of the Federal Council of Churches, and, later, Horton's collaborator on

---

[46]"A Declaration by Members of a Group Gathered at a Round Table During April and May, 1932 at the United Church of Hyde Park Chicago," RHF.

the "Greenwich Plan of Union." *Taking A City* presented the Church with the task of converting "this city [Chicago] . . . into the still more stupendous city of God." Differing from an earlier emphasis on the centrality of the individual leader in this process of converting society, Horton now envisioned the need for a whole army of saints—the Church—to bring about social transformation.[47] In a review of *Taking A City*, one writer remarked of Horton:

> He has all of Barth's faith without Barth's archaic thought pattern. He is a modernist with momentum. . . . And he can strike boldly for a new and decent social order without preaching hate.

Another reviewer announced:

> Chicago has done something for Doug Horton. . . . To the character of the scholar and theologian ministering with quiet sincerity to a suburban community he has added that of an inspired prophet going out to meet life at the crossroads.[48]

The popularity of *Taking A City* in 1934 led in the following year to the publication of a second book of sermons called *The Art of Living*. These sermons, too, focused on "the need for the redemption of neighborhoods and society as a whole." The book was published by United Church of Hyde Park on the recommendation of one its members, Professor Matthew Spinka of the Chicago Theological Seminary. Also at Spinka's suggestion, all profits from the book were donated to Howell House and similar institutions in Chicago that were dedicated to "the upbuilding of humanity in body, mind, spirit, and brotherhood."[49]

---

[47]Horton's first book, *Out Into Life*, offered young men a manual of career choices—from agriculture to the Christian ministry and all occupations in between. The thesis of the book was that young men exercised Christian stewardship in their chosen professions; therefore, the choice of profession—coupled with a sense of calling—was a crucial matter. Compare Douglas Horton, *Out Into Life* (New York: Abingdon, 1924) and idem, *Taking a City* (New York: Harpers, 1934) 1–13.

[48]"Taking a City," review of *Taking a City* by Douglas Horton, *The Christian Leader*, 24 November 1934, and "Taking a City," review of *Taking a City* by Douglas Horton, *Advance*, 22 November 1934.

[49]Douglas Horton, *The Art of Living Today* (Chicago: United Church of Hyde Park, 1935) 5.

The concern for social justice, which Horton always contended was a hallmark of the Congregational tradition, came to the fore in an incident first recorded in the Chicago papers and later reproduced in the *Christian Century* and many of the nation's papers as well. The "World War Adjusted Compensation Act" was a popular measure in Congress in the midst of the U.S. economic depression of 1929–1933. Passed in early 1936, it granted bonus pay to all those who had served in the World War. Horton qualified for the bonus by virtue of his mission aboard the U.S.S. *Michigan* in 1917 and 1918. But Horton asked in a sermon and in subsequent articles what the bonus had to do with the *summum bonum*, that is, the supreme good. Horton argued that veterans should not be given additional compensation simply because they had served in the military; rather, aid should be offered to those who were truly in need. Because the government was unwilling to adopt such a radical measure, Horton announced to his congregation that he would give his bonus to the institution he most trusted "of all the institutions of the world, whether they be states or nations, groups economic or political, or any other: the Christian Church."[50]

Horton's national reputation led to his involvement in 1936 with the Federal Council of Churches' "National Preaching Mission," a nationwide mission to the mainline Protestant churches. A typical four-day mission involved fifteen or more ministers speaking and leading discussions. The program combined an emphasis on social ministry with other meetings that focused on spiritual themes. Large rallies featuring nationally known preachers such as Horton were held in the evenings, usually in a town's or city's largest auditorium. Although the National Preaching Mission did not involve many unchurched people, it did revive "the evangelistic spirit of many local churches, especially their pastors, and did something to offset the defeatist mood current during the depression," according to Samuel McCrea Cavert.[51] The enterprise was so successful that it was repeated in 1937.

---

[50]Douglas Horton, "Bonus and *Summum Bonum*" (sermon manuscript, n.d. [2 February 1936]), CDH. See also "The Veteran and His Bonus," *Christian Century*, 19 February 1936, 286–87, and Douglas Horton, "A Veteran's Reaction to the Bonus," *Character*, March–April 1936, 7–8, 31–32.

[51]Cavert, *The American Churches in the Ecumenical Movement*, 154.

While Horton became recognized as a leading Protestant minister, he was also intimately involved with the affairs of Congregationalism on both sides of the Atlantic, particularly as these pertained to the emerging ecumenical movement. During the summer of 1932 he was guest preacher at the City Temple in London, a position held on several previous occasions by Cadman. A certain prestige attached itself to Americans who preached at the City Temple. In Sinclair Lewis's 1927 novel *Elmer Gantry*, the famous Rev. Dr. G. Prosper Edwards basks in glory "from having sermonized in the City Temple," for according to Dr. Edwards, "American clergymen [divided] into just two classes—those who could be invited to a London church and those who couldn't." In 1932 Horton attained that privileged status. His larger mission that summer was twofold: to begin preliminary conversations toward planning the next meeting of the International Congregational Conference in Boston in 1940, and to discuss the offer made to him by Albert Peel to become the American editor of the London-based journal, *The Congregational Quarterly*.[52]

Horton was also an emerging leader in the Congregational denomination. He had begun serving on the Prudential Board of the American Board of Commissioners for Foreign Missions in the mid-1920s, when he was still in Brookline. In 1934 he led a seminar on the theme "Current Theological Questions" at the denomination's biennial General Council meeting in Oberlin, Ohio. A significant portion of Horton's seminar was devoted to a recent report by the Commission on Interchurch Relations and Christian Unity that rejected a proposal to join in a merger with the Unitarians and Universalists.[53] The seminar's attention turned toward broader approaches to church unity including the Faith and Order movement. In *Advance*, the denomination's national publication, Horton's abilities as a leader were singled out: "Douglas Horton makes a seminar what a seminar should be—and is, literally—a place where a

[52]Sinclair Lewis, *Elmer Gantry* (New York: Harcourt and Brace, 1927) 401. Horton describes the events of his London summer in a series of letters to Carol Williams Horton, 2–22 July 1932, RHF. One of Horton's sermons, "A World of Persons," was published in *The City Temple Tidings*, 10/117, n.d. [circa July 1932] 149–55. Horton subsequently served as the American editor of the *Congregational Quarterly*.

[53]The proposal was turned down despite the strong historical ties between Congregationalism and Unitarianism (as Horton had praised them in his speech in Lowell, Massachusetts, in 1930). The Congregational propensity for inclusiveness did not supersede an "essential" unity in Christ—whose divinity the Unitarians in general could not affirm. See Harvey, "Individualism and Ecumenical Thought," 88–92.

seed is nurtured."[54] When he attended the next General Council meeting in 1936, Horton was recognized as an important leader within the denomination and on the international scene.

The General Council met at Mount Holyoke in 1936, where the honorary moderator, S. Parkes Cadman, delivered a paper on "The Nature and Function of the Christian Church," the last major address of his life.[55] Cadman spoke of the Church not as one particular denomination but as the "Church Universal," which he described as *the congregation of all souls reborn in Christ and gathered out of every nation and kindred, fused into one spiritual homogeneity broadly and securely founded upon the teachings of her Living Head.* Cadman did not stop with descriptions of this Universal Church as a mere spiritual force in the world. He anticipated the day "when all believers shall unite in one Lord and one Church . . . because a divided Church can no longer do God's work in the world."[56]

In a sense, Cadman was returning to a theme he had developed in the early 1920s when he had called for the unification of Protestantism and had foreseen the Church of the future as a corporate whole, elastic enough to accommodate difference in nonessentials, with a simple but catholic doctrine, a common worship, a mission which has no boundaries in a world which the Lord of all has redeemed.[57] Although Cadman's convictions had been chastened by the war and the Depression, his vision had been sharpened by years of involvement as president of the Federal Council of Churches, and as a leader in the Life and Work as well as in the Faith and Order movements. In words that fully resonated with Horton's call to convert Chicago into the "holy city of God,"[58] Cadman called on the assembled church to bring into being "a recreated Church and State, united as soul and body in justice and righteousness." There was a time, he suggested, "when the Church was the visible witness of a Divine Order covering the whole life of man."[59] Cadman's parting chal-

[54]Carl Heath Kopf, "Notes of a Neophyte at Oberlin," *Advance*, 18 November 1934, 579.

[55]In a little over a month after he delivered this address, Cadman died.

[56]S. Parkes Cadman, "The Nature and Function of the Christian Church," *Advance*, 1 July 1936, 453. Emphasis in the original.

[57]S. Parkes Cadman, "Can a Divided Church Meet the Challenge of the Present World Crisis?," in Lynch, ed., *The Problem of Christian Unity*, 10.

[58]See the discussion earlier in this chapter of Horton's book *Taking a City*.

[59]Cadman, "The Nature and Function of the Christian Church," 462.

lenge to the General Council in 1936 was to become that Church once again.

Cadman's rousing address combined old Social Gospel values with sensibilities nurtured in the burgeoning ecumenical movement. He only lacked a plan for bringing into being a united Church. This plan his protégé, Douglas Horton, soon supplied.

Beginning in the winter of 1933 and continuing for three more winters, a group of Congregational and Episcopal ministers met in Chicago to discover the "common convictions and differences" that prevailed between their communions. As the conversations progressed, the men began to formulate a theory of Church union, which, they believed, "point[ed] a way to the restoration of unity to the now divided body of Christ."[60] Among those who participated in the conversations were Frederick Clifton Grant, an Episcopal priest and a professor at Seabury-Western Theological Seminary (his son Robert married Horton's daughter Margaret), and the Congregationalists Wilhelm Pauck, from Horton's church, and Arthur Cushman McGiffert, president of the Chicago Theological Seminary. Douglas Horton served as secretary for the group of twenty and acted as editor of their report, *The Basic Formula for Church Union*.

The report argued that a disunited Church offered no real hope to a world torn apart by war and economic depression. At the heart of *The Basic Formula* was the conviction that "the essential, inner, and still unbroken unity of Christians in Christ deserve[d] and really require[d] an adequate manifestation in the world." The authors adopted with appropriate attribution the watchwords of Rupertus Meldenius: "in essentials unity, in non-essentials, liberty, in all things charity." They claimed that visible "unity" was essential to the Church. To manifest this unity, they concluded, was "the will of God for this generation."[61]

The Basic Formula proceeded from the conviction that all the participants in the conversation (and, by implication, their two denominations) were in fundamental agreement in matters of theology. Aside from

[60]Horton, ed., *The Basic Formula for Church Union*, 7–8.

[61]Ibid., 11–12, 15. Rupertus Meldenius was a pseudonym for the German Lutheran theologian, Peter Meiderlin (1582–1651). At the time of the Thirty Years' War, he wrote a small tract in Latin admonishing theologians in their disputes not to forget moderation and love. "Meiderlin is to be regarded as the originator of the phrase in question, since so far as is known it occurs nowhere any earlier than in his tract." See the *Schaff-Herzog Religious Encyclopedia* (New York: Scribners, 1917) 287.

loyalty to Christ and to the principle of unity through him, numerous variations were possible: in polity, in worship, in confessional formulation. The authors attempted to strike a balance between what they called "the individual principle" and "the collective principle," or what Congregationalists had traditionally characterized as the relationship between "freedom" and "fellowship." In the matter of Episcopal polity, for example, they contended that a variety of parties coexisted within the church. They were able to stay together because of a flexible relationship between the carefully worded formulations that all Episcopalians accepted in principle and the glosses applied to those formulations by different schools of thought.

To illustrate this point, the authors cited the official formula from the *Book of Common Prayer*: "No man shall be accounted or taken to be a lawful Bishop, Priest, or Deacon . . . except he hath had Episcopal Consecration or Ordination." They pointed out that an Anglo-Catholic would "gloss" this passage to mean "without bishops there can be no true Church, nor any valid ministry or sacraments." But an Evangelical Episcopalian would interpret the passage to mean "merely that the Church of England requires for herself one type of organization and ministry, while tacitly assuming that in other churches another form of ministry and ordination might prevail without the sacrifice of validity" as a truly Christian ministry. If these differences could be bridged within one denomination, the authors insisted, they could certainly be bridged across denominational lines "toward the great end of gathering together the fragments of the body of Christ."[62]

The Basic Formula for Church Union was submitted as a report to the Congregational Association and the Episcopal Diocese of Chicago. In his reply to the report, Bishop George Stewart suggested that the authors presumed a flexibility in the Episcopal system that did not exist.[63] In fact, no evidence suggests that any churches, locally or at the national level, used *The Basic Formula* as a blueprint for uniting. Still, *The Basic Formula* is significant inasmuch as it articulated the principles of visible unity that Horton carried with him after he left United Church in 1938 to assume his duties as the chief officer of the Congregational Christian Churches.

[62]Horton, ed., *Basic Formula*, 52, 87.
[63]George Stewart to Horton, 1935, CDH.

If the *Lusitania* symbolized the broken condition of the world after 1914, Horton and his collaborators on *The Basic Formula* looked toward a united Church to provide a new symbol of hope on uncertain seas—even as the storm clouds of war were gathering over Central Europe. The final paragraph of *The Basic Formula* evoked this symbol and conjured that hope. Its Latin language and naval terminology, meanwhile, betray the hand of the former naval chaplain:

> The ship *Ecclesia Christi* has been broken on the treacherous reefs that have beset her course during the last centuries. Her canvas is torn, her masts and yard shattered; she has been sorely beset by many winds. But in the providence of God she has at least survived. Now there is a need for many hands—our hands—to put her on the way again for a new launching; a call to mend the sails, repair the spars, and make her once more fit for her voyage. . . . On she will move through storm or calm, toward her unseen distant goal, her sails filled with the breath of God, her ship's company ready at all times for high adventure, her course set for all of civilization to follow.[64]

Shortly after those words were written, in early September 1938, Douglas Horton and his wife, Carol, set sail from San Francisco on a voyage around the world. Horton had been elected the new minister and secretary of the General Council of the Congregational Christian Churches. The journey's purpose was to meet with Congregational missionaries abroad, to attend the International Missionary Conference in Madras, and to visit churches affiliated with the International Congregational Council in places such as Ceylon, Turkey, and Czechoslovakia. Along the way, Horton became involved in a plan for the American churches to mediate the conflict between Japan and China. He met with Gandhi and discussed the application of Christian principles to the problems of social justice in the world. The Hortons traveled to Prague, where they offered their help to several Jewish families seeking to escape from the Nazis who occupied their country. The example of the missionaries in particular, suggested to Horton that if doctrinal differences could be set aside, the churches could be united and the Church would become a force to be reckoned with in the world. Indeed, Horton was convinced

[64]Horton, ed., *Basic Formula*, 88.

that a united Church was the only thing that could save the world from its current calamitous course. This conviction was at the heart of Horton's efforts to bring into being the United Church of Christ.[65]

[65]Carol Williams Horton kept a journal throughout most of the trip. It offers a fascinating glimpse of the networks of church and family that welcomed the Hortons throughout their travels around the world. See Carol Williams Horton, Diaries, 1938–1939 (3 vols.), RHF.

Minister and Secretary of the General Council

Horton was elected Minister and Secretary of the General Council of the Congregational and Christian Churches during the Council's biennial meeting in 1938 in Beloit, Wisconsin. The addition of the word "minister" to the executive officer's title was made at Horton's personal request to emphasize that the duties he was assuming were to be regarded "in a spiritual light."[1] During the term of Horton's predecessor, Charles E. Burton (1921–1938), the secretary's office had served as a hub for the exchange of general information among the Congregational churches and for the orchestration of national meetings of the various state superintendents and the denomination's agencies and boards.[2] The secretary was not the presiding officer at the biennial meetings of the General Council; this position was held by an elected moderator, either a prominent pastor or layperson. The moderator then served on the executive committee, which functioned as the General Council *ad interim* but met irregularly between General Council meetings. Soon after Douglas Horton took

---

[1]"The Minister of the General Council," *Advance*, 1 February 1938, 97.

[2]Charles E. Burton served as secretary of the National Home Missionary Societies from 1914 to 1921. He was Secretary of the National Council of Congregational Churches when they united with the Christian Church in 1931. Thereafter he was Secretary of the Congregational and Christian Churches. (Although the "and" was not dropped from the denomination's official title until 1942, I have followed the standard anachronistic practice of referring to the "Congregational Christian Churches" in this discussion).

office, however, the executive committee (now functioning like a corporate board of directors) assumed a much more prominent leadership role in the expanding work of the denomination. And the denomination's administrators, chief among them Horton himself, assumed an increasingly significant — and powerful — role in the management of the denomination's affairs.

As church historian C. Conrad Wright has suggested, the broad change in denominational bureaucracies during this period of American religious history is a much-neglected and much-needed area of study.[3] The next two chapters do not purport to be that study; rather, they represent an exploration of the tensions that arose during the Horton era as the General Council's role expanded and the office of secretary and minister assumed more power. This drama was played out in a variety of venues;[4] in particular, conflict arose around efforts to create the United Church of Christ by uniting the Congregational Christian Churches with the Evangelical and Reformed Church. This attempt followed logically, and perhaps inevitably, on the heels of Horton's *Basic Formula*, the plan devised in Chicago as a blueprint for uniting Protestant churches.

From the beginning, voices were raised in opposition to union. Horton dismissed most of these, presuming that if the persons involved had more information concerning the great ends to be achieved they would support the United Church. For example, since many members of the Evangelical and Reformed Church were ethnically German, some of the union's opponents were motivated by fear or hatred — sentiments not wholly discouraged in the American culture at large during the World War II era. Horton, of course, saw union as a way for the Church to get beyond such prejudices and, at a time of deep division, to put the world back together again.

This "ecumenical impulse" to put the world together eventually encountered far more serious opposition from various quarters within the

---

[3]C. Conrad Wright, "The Growth of Denominational Bureaucracies: A Neglected Aspect of American Church History," *Harvard Theological Review* 77 (1984) 177–94.

[4]The debate over the Committee for Social Action is one significant site of the power struggle. This conflict is examined carefully by Cyrus Ransom Pangborn in his doctoral dissertation "Free Churches and Social Change: A Critical Study of the Council for Social Action of the Congregational Christian Churches of the United States of America" (Ph.D. diss., Columbia University, 1951). Unfortunately, Pangborn's period of study ends in 1950, shortly before anti-CSA and anti-Union forces united their critical voices in opposition to the "leaders" of the denomination.

Congregational Christian denomination. These opponents argued that ecumenism, at least in the proposed form of organic union, would tear apart the fellowship that had prevailed historically in the denomination. Horton's efforts to appease this minority were unsuccessful. Furthermore, even though the opponents of union raised significant questions concerning denominational history, polity, and identity, these important matters were subsumed in a conflict of personalities. This conflict reached a temporary conclusion in a New York courtroom after one church sued to prevent the union from taking place. Ironically, that church was the Cadman Memorial Church in Brooklyn, a congregation that resulted from the merger of Horton's childhood congregation, Central Congregational Church, with several other Brooklyn congregations. Thus, the cherished name of Horton's mentor became a source of torment for Horton and other supporters of union at the midpoint of the twentieth century.

Turning Ecumenical Theory into Practice

As alluded to earlier, after his seven-year tenure as minister of United Church in Chicago and before assuming his new duties as minister and secretary of the Congregational Christian Churches, Horton embarked on a sabbatical with his wife in 1938. They traveled around the world, "meeting Congregationalists in every continent" and deepening Horton's ecumenical perspective.[5] During this tour, Horton attended the meeting of the International Missionary Council in Madras. It was the last ecumenical gathering over which the aged John R. Mott was to preside.[6] Mott had been a figure of continuity in the ecumenical movement, a link to the Edinburgh Conference and to Horton's early mentors in ecumenism, including Mackenzie and Cadman. In Madras, Horton chaired one of the International Missionary Council's commissions, as did Frederick Field Goodsell (Horton's new colleague and secretary of the American Board of Commissioners for Foreign Missions) and Henry Pitney Van Dusen, later president of Union Theological Seminary in New York. (Nearly a decade later, in 1948, Horton would begin lecturing on Congregational polity at Union.) This international dimen-

[5]Albert Peel and Douglas Horton, *International Congregationalism* (London: Independent, 1949) 58–59.

[6]Cavert, *The American Churches in the Ecumenical Movement*, 168.

sion to the ecumenical movement is one that Horton took for granted in his work as minister and secretary. But most of his subsequent opponents in the denomination did not travel in the same cosmopolitan circles as he did—nor were they convinced of the need for anyone to do so.

Back in the United States, the forty-nine-year-old Horton first addressed the General Council of the Congregational Christian Churches as its minister and secretary on 13 August 1940, in Berkeley, California. Three themes from his address would remain central to Horton and his denomination for the next fifteen years: theology, Congregational identity, and ecumenism. Indeed, the title of his speech could well serve as a summary of Horton's tenure: "Toward an Understanding of Congregationalism."[7]

The speech began with reference to the origins of the Christian community and its growing "apprehension" of God as Father, Son, and Holy Spirit. Horton drew parallels from this trinitarian formula, common to all Christians, to the "three facts of Congregational life," namely faith, freedom, and fellowship. Horton insisted that the three must be held together in a dynamic tension. Where faith dropped off, God the Father was forgotten and the community turned to humanism. Where fellowship among churches was not maintained, the community became separated from itself. To sound a warning that would reverberate throughout the next fifteen years of his career, Horton criticized those who "break up into the atomic kind of churches of which I fear Congregationalism in the last generation or so has given some illustration." Finally, he argued, where freedom was sacrificed, the churches became authoritarian and traditionalist.[8]

After discussing the nature of congregationalism, Horton moved to an intriguing parenthetical comment that seems to have received little notice at the time. He drew attention to the "sesquipedalian monster, Con-gre-ga-tion-al-ism," that had been the focus of his address so far. This was not a word one could pray, he claimed. In his preparations for the General Council meeting, therefore, Horton realized that he needed "a name for our churches which would suggest their togetherness." As

---

[7]Douglas Horton, "Toward an Understanding of Congregationalism: A Preface to the Council," *Minutes of the General Council, 1940* (New York: Congregational Christian Churches, 1940) 57–70.

[8]Ibid., 57–58.

he told the gathered Congregationalists, he had rejected the word "churches"—which did not express the unity of the fellowship—and "in the quiet of my study I therefore crossed the Rubicon which some of you have long since left behind you: I wrote a prayer for the Congregational and Christian Church."[9] Throughout the rest of his address, then, Horton referred to the denomination in the singular rather than the plural—not as a collection of many churches, in other words, but as one church. Although this ecclesiological affirmation was commonplace among the ecumenical leaders with whom Horton circulated, it was destined to become a point of controversy in his own denomination during the ensuing decade.

The remainder of the speech identified the state of the denomination and signaled existing needs and opportunities. Horton called for stronger organization, stressed the need for well-educated ministers, and expressed the desire for a common statement of faith "understandable by every intelligent layman." Under the rubric "our responsibilities to others," Horton identified encouragement of the missionary impulse to foreign lands and the ecumenical impulse from foreign lands as the two most significant activities that the denomination could undertake for the welfare of the world. Reflecting on his own recent world travels, he asserted: "[T]he only hope of the world is . . . the establishment of a world Christian community." Horton, remaining consistent with his thinking since the onset of World War I, argued that Christian community was the way to prevent "the emergence to power of any who think merely in terms of national welfare." While he acknowledged that the record of the Congregational Christian denomination was exemplary when it came to participation in cooperative agencies like the Federal Council of Churches and the emerging World Council, Horton insisted that mere cooperation was no longer enough. He announced that "the churches must grow together." Toward that end, Horton recommended the acceptance of a proposal from the denomination's Commission on Interchurch Relations and Christian Unity to invite official visitors from other denominations to future biennial gatherings of the General Council. The churches "cannot grow together unless they see something of each other officially," Horton said.[10] Within two years, delegates from

[9]Ibid., 59.
[10]Ibid., 65–67.

the Evangelical and Reformed Church were in attendance at the General Council meeting in Durham, New Hampshire.

When Douglas Horton first called for the exchange of delegates at denominational gatherings, an intimation of official contact between leaders of the Congregational and Christian Churches and the Evangelical and Reformed Church had already taken place. In a letter of 7 December 1939 to Louis Goebel, president of the Evangelical and Reformed Church, Horton noted: "Dr. Press of Eden Seminary has just written me of his correspondence with you concerning an informal discussion between representatives of your church and ours, looking to a closer rapprochement."[11]

Horton and Goebel met in New York City in January 1940. Horton had served as minister and secretary of the General Council for a little more than a year. Meanwhile, the Evangelical and Reformed Church was still engaged in the process of writing a constitution for the new denomination whose union was inaugurated in 1934 between the Lutheran-leaning Evangelical Synod of North America and the Reformed Church in the United States. Nevertheless, conversations toward union between the new partners advanced apace during the early years of the decade. By 1942 a "Joint Committee on Union" had prepared a formula for union. Several drafts of this "Basis of Union" were composed before the plan to create a new denomination, the United Church of Christ, was broadcast to the members of the two denominations.

It is remarkable how swiftly Horton and his partners in ecumenism moved during this early stage of the enterprise, particularly in light of the protracted negotiations that occurred later. On the one hand, Horton and his collaborators enjoyed full autonomy in their efforts. They proceeded unhindered until they had a proposal to place before their respective denominations. On the other hand, the nation's attention was focused on World War II, not the activities of denominational committees. Moreover, the effort to unite with *the* quintessential American denomination was probably welcome relief to members of the Evangelical and Reformed Church, whose historical ties to Germany were suspect in time of war.

The "Basis of Union" set forth the principles that would guide the new denomination: it outlined the faith "held generally" and in common by the two denominations and it described the organization of the new

---

[11]Horton to Louis Goebel, 7 December 1939, LLG.

church at the local, state, and national levels. The preamble to the document captured the sense of mission and urgency shared by the members of the committee as representatives of their denominations. It read in part:

> We [representatives], moved by the conviction that we are united in spirit and purpose and are in agreement on the substance of the Christian faith and the essential character of the Christian life; Affirming our devotion to one God . . . and our membership in one holy catholic Church, which is greater than any single Church and than all the Churches together; Believing that denominations exist not for themselves but as parts of that Church, within which each denomination is to live and labor and, if need be, die: and Confronting the divisions and hostilities of our world, and hearing with a deepened sense of responsibility the prayer of our Lord "that they may all be one"; Do now declare ourselves to be one body.[12]

Early, but relatively minor, opposition arose among the Congregational Christian Churches around the time of the General Council meeting in June 1944 in Grand Rapids, Michigan. A group of "fundamentalist" congregations (under the direction of Hilmer Sandine of the Temple Bar College in Minneapolis) threatened to leave the denomination, should union with the Evangelical and Reformed Church be pursued.[13] Various liberal church leaders on the other end of the ideological spectrum felt that the principle of congregational freedom would be compromised in a union with the Evangelical and Reformed Church. Theodore Faville, superintendent of the Wisconsin Conference, stated in a letter to Horton dated 23 March 1943: "[The Evangelical and Reformed people] are . . . reported by one who knows them better than I do to be largely Fundamentalist. We have enough Fundamentalists in our Congregationalism." Horton's response, particularly in light of his early association with the work of Barth, is revealing. Referring to the Evangelical and Reformed seminary in Wisconsin, Horton noted:

---

[12]"The Basis of Union of the Congregational Christian Churches and the Evangelical and Reformed Church," 1947; repr. in Hanns Peter Keiling, *Die Entstehung der United Church of Christ* (Berlin: Lettner, 1969) 236–53.

[13]This group left in 1947 to become the Conservative Congregational Christian Fellowship.

> If only the Mission House at Sheboygan and the churches it has established were Fundamentalist in character, the situation would almost be better than it is. Their leaders are more than Fundamentalist: they are for the most part well-educated, but they are largely given to the Barthian viewpoint. They constitute the headache of the present Evangelical and Reformed Church, and I fear they will be a headache in any denomination of which they are members.[14]

A month later, Theodore Shipherd, a pastor in Norwich, Connecticut, quoted "a seasoned Congregational minister who came out of the Evangelical group" as saying: "Some of the [Evangelical and Reformed] clergy . . . carry the shepherd-sheep idea to allegorical extremes. Sheep, after all, are dumb brutes. It usually takes a couple of generations of American tempering to get a German away from the patriarchal idea, whether in the family or the church."[15]

Ward Klopp, pastor of the First Congregational Church in Durand, Michigan, carried the ethnic implications of Shipherd's quote concerning America's wartime enemies to an extreme. With the war in Europe coming to a close, Klopp characterized the Evangelical and Reformed Church members as religionists possessed of a piety that "fights for its convictions." Thus, even though the Congregationalists were stronger numerically, if they united with the Evangelical and Reformed Church, they would be swallowed up by the Evangelical and Reformed pastors, for "their men with their dogmatic confidence will win their way into the best pulpits." As for the General Council's assertion that the two denominations were alike in their thinking, Klopp noted that the Congregationalists were inheritors of the Social Gospel and took a keen interest in the affairs of the state. The Evangelical and Reformed Church, by contrast, stayed away from politics and pursued an "individualistic ethic" that resulted in the establishment of facilities such as hospitals and homes for the aged. Klopp's prejudices were excited when he discovered that the Evangelical and Reformed Church supported two hospitals for people with epilepsy:

---

[14]Horton to Theodore Faville, 21 April 1943, BGC.
[15]Theodore Shipherd to Horton, 12 May 1943, BGC.

I would look over very carefully an organization that admitted it required two hospitals to take care of their epileptic patients. The modern psychiatrist recognizes a close
relation between wrong types of religion and epilepsy. A
religion that is negative in its approach, that emphasizes
repression rather than expression, will be productive of the
frustrations and repressions that result in epilepsy. Congregationalists do not have epileptic institutions because
there is no need for such among our membership. . . .
[Here] you have an indication of a basic divergence that
thoughtful people will consider carefully before marrying
into such a group.[16]

A few months later, in an open letter addressed to the "Friends of
Congregationalism," Klopp criticized Horton, noting that Horton was a
self-confessed "admirer of Karl Barth." Klopp went on to declare that
the whole union movement was neo-Barthian: a return to the worn-out
notion that human beings are "damnable before God," "completely dominated by evil," and "naturally vicious." With rhetorical flair and patri-
otic zeal, Klopp asked: "Are Congregationalists at the hour of greatest
victory for human liberty and freedom in history going to turn to the
Teutonic tradition and philosophy which is the negation of all that our
men have died for on the battlefields of the world?"[17]

In his responses to letters like these, Horton was characteristically
patient as well as confident that with further contact between the two
communions, misunderstandings and misrepresentations would give way
to mutual affirmation. His letter of 4 June 1945 to Klopp closed on a
typically diplomatic note:

I am greatly moved that you have taken the trouble to do
so much thinking along these lines. I hope you will carry
on—and I am convinced that a wider acquaintance would
give you a different picture of the group in its entirety.[18]

During the war years and for a while afterwards, the opponents of
union were disorganized. They often resorted to the anti-German rhetoric
of the time. And in their letters and pamphlets, the opponents tended

[16]Ward Klopp to Horton, 26 May 1945, BGC.
[17]Ward Klopp, "A Letter to the Friends of Congregationalism," 7 September 1945,
BGC.
[18]Horton to Ward Klopp, 4 June 1945, BGC.

to reveal a lack of awareness concerning the basic facts of the union process. They seemed harmless — even silly. But by 1947, the situation changed.

The Developing Controversy in the Quest for Union

A joint committee of Evangelical and Reformed and Congregational Christian delegates composed seven drafts of the "Basis of Union" between March 1943 and November 1946. Finally, in January 1947, an eighth draft was prepared and presented to the governing bodies of the two denominations for their official approval. The "Procedures" section of the document spelled out the method for ratifying the *Basis of Union* in the Congregational Christian Churches:

> In late June of 1948, at the regular meeting of the General Council [in Oberlin], the delegates will vote on the basis of previous votes taken by the Conferences, Associations, churches and members, on the question of effecting the Union. It is recommended that the General Council vote approval of the Union if seventy-five percent of the Conferences voting, seventy-five percent of the Associations voting, seventy-five percent of the churches voting, and seventy-five percent of the members voting have already approved the Basis of Union.[19]

The June 1948 date for ratification and the 75 percent figure, repeated four times in the recommendation, became key points of contention in the unfolding drama among the Congregational Christian Churches.

In July 1947, the General Synod of the Evangelical and Reformed Church adopted the *Basis of Union* by a vote of 281 to 23. And once the Evangelical and Reformed Church had expressed a desire for union in the form of a document and scheduled a uniting synod for November 1948 — pending the approval of union by the Congregational Christian Churches — opposition to the merger among the Congregational Christian Churches crystallized. One group of opponents gathered together in Evanston, Illinois, on 4–5 November 1947 to articulate opposition to

---

[19]*The Basis of Union* (8th draft; 22 January 1947; pamphlet) 3, BGC. The significance of the precise wording became a central issue in the debate between pro- and antiunionists.

the *Basis of Union*.[20] After lengthy deliberations, the 190 participants—
subsequently called "the Evanston group"—summarized their concerns
in a pamphlet that was circulated widely throughout the denomination.
They announced:

> We reject the present Basis of Union. It is a defective
> instrument for accomplishing its purposes of organic union.
> We believe the kind of union it proposes is short-sighted
> and ill-timed. We hold that the genius of Congregational-
> ism calls for a federative rather than an organic union of
> churches.[21]

The document also challenged the possibility of organic merger on
legal grounds, claiming that the very concept was contrary to congregational principles. In Congregationalism, the writers argued, only
individual churches were empowered to act on their own behalf. No
national organization could act for them. The Evanston group was
committed to ensuring that the church-by-church votes scheduled to
occur before 1 April 1948 would go against the merger.

Innocently, though perhaps ominously, a letter from Dr. Howard Conn,
dated 18 December, arrived at Horton's office during the Advent season
of 1946. It contained a request for guidance concerning the drafting of
bylaws for the young Conn's new church, the Plymouth Congregational
Church in Minneapolis. Some attention was given to the provisions
needed "for the dismissal of a minister." A minor controversy existed in
the congregation over the percentage of votes needed to effect the
minister's departure: Should the bylaws mention that matter at all?
Should a two-thirds vote be required? Or only a majority vote? Conn
requested specifically: "If the General Council publishes any standard
church manual or bylaws which could be used as a guide," his church
would welcome copies of these. Here the minister and secretary's role
as arbiter of that which was practiced generally among the Congregational Christian Churches was acknowledged and relied upon. Following an extended report on the financial and membership gains the con-

---

[20]Another group that began around the same time was the League to Uphold Congregational Principles. See Louis H. Gunnemann, *The Shaping of the United Church of
Christ* (New York: United Church Press, 1977) 30.

[21]"The Evanston Meeting, November 4 and 5, 1947," repr. in Malcolm Burton,
Disorders in the Kingdom (New York: Vantage, 1980) 292–307.

gregation had attained under Conn's ministration during the previous two years, a closing remark registered Conn's opposition to the proposed merger on two counts:

> (1) It is an unwarranted sacrifice of the historic contribution of Congregationalism whose life-story constitutes one of the major trends in American religious life; and (2) it is an unrealistic approach to the problem of church unity.

Conn then stated his preference for a federation of all churches "with open communion" nationally and with no change of denominational identity—merely the adoption of a broader affiliation—for the local congregation.[22]

In his 5 January 1947 reply to Conn, Horton enclosed a suggested form of church bylaws and noted that only a majority vote was needed "to invite the resignation of the minister." He continued: "This represents the general precedent and would undoubtedly be the standard procedure if no mention of the matter were made in the Constitution at all." The exchange suggests something about the nature of the fellowship that prevailed among the Congregational Christian Churches at the time: the general practice, unless specified otherwise, was presumed to be operative throughout the denomination. The "freedom" that characterized individual congregations was exercised in the context of a broad "fellowship."

Horton dedicated the remainder of his reply to Conn to a discussion of the union proposal. He argued that no quality of congregationalism would be lost in the union with the Evangelical and Reformed Church: "If I thought that we should lose a jot or tittle of anything that we have stood for in the past by uniting . . . I would be unalterably opposed to it," he wrote. As for the advantages of cooperative unity over the type of denominational unity that the Evangelical and Reformed Church and the Congregational Christian Churches were considering, Horton suggested that the situation confronting the Congregational Christian Churches was better represented as "both/and" rather than "either/or." He argued that the cooperative movement had advanced because of strong denominations—a gift the united church would bring to organizations

---

[22]Howard Conn to Horton, 18 December 1946, BGC. Horton had preached at Conn's ordination service at Plymouth Church in 1945.

such as the Federal Council of Churches and the World Council of Churches. In an addendum to the letter, Horton invited Conn to attend an upcoming meeting of the Joint Committee on Union, scheduled for the following month, February 1947, in Cleveland.[23]

Conn's casual reference to the merger bespeaks an indifference to it that was typical of the majority of Congregational Christian churches in the years following World War II. Meanwhile, Horton's naïve optimism about the merger's qualities was also typical of those denominational leaders who had been involved in discussions with Evangelical and Reformed Church leaders since 1942. Horton's closing note to Conn, reminiscent of his benediction to Ward Klopp, suggests that if only Conn had all the facts before him, he would embrace the union cause. Unfortunately, Conn was unable to attend the committee meeting in 1946. By 1948, however, he would have occasion to attend such meetings. His opinions about the merger would be challenged and changed. And his newfound alliance with Horton would have unfortunate consequences — at least for the latter.

Conn's early (1946) remarks to Horton sounded some of the themes that emerged from the Evanston group: in particular, the appeal to the "genius" of historic Congregationalism and the preference for federation as a union strategy. This link is not surprising inasmuch as Stanley Gillam, one of the leaders at Evanston, was also a prominent member of Conn's Plymouth Congregational Church. Gillam may have exercised a degree of influence over his pastor; or, to put it differently, Conn might have been anxious to secure the approval of this prominent parishioner in matters concerning the merger. In any case, the Horton-Conn correspondence reveals a theme that reemerged throughout the merger negotiations: powerful members of individual churches had views that opposed or challenged their pastors' views. In the end, this factor along with a variety of others conspired to set in motion a disastrous breakdown in communications about the merger among Congregational Christian leaders.

Shortly after the Evanston meeting in 1947, Conn wrote an article scheduled for publication in the February 1948 issue of *Congregational Minnesota* in which he expressed his opposition to the merger. But his views changed by January 1948. That month, Conn attended the mid-winter meeting of the Congregational Christian Churches' Missions

[23]Horton to Howard Conn, 5 January 1947, BGC.

Council; he underwent a conversion experience after reading the "Walton Report," later called "Interpretations." The report offered a favorable commentary on the *Basis of Union* written by some of those who initially had opposed it. The "Interpretations" applied what might be called an aggressive "Congregational hermeneutic" to the *Basis of Union*. Its authors chose to interpret the agreement as favoring free church polity, in general, and the importance of local autonomy in particular. The *Basis of Union*, they argued, secured the rights of congregations and boards, and thus provided protection against any authoritarian or centralized conception of church order. Characteristic of the "Interpretations" was Paragraph F:

> Congregational Christian churches do not go out of existence at the time of the union of the two communions. In consummating this union the Congregational Christian Churches and the Evangelical and Reformed Church are uniting without break in their respective historic continuities.[24]

The new interpretation qualified—or even contradicted—the more outright unitive commitment presented in the preamble to the *Basis of Union*. The preamble had announced that the two denominations, "if need be," were willing to "die" in order to be united. But the "Interpretations," if adopted, would ensure not only that local churches could not be controlled by the United Church, but that they also did not need to change at all to become a part of the United Church. The "Interpretations" were designed specifically to guarantee that Congregationalism would undergo no "death" (or even "near-death") experience in the merged church.

Conn, among other supporters of the Evanston viewpoint, was persuaded that union *in accordance with* the "Interpretations" was desirable.[25] He returned to Minneapolis "convinced that Christian statesmanship requires that we do all we can to consummate this merger." Conn therefore wrote an open letter "To the Congregational Ministers of Minnesota" as a way to warn them of his change of mind before his *Congre-*

---

[24]"The Interpretations of the Basis of Union" in Keiling, *Die Entstehung*, 252.

[25]As Horton later reported to Goebel (president of the Evangelical and Reformed Church), the document had "an electric effect" on the entire company gathered at Grand Rapids. Horton to Louis Goebel, 2 February 1948, LLG.

gational Minnesota article appeared in print.[26] As a new insider to the union cause, Conn received a letter of praise from Horton, who outlined his appreciation of Conn's courage in making a public retraction of his previous antiunion stance.

Conn was left with the delicate problem of having an active antiunionist in his congregation in the person of Stanley Gillam. But now, as an ally of Douglas Horton, he could offer his parishioner the chief executive's ear, as it were: a direct line of communication with the minister and secretary of the General Council. In his new capacity as courier, Conn relayed a variety of concerns from Gillam to Horton. One in particular had to do with the proposed *Basis of Union*. Gillam, one of many lawyers in the Evanston group, argued that the union as described in the *Basis* was not based on Congregational principles. Therefore, any church that entered into the union would leave the Congregational fold and surrender its Congregational identity. He urged the alteration of the *Basis* to ensure that the principle of Congregationalism would be carried intact into the new union. In his response, Horton assured Conn that his parishoner's objections to the merger were unfounded. What Horton had not anticipated was that Conn would give the letter directly to Gillam. This letter, dated 9 February 1948, became central to the subsequent controversy.

In his reply to Conn, Horton noted that the agreement could not be altered before the impending vote on it among the Congregational Christian churches because the Evangelical and Reformed Church had already voted its approval of the existing *Basis*. Altering the *Basis* at this point would be tantamount to starting over again and would delay union for at least three years, until the Evangelical and Reformed General Synod could vote on a new agreement. With specific reference to Gillam's objection that the proposed union was legally impossible according to the principles of Congregationalism, Horton made six points: 1) The General Council's own lawyer, Loren Wood, "believes the Basis to be thoroughly Congregational." 2) Chief Justice William Maltbie of the Supreme Court of Connecticut concurred with this assessment. 3) Despite the reasoned contrary opinion of a respected lawyer, Harold S. Davis of Boston, Horton argued that Davis began with a definition of Congregationalism that was unacceptable:

[26]Howard Conn, "To the Congregational Ministers of Minnesota," mimeographed letter dated 31 January 1948, BGC.

> viz, that Congregationalism is the polity of churches joined in a fellowship of such a type that the fellowship itself cannot act. His [Davis's] own words are: ". . . the Congregational 'denomination' is not an entity capable of taking action of any kind."

This misunderstanding of Congregationalism, Horton continued, also tainted the approach taken by Joseph Fackenthal, "a Brooklyn business man who studied law in his youth." 4) Moreover, the position that Davis held would have no standing in a court of law (Horton surmised). 5) The new entity, the United Church of Christ, would retain the polity that prevailed *in fact* among the Congregational Christian Churches: "freedom with fellowship" as opposed to freedom without the principle of fellowship. Horton noted that "we cannot keep people from suing us on this score if they want to (though I know of no one who intends to do so) but we are so sure of our ground that we have not the slightest apprehension regarding the result of such a suit." Finally, and with drastic consequences later, 6) Horton wrote that a reasoned reading on the part of Stanley Gillam would come out "where Judge Maltbie and all the other grade-A lawyers have come out," i.e., that the *Basis* was thoroughly Congregational. Horton concluded his letter by warning that it would be unfair to insist that " 'the new denomination is going to be completely Congregational' — period." Rather, members of the Evangelical and Reformed Church would contribute their values to the new church, and the Congregational Christians would contribute "the idea of the self-governing church in fellowship with other similar churches."[27]

Conn handed over Horton's letter to Stanley Gillam. Whether Gillam studied Horton's argument concerning the nature of congregationalism is not clear; what is clear, however, is that Gillam focused on Horton's characterization of Fackenthal and on Horton's reference to "grade-A lawyers." Gillam copied the letter in some form and quickly distributed it to a number of colleagues, who registered their offense in letters to Horton. The rumor of litigation from Fackenthal and a confrontational visit to Horton's office by the moderator of Fackenthal's congregation followed quickly thereafter. Horton's character was under attack, as it would be throughout his tenure as minister and secretary of the General Council.

[27]Horton to Howard Conn, 9 February 1948, BGC.

At the center of this particular maelstrom was Joseph Diehl Fackenthal, vice president of the Traprock Corporation and a trustee of the Cadman Memorial Church in Brooklyn. It is a great irony that Horton became embroiled in a controversy with the church of his childhood and youth. The debates over the merger eventually placed the Horton name in opposition to the Cadman name, and it placed the Cadman name in opposition to church union—despite Cadman's repeated pleas for church unification throughout his career. Even the tension between Fackenthal and Horton had an internecine quality to it, for Fackenthal's father, Michael, had served for many years as a deacon at Central Congregational Church alongside Horton's father, Byron.[28]

Fackenthal's position came to Horton's attention in a publication that received wide distribution after it was presented initially at the Evanston meeting by Raymond Fiero, moderator of Cadman Memorial Church. Fackenthal argued that "certain underlying legal matters" made dubious the prospect of union between the Congregational Christian Churches and the Evangelical and Reformed Church. Beginning with the premise concerning the inviolable autonomy of the local church as Church, Fackenthal argued 1) any merger between "The Congregational Church" [sic] and any other body was impossible, given that only individual churches existed in true Congregationalism; 2) any church that did consent to the merger would, by definition, cease to be a Congregational Church; 3) unless all of the churches moved into the new union, the funds held in trust for the Congregational churches by various boards, mission agencies, pension plans, and so on, would not go into the merger; and 4) members of the new church would not be entitled to the privileges afforded Congregational church members, such as admission to the "Congregational Home for the Aged."[29]

Lawyers for the General Council reviewed Fackenthal's argument and dismissed it. But the Council's legal arguments were not what Gillam— and subsequently, Fackenthal—focused on in Horton's 9 February 1948 letter to Conn. Rather, they became incensed by the reference to Fackenthal as "a Brooklyn business man who studied law in his youth" and the suggestion that "grade-A lawyers" were all of one mind regard-

---

[28]It is curious that Horton never commented on these developments. Horton's relationship to the Fackenthal family and Cadman's advocacy of church union are discussed in chapter 1.

[29]Joseph Fackenthal to Ray Fiero, 23 October 1947, BGC.

ing the Congregational nature of the *Basis of Union*. These were breaches of traditional "fellowship" at the very least, and probably grounds for a libel suit—or so suggested the injured parties.[30]

Eight days after Horton's letter was sent to Conn, the moderator of Fackenthal's congregation, Raymond Fiero, visited Horton's office in an effort to alleviate the mounting tension between Fackenthal and Horton. Apparently Fackenthal had threatened "drastic" (in all likelihood, legal) action against Horton; therefore, Horton took the precaution of making a tape recording of his portion of the conversation with Fiero so that his exact words would be available for public scrutiny. The transcript of the meeting begins: "The following is a recording, so that every word I speak will be available to anybody that wants to hear it." In the ensuing five closely-typed pages of transcript, Horton established that Fackenthal lived in Brooklyn, that he studied law "in his young manhood," and that his business was the Traprock Company. Horton insisted that this was all he had ever said about Fackenthal in his correspondence with Conn. In addition, Horton told Fiero that he dashed off the controversial letter late at night without the aid of a secretary, and he had no intention of belittling Fackenthal's reputation in any way.

The whole controversy, as Horton summarized it in his conversation with Fiero, happened this way: "This was a private letter to a private individual. He [Conn] gave it to a friend, Mr. Stanley Gillam. What Mr. Gillam did with it, I don't know." Horton stated that he had nothing against Conn sharing a copy of the entire letter with Fackenthal—as he had apparently done—but that, for the time being and as a resolution to the current crisis, he hoped that Fiero would show Fackenthal only the pertinent and exact quotation: "It is from the same angle that Mr. Fackenthal, a Brooklyn business man who studied law in his youth approaches the matter." In closing, Horton cited the adage, "the least said, soonest mended." After all the acrimony that had been generated already, Horton's desire was to have everyone concerned behave in a "gentlemanly fashion" toward one another.[31]

---

[30]Harold S. Davis, "Memorandum on the 'Basis of Union,' " 6 November 1947, BGC; Charles L. Merrill, "Comment on Mr. Harold S. Davis' 'Memorandum' on the 'Basis of Union,' " 27 February 1948, BGC. See also the letter from Wm. M. Maltbie to Horton, 6 December 1947, BGC.

[31]"Transcript of a Conversation Between Douglas Horton and Raymond Fiero," 17 February 1948, BGC.

The meeting with Fiero did not settle the matter. Horton received a number of letters from various lawyers who had also seen or heard of "the Conn letter." Rollo Hunt, of the firm Hunt, Palmer, and Hood in Duluth, Minnesota, sent a five-page letter to Horton on 18 February 1948. Hunt challenged Horton's ability to say anything about the legal aspects of Fackenthal's critique. He accused "the princes of the Congregational Church [sic] of doing more harm to the Congregational Church [by misleading the membership concerning the union] than could be repaired in a decade." He spent most of his letter describing the qualities of "grade-A lawyers" as understood by the *Martindale-Hubbell Law Directory*. By the directory's standards, Davis, Palmer Edmunds (one who had taken exception to the proposed merger), and Hunt himself were all Harvard Law School–trained "grade–A lawyers." Not all "grade–A lawyers" had reached the conclusion, in other words, that the proposed merger was legally sound. Hunt concluded by harshly berating Horton for "shooting from the hip": "There has been entirely too much of this supercilious, paternalistic . . . type of argument and innuendoes thrown around."[32]

On 3 March, Dring Needham, a lawyer in the Des Moines law firm of Emert, James, Needham, and Lidgren, and the moderator of the Iowa Conference, sent a letter to Horton requesting verification of the quote concerning Gillam and "grade-A lawyers." Horton refrained from affirming or denying the quote. Needham took this as a sign that he had the correct quotation, and so on 16 March he wrote a lengthy letter describing his personal objections to the proposed merger. He argued in particular that the *Basis of Union* granted power to people to whom it should not be given, i.e., church bureaucrats:

> I have given considerable time to the discussion and study of the Basis of Union. If I think executives will assume powers that it does not give, I am fearful. If I think, without proof, that executives are ambitious for more power, and want to assume power in all doubtful cases, I am suspicious although I could even be right. But if I think the Basis of Union gives power where power should not be given, which I do, that is not fear and that is not suspicion. It is my opinion arrived at after months of thought

[32]Rollo Hunt to Horton, 18 February 1948, BGC.

and study, and it simply strengthens my position to try to pass it off as a product of fear and suspicion.[33]

Horton's gracious reply to all of this concluded: "there is a middle way between the two extremes—a continuance of the Congregational Christian idea and an enlargement of it, but with the safeguards you rightly (it seems to me) say are needed."[34] Horton assumed that any reasonable person who was familiar with Congregational polity or history as recorded in books like Barton's *Laws of Congregationalism* (1913) or the Atkins and Fagley volume *History of American Congregationalism* (1942) would accept the desirability and the legality of the proposed *Basis of Union*.

This facile assumption was calmly challenged by Harold S. Davis of the prominent Boston law firm of Palmer, Dodge, Chase, and Davis. As he pointed out in his letter of 4 March 1948 to Horton, Davis was not a stranger to Congregational lore. His father had been the minister of the Union Congregational Church in Worcester, Massachusetts. A Unitarian faction had attempted to oust his great-grandfather, the Rev. Samuel Stearns, from the First Parish in Bedford, Massachusetts. The Unitarians were unsuccessful in their effort, and the ensuing court decision, *Stearns v First Parish in Bedford*, became recognized "as a leading authority on the function and powers of councils under the Congregational polity."[35] Indeed, childhood exposure to Barton's *Laws of Congregationalism* engendered in Davis a lifelong fascination with Congregational polity. Hence, Davis had served as legal advisor to the Massachusetts Conference of the Congregational Churches for twenty years and as clerk of Old South Church in Boston for almost thirty years. Still, he stood behind the objections he raised originally in his 6 November 1947 "Memorandum on the 'Basis of Union.' "[36]

Setting aside the issue of personalities that had arisen after the distribution of the Conn letter (Davis had received a copy from Rollo Hunt),[37]

[33]Dring Needham to Horton, 3 March 1948 and 16 March 1948, BGC.

[34]Horton to Dring Needham, 19 March 1948, BGC.

[35]Harold S. Davis to Horton, 4 March 1948, BGC.

[36]Harold S. Davis, "Memorandum on the 'Basis of Union.' " The memorandum was circulated among partisans against the *Basis of Union*. Horton referred to Davis's position in his 9 February 1948 letter to Conn.

[37]"I have examined once more the copy [of the Conn letter] which Mr. Hunt sent me and which I take to be correct. I do not see how either he or I could avoid drawing the

Davis elaborated on his objection to the proposed plan to unite:

> I think our diversity of views on this point arises from the fact that we are, as it were, speaking different languages. To a lawyer, the idea of legally significant action by or in behalf of an abstraction called "denomination," or "fellowship," or whatever it may be is as strange as the idea that iron tends to contract when heated would be to a physicist. It is undoubtedly true that the Congregational Churches have always maintained a high degree of "fellowship"—that is, of cordial diplomatic relations such as obtain between friendly nations—but this "fellowship" is much like the family of nations; either may be an entity in the metaphysical sense, but neither is such in the eyes of the law.

Davis's position is quoted at length here because the issue at stake—whether a legal entity known as the Congregational Christian Churches existed—became the matter of central significance in the ensuing court debates. Indeed, this critique may have been behind Horton's effort to establish ecclesiastical, and therefore legal, status for the General Council itself in his speech *Of Equability and Perseverance in Well Doing* and in his subsequent book *Congregationalism: A Study in Polity*.[38]

Davis wished to demonstrate that beyond personalities the question of merger presented legal and polity issues that could not be glossed over. He suggested that an effort to alter the proposal before the churches by way of compromise would be inappropriate "until the sense of the Churches has been ascertained." In response to Horton's invitation to work with other church leaders to sort out the confusion, Davis noted that his involvement would suggest a kind of support for the union movement on his part that he was not ready to give.[39]

The excitement generated by the inadvertent broadcast of Horton's letter to Conn slowly dispersed into crannies of the Congregational de-

---

inferences which we did draw. I now have, however, your insurance that the letter was so worded *per incuriam* [through carelessness] and that you did not intend the implications to which the language gives rise. Between gentlemen such an assurance is conclusive." Harold S. Davis to Horton, 4 March 1948, BGC.

[38]For further discussion, see chapter 4. Douglas Horton, *Of Equability and Perseverance in Well Doing* (26 June 1950; pamphlet); idem, *Congregationalism: A Study in Polity* (London: Independent, 1952).

[39]Harold S. Davis to Horton, 4 March 1948; see also Horton to Harold S. Davis, 27 February 1948, BGC.

nomination. Horton sent a letter to Fackenthal on 26 February in which he apologized for "the infelicity of my phrase."[40] Conn, meanwhile, expressed his appreciation for the opportunity to correspond with Horton despite the odd circumstances surrounding the Fackenthal imbroglio. Conn also registered his disappointment in the denomination, at least with reference to the recent unpleasantness, lamenting: "I had supposed that we were an intellectual and liberal people, interested in Christian unity, and that we could discuss controversial subjects without acrimony. I am discovering for how many of our people that is not true."[41]

Conn was correct about the acrimony. The Evanston group had been circulating antiunion material among Congregational Christian ministers and churches for months. A similar campaign was being waged by Malcolm Burton, a prodigious pamphleteer and son of Horton's predecessor on the General Council.[42] Then in early March, the Evanston group sent a letter to Evangelical and Reformed ministers suggesting that they would have to submit to Congregational polity—in particular, its emphasis on the autonomy of the local church—if they wanted the merger to succeed. (At the same time, the Evanston group was arguing in Congregational Christian circles that the Congregational "way" would be completely lost were the merger to take effect.) Gerhard Grauer, pastor of Saint Paul's Evangelical and Reformed Church in Chicago, wrote to Horton to express his concern and the concern of many others in the Evangelical and Reformed Church. Grauer was particularly troubled by the narrow "sectarian view" advocated by the opponents of union. He wondered if the Evanston group, as well as their followers in the Congregational Christian Churches, knew "what the term ecumenical church means?"[43] Conn, perhaps convinced that a scandal greater than the one he had engendered was now at hand, took the Evanston group's latest action as the catalyst for his own abandonment of the union cause (after three short months of disastrous advocacy). Although he did not want to

[40]Horton to Joseph Fackenthal, 26 February 1948, BGC.

[41]Howard Conn to Horton, 26 February 1948, BGC; see also Howard Conn to Horton, 2 March 1948, BGC.

[42]Malcolm Burton was the chief propagandist against Horton and the united church, probably in that order. Burton's numerous books and pamphlets must be read carefully to separate vitriol from verity. Particularly helpful is Burton's frequent inclusion of the source documents related to the events he exuberantly describes.

[43]Gerhard Grauer to Horton, 3 March 1948, BGC.

admit defeat for the merger, he did allow that "Evanston has done a rather thorough job of destroying the spiritual quality which would make Merger effective."[44]

Through it all, Horton remained optimistic about the prospect for union. He was convinced that the detractors represented a small minority among the Congregational Christians. In letter after letter he expressed his confidence that the Congregational Christian Churches would vote overwhelmingly for the merger by the upcoming deadline of 1 April 1948. Despite his optimism, however, Horton's own projection of the "pro-union" vote decreased as 1 April approached. On 18 February, Horton estimated that 88 percent of the churches would vote for union; one week later, on 25 February, he tempered this estimate to roughly 80 percent; one month later, on 26 March, he discussed with a Brooklyn lawyer what might happen if fewer than 75 percent of the churches should vote for approval.[45] Horton refrained from taking assaults on his own character personally, and he stood by his belief in the reasonableness of the union proposal to all who would take the time to study the *Basis of Union* carefully. But when he gathered with his fellow members on the executive committee toward the end of April, his unwavering—perhaps even imperial—enthusiasm was overruled.

The Cadman Decision and the Contest for Congregationalism

At their April 1948 meeting in Buck Hill Falls, Pennsylvania, the executive committee of the General Council determined not to recommend the *Basis of Union* for a vote at the upcoming General Council meeting in Oberlin: the vote among the participating congregations was falling short of the 75 percent approval figure; actual participation in the process throughout the denomination was minimal; and opposition to the union was relentless. If the coincidence of a major church union with the 1948 Amsterdam inauguration of the World Council of Churches had been the unarticulated hope of the unionists, that hope was now surrendered. The "Interpretations" that had once so impressed Howard

---

[44]Howard Conn to Horton, 11 March 1948, BGC.

[45]Horton to Walter Ross, 18 February 1948, BGC; Horton to William Lampe, 25 February 1948, BGC; Horton to Harold Warner, 26 March 1948, BGC.

Conn were in circulation, converting some skeptics among the Congregationalists to the union cause. Still, the "Interpretations" were problematic, for, as Horton and various members of the executive council were well aware, they remained a thorn in the side of the Evangelical and Reformed people, who felt the "Interpretations" did "even more to Congregationalize" the *Basis of Union*.[46] The executive committee decided that it would not be prudent for the committee itself to bring forward any merger proposals at the Oberlin General Council meeting. However, they did leave open one possibility, should the spirit of union hover over the gathering. As Horton remarked: "Well, there is nothing to prevent somebody from making a motion from the floor to go ahead."[47]

The General Council met in Oberlin in June 1948. When the discussion about the future of church union came up, a new plan was proposed from the floor: the "Interpretations" would be adopted officially as a portion of the *Basis of Union* and the entire proposal would be resubmitted to the congregations. The inclusion of the "Interpretations" into the foundational document satisfied the concern of some members of the Evanston group, who felt that the character of Congregationalism would be guaranteed sufficiently in the new church. Having successfully prevented the uninterpreted *Basis of Union* from being adopted, they disbanded. Still, many members of the Evanston group remained unconvinced by the new state of affairs and formed other opposition groups, most notably the Committee for the Continuation of Congregational Principles.

Again, the 75 percent recommendation for approval figured prominently in the discussion. In a pamphlet distributed by the General Council after the Oberlin meeting, titled *Brief Summary of the Basis of Union by a Layman*, the matter was stated this way: "The union will be consummated by the General Council of the Congregational Christian Churches . . . only on condition that the 'Basis of Union' has been previously approved by not less than seventy-five per cent (75%) of the members, churches, associations, and conferences voting on the issue."[48] Although he would later point out that this was merely a layperson's helpful description of the plan but not an official statement about it from

---

[46]Louis Goebel to Horton, 2 February 1948, LLG.

[47]Burton, *Disorders in the Kingdom*, 223.

[48]*Brief Summary of the Basis of Union by a Layman* (1948; pamphlet), point 10.

the General Council, Douglas Horton nevertheless appeared to accept the 75 percent figure for a time as a *sine qua non* for effecting the union. In a personal letter to Louis Goebel dated 11 November 1948, Horton conceded that the union would have to be reconsidered if that figure were not reached by January 1949: "A second contingency in which the whole matter would go back to our General Council would be the event of our not securing an affirmative vote of 75% of our churches." Horton then admitted: "If the matter should come back to our General Council . . . we should have to decide upon some course alternative to the one we have taken."[49]

At Oberlin it was resolved that a special meeting of the General Council would be convened in Cleveland to deal exclusively with the union matter. At that meeting on 4 February 1949, the "Committee of Fifteen," which had been appointed to oversee the voting process, reported that 72.8 percent of the churches had voted in favor of the union. In spite of this shortfall from the 75 percent figure, which had been broadcast generally since 1947, the Committee recommended that the General Council proceed toward union with the Evangelical and Reformed Church. After vigorous debate, the Council voted 757 to 172 in favor of the motion. In justifying this apparent change in rules, the Council underlined a distinction between the words "recommend" and "require." As Douglas Horton noted later in a letter to a merger opponent from Minneapolis:

> Our Commission on Interchurch Relations recommended that the General Council go ahead with the union if 75% of the churches approved it, but neither the General Council nor the Executive Committee ever accepted this recommendation (and even the recommendation did not say that the General Council should *not* go ahead if 75% of the churches did *not* approve).[50]

Whether or not Horton himself had forced the resolution through,[51] the executive committee of the General Council decided that the vote was close enough to the established figure to proceed and that the man-

---

[49]Horton to Louis Goebel, 11 November 1948, LLG.

[50]Horton to J. Gordon Bennett, 22 July 1949, BGC.

[51]Burton's *Disorders in the Kingdom* focuses on Horton's alleged manipulative role behind the scenes. A major theme of the book is signaled in the opening sentence of

date from the General Council was clear. No further concessions would be made to the opponents of the union, for, as Horton had confided to the Evangelical and Reformed Church's Goebel prior to the Oberlin meeting,"we have reached the limit of our capacity to come to terms with our minorities." The General Council was determined to proceed.[52] The green light of union at the end of the pier was almost within reach.

And so it was that Douglas Horton's hometown church stepped out-side the bounds of St. Paul's prohibition to the Corinthians and under-took a lawsuit in the secular courts.[53] Given the brouhaha that Horton kicked up inadvertently with his reference to "grade-A lawyers" in the Conn affair, it is perhaps not surprising that the church that counted Fackenthal and Fiero among its lay leadership would be the one to ini-tiate the proceedings — perhaps with the additional motive of proving its sophistication in the legal sphere. The lawsuit was filed in the New York Supreme Court (actually the state's lowest court) by the firm of Davies, Hardy, Schenk, and Soons on 19 April 1949, on behalf of the Cadman Memorial Church Society, the Cadman Memorial Church, and "other Congregational Christian Churches similarly situated."[54] The arguments in the case *Cadman v Kenyon* began on 14 November 1949; the named participants were the Cadman Memorial Church and Helen Kenyon, then moderator of the denomination.

The Cadman attorneys argued that the General Council had no au-thority to act on behalf of any of the Congregational Christian Churches; nor could it, as a representative body, unite itself with the Evangelical and Reformed Church. The General Council served the churches. If fewer than all of the churches approved of its proposed actions, those actions

---

Chapter 3, titled "Some of the Principal Personalities." Burton asserts: "The one indi-vidual most responsible for pushing the union through was undoubtedly Douglas Horton" (p. 30).

[52]Horton to Louis Goebel, 11 November 1948, LLG.

[53]"Dare any of you," writes Paul in 1 Corinthians, "having a matter against another, go to law before the unjust and not before the saints? I speak to your shame. Is it so that there is not a wise man among you? No, not one that shall be able to judge between his brethren? But brother goeth to law with brother.... Now, therefore, there is utterly a fault among you" (6:1, 5–6). This passage was referred to frequently throughout the period of court proceedings. See Keiling, *Die Entstehung*, 141.

[54]*Cadman Memorial Congregational Society v Kenyon*, 26 January 1950. The original decision does not bear an identifying number; the decision was later designated as 95 N.Y.S.2d 133.

could not be pursued. Particular focus was given to the property rights of individual congregations and monies granted by the churches to the denomination's "agencies"—that is, boards and instrumentalities. The denomination's lawyers maintained that the General Council had authority and power to act on its own behalf as an autonomous body in spiritual fellowship with the Congregational Christian Churches. Funds granted to the General Council and the agencies and boards were gifts to be used to further the denomination's interests—which these bodies were empowered to determine.

Behind the arguments on either side were conflicting conceptions of the nature of the Congregational Christian denomination. According to Cadman Memorial Church, the denomination was significantly called the Congregational Christian *Churches.* All decision-making power rested in the local congregations, the fundamental unit of the Church. No agency of the churches had any real power to do anything that any of the churches objected to. The General Council's argument was based on an understanding of the nature of Congregationalism particularly as it had developed during the twentieth century. By this theory, the General Council had the right and the power to act for itself and the churches were free to decide whether or not they wished to follow the Council's lead. When Horton was pressed on this particular issue by Judge Steinbrink, the following exchange (circulated widely by the antimerger forces) occurred. The reference is to the significance of the 75 percent vote figure as a prerequisite to union:

Court: But you now say that it didn't make a
         particle of difference which way the churches
         voted, because the Council had the power [to
         unite with the Evangelical and Reformed
         Church]?
Horton: For itself.
Court: For itself, even though the majority were
         against it?
Horton: That's theoretically possible.[55]

---

[55]Malcom Burton, *Understanding the Fundamentals of the Merger Trial* (Committee for the Continuation of the Congregational Christian Churches: 9 May 1950; pamphlet), 2, BGC.

In particular, Horton argued that the General Council had power to operate within its own sphere and was autonomous. This argument was built into the *Basis of Union*. Freedom to act was given the Council as it was to all other Congregational bodies. Even if all the churches were against the union, the General Council had legally—that is, by church polity—the right to pursue merger. Because of the responsibility in fellowship (a moral, but not a legal, restraint on freedom), Horton claimed, this kind of unilateral action would never happen. But, he maintained, it was allowed to happen.

Horton was cautiously optimistic about the General Council's chances of obtaining a positive verdict in *Cadman v Kenyon*. The General Council had received permission from the court to make tentative plans for a uniting conference in June 1950. And in a letter to William T. Scott, the superintendent of the Southern Convention of the Congregational Christian Churches, Horton discussed the steps to be taken by the conferences in anticipation of the merger: "We should make all plans possible in a decent and orderly way, without waste of time but without haste. Our attorney . . . believes that the uniting meeting may be held in Cleveland on the 26 of June."[56] The letter to Scott was written on 24 January, the same day that hearings in the Cadman case were concluded. Judge Steinbrink announced to the court on that day that he would be prepared to deliver his decision orally two days hence. And within two days, Horton's hopes for a significant church union at the midpoint of the "Christian century" were dashed. On 26 January, Judge Steinbrink called the *Basis of Union* a "conglomeration of confusion and conflicting statements with a cacophony of ideas." Furthermore, he ruled that the General Council "has not now, and never had power or authority" to act on behalf of the Congregational Christian Churches.[57]

When the written judgement appeared a month later, it was clear that Judge Steinbrink had sided entirely with the plaintiffs. In a lengthy decision, he "ordered, declared and adjudged," among other things, that 1) the General Council had neither the power nor the authority to act on behalf of "the separate Congregational Christian Churches." 2) Votes taken for or against the " 'Basis of Union' with or without 'Interpretations' " committed no one to become a member of the United Church of Christ. 3) The polity of the Congregational Christian Churches was "that system of

[56]Horton to William T. Scott, 22 December 1949, BGC.
[57]Quoted in "Merger Deferred," *Time*, 6 February 1950.

church organization which recognizes the autonomy of the local church in all matters temporal and spiritual." 4) All funds held in trust by the General Council and the various boards and agencies of the Congregational Christian Churches were intended for the benefit of those churches alone—"for the purpose of carrying out and aiding the Christian way of life through the basic principles, usages, and polity of the Congregational Christian Churches"—and hence those funds could not be put to other purposes. In addition, Judge Steinbrink decreed that the General Council was permanently "enjoined and restrained from carrying out or consummating" the *Basis of Union* either on the churches' behalf or its own behalf; that funds of the General Council could not be used for the purpose of promoting union; and that all persons inside and outside the Congregational Christian fellowship were prohibited from aiding or cooperating with the General Council in any union activities.[58]

Between the announcements of the oral and written decisions, Horton's position wavered on what recourse the General Council ought to pursue. Already on 1 February, in a letter to his former parishioner Wilhelm Pauck, Horton spoke of "the absolute necessity of appeal." He identified three ways in which the Steinbrink decision proved menacing:

> (1) We as a denomination are menaced because our fellowship is broken up. Servants cannot be part of a fellowship, and the decision plainly makes all other bodies the servants of the local churches. When two or three are gathered together in the Cadman Church, the Lord is in the midst of them—but not so when two or three are gathered in the General Council! (2) American Protestantism is menaced because hereafter denominations cannot legally unite except by the unanimous consent [of all the churches]. (3) All organized American religion is menaced because, if the state can reach in and fix our polity, it can do so in regard to any group, Catholic, Jewish, or Protestant.[59]

Horton noted, however, in a letter sent to Dr. Frederick R. Meek of Old South Church in Boston two days before the written decision was rendered, that although the vast majority seemed to favor an appeal as "the only way out," he would not favor the process unless "it was a

[58]*Cadman v Kenyon*, 20 February 1950.
[59]Horton to Wilhelm Pauck, 27 January 1950, BGC.

very bad judgement indeed." Horton argued that it would be better to "reform" the denomination itself so that false perceptions of essential Congregationalism, such as those held by Judge Steinbrink, would not be perpetuated, and "so as to become what we thought we were."[60]

On the third day after the written decision was handed down, the denomination's Committee of Lawyers submitted its report to the Procedures Committee of the General Council. The three lawyers were unanimous in their recommendation to appeal the Steinbrink decision. They enumerated twelve points of objection falling along the lines Horton had outlined in his letter to Pauck. Particular emphasis was placed on the disastrous consequences to the movement for unity among Protestant denominations and the impediment to growth placed on churches sharing a polity similar to that of the Congregational Christian Churches.[61]

Meanwhile, the mainline religious press also expressed its concern. Henry Pitney Van Dusen, president of Union Theological Seminary in New York, focused on the damage done to the ecumenical movement. In his *Christianity and Crisis* article "A Blow to Christian Unity," Van Dusen noted that "Congregationalism has been in the forefront of almost every movement for the larger unity of Christ's church" and that the Steinbrink decision made the whole movement impossible.[62] A *Christian Century* article two months later characterized the court's decision as a dangerous infringement on religious freedom. A follow-up article appeared in the next issue on the significant topic, "What Are the Principles of Congregationalism?"[63] Horton had investigated this matter a decade earlier in Berkeley; he would take it up again at the biennial meeting of the General Council in June in Cleveland.

---

[60]Horton to Frederick Meek, 6 February 1950, BGC. Dr. Meek had been an early and influential opponent of the union. With the addition of the "Interpretations," he became a cautious supporter who would, perhaps, welcome Horton's approach as outlined in this letter. Meek's significant parishioner, Harold Davis, figured in the "grade-A lawyer" fiasco.

[61]Loren N. Wood, Gurney Edwards, and David K. Ford, "Report of Lawyers Committee," 23 February 1950, BGC.

[62]Henry Pitney Van Dusen, "A Blow to Christian Unity," *Christianity and Crisis*, 20 March 1950, 25–26.

[63]"Religious Liberty Denied to Congregationalists," *Christian Century*, 31 May 1950, 670–72; "What Are the Principles of Congregationalism?," *Christian Century*, 7 June 1950, 694–96.

*   *   *

Horton came to the role of minister and secretary of the General Council as an activist in the international ecumenical movement. He was shaped by the conviction that the Church was called to visible unity as a way to confront, in the words of the *Basis of Union*, "the divisions and hostilities of our world." As an international leader, Horton was very successful in advancing the cause of cooperation and union within the larger Congregational family and among many denominations. At the same time that opposition to union was mounting within the Congregational Christian Churches, for example, Horton was involved in preparations for the first assembly of the World Council of Churches in Amsterdam. One year after that assembly, in 1949, Horton was elected moderator of the International Congregational Council (ICC). Under his leadership, the ICC ended its practice of meeting on an *ad hoc* basis every ten years or so and established permanent officers. Horton's responsibility as moderator of the ICC was to serve as a link among Congregational churches around the world: to visit them on behalf of the ICC and to offer them support, particularly in the cause of church unity.

These signs of ecumenical advance stood in sharp contrast to the seemingly minor and often petty opposition that Horton encountered within his own denomination in relation to the plan to unite with the Evangelical and Reformed Church. Horton's careless characterization of Fackenthal's position, Fackenthal's personal attack, and Conn's confusion were all part of a general atmosphere in the denomination that focused on personalities and prejudices. Perhaps for this reason, Douglas Horton tended to underestimate the opposition. If nothing else, the Cadman case demonstrated the strength of the opponents and the seriousness of their case against uniting. It also called into question Horton's basic presuppositions about the ecumenical character of Congregationalism—a matter that was never fully addressed during the protracted union conversations, as the continuing conflict within the Congregational Christian Churches demonstrated.

CHAPTER FOUR

The United Church of Christ Resurrected

T he plan to unite the Evangelical and Reformed Church and the Congregational Christian Churches advanced because the leaders of both denominations remained convinced of the necessity for church union. Negotiations began during World War II; the effort continued into the Cold War era. The unity of the churches, according to many in the ecumenical movement, could be the one sign of hope in a world that was not only fragmented, but also bent on self-destruction—as the charred remains of Hiroshima signaled.

In October 1945, Horton served as chairman of the first American civilian deputation to travel to Japan following the war. President Harry Truman wrote to Horton: "if Japan is to evolve into a peaceful nation, with an internationalistic as against a nationalistic outlook, she must understand the religious forces of the world. . . . Your deputation should in a large measure aid in solving this fundamental problem facing Japan."[1] At the conclusion of his visit, Horton composed the deputation's report. In response to the destruction that was everywhere present in Japan, Horton offered one solution: "this is the theme which we bring home to our American Christian friends and to our Christian friends throughout the whole world. Oneness in Christ—it is the hope of humanity."[2]

[1]Harry S. Truman to Horton, 16 October 1945, CDH.
[2]Douglas Horton, et al., *The Return to Japan: Report of the Christian Deputation to Japan* (New York: Friendship, 1945) 60.

Horton shared this conviction about unity with his counterparts in the Evangelical and Reformed Church. It enabled them to contemplate together what would become a first in the history of American Christianity: a denominational union across confessional and polity borders. The Evangelical and Reformed Church was theologically Lutheran and Reformed; creeds from both traditions were taught and revered throughout the denomination. The church polity was essentially presbyterian. The Congregational Christian Churches, on the other hand, were free churches without, at least in principle, any specific confessional identity. Their polity was congregational. But a large and vocal minority within Horton's own denomination did not make the automatic connection that he did between visible unity in Christ and the transformation of the world into the kingdom of heaven. The urgency of the situation was not at all self-evident to Horton's opponents. As a consequence, neither the prounion nor the antimerger forces within the Congregational Christian denomination really understood the other. This lack of mutual understanding fueled the conflict that had reached a temporary conclusion with the *Cadman v Kenyon* decision in early 1950.

Ultimately, in the debate leading up to the Cadman decision, Horton's effort to appease the minority had given way to the majority's rule, in part because Horton's own history and polity arguments were not generally convincing. Important issues of Congregational history and polity were at stake in this debate, but these were never resolved. Thus, despite an official denominational union, a dubious ecclesiology and other conflicts were carried eventually into the merger by the Congregational Christian Churches.

(Re)defining Congregationalism

As the General Council's lawyers chose to cast the matter, Judge Steinbrink's decision was a case of state interference in church affairs. The separation of church and state, accordingly, had been breached.[3] Meanwhile, in publications such as the *Christian Century*, numerous articles considered the implications of the decision for the future of ecumenism, in general, and for the Congregational Christian Churches as a denomination, in particular. It was against this backdrop that Horton

---

[3]The General Council's appeal of *Cadman v Kenyon* was based on the presumption of this breach.

addressed the internal problem concerning the nature of American Congregationalism at the General Council meeting in Oberlin in 1950.

Horton titled his address to the General Council, *Of Equability and Perseverance in Well Doing*. These words appealed to the collective memory of Congregationalists with a famous phrase from the saintly John Robinson, the revered Congregational minister of Scrooby, England, and later Leyden, Holland. Horton drew upon the Cold War atmosphere that pervaded the nation in the aftermath of the Soviet Union's recent bomb detonation in September 1949. He introduced his topic with a discussion of the "dangerous opportunity" that confronted all Congregational Christians "with ramifications both for American Protestantism today and our whole future." He continued:

> The issue is of the nature of uranium and helium. That is to say, its value depends upon how we handle it. We can use it to destroy our fissionable fellowship and others with us, or we can deal with it so constructively, that our own churches and the larger Church of Christ will through us be blessed by it. The issue is as to the structure of the Congregational Christian denomination.[4]

Horton presented the options for the Church in parallel to those that faced the world. On the one hand, there was the struggle between the "free" and the "communist" worlds — a struggle brought home through the investigations of the House Committee on Un-American Activities. On the other hand, there was the hope for greater understanding that the emerging United Nations represented. The universal Church, too, had to choose between schism or greater Church unity. Horton recommended historic Congregationalism as the natural form for the Church of the future because of its flexibility, which Horton saw as Congregationalism's gift to the ecumenical movement. But the "comforting communal blur of spirit" that pervaded the American denomination itself could persist no longer. The time had come to delineate precisely what congregationalism was.

---

[4]Horton, *Of Equability and Perseverance*, 1. Philip Schaff, in serendipitous anticipation of Horton's address, announced shortly after his arrival in the United States in 1844 that the inner logic of congregationalism led to complete "atomism." Doubtless Schaff did not fully expect that his nineteenth-century critique of Congregationalism's polity problems would be examined, finally, during the "atomic age" (*The Principle of Protestantism*, 121).

Perhaps with reference to Kierkegaard's notion of "Religion A" and "Religion B" — where Religion A was a kind of religiosity that pervaded Christendom but did not attain to the essential Christianity of Religion B — Horton drew a distinction between "Congregationalism A" and "Congregationalism B."[5] Both kinds of congregationalism shared two factors: they both insisted that the local church had control over its own affairs and they both allowed for no authority (save Christ) over the local church. The issue of control was crucial in Horton's deliberation. In Congregationalism A, the "organizations of fellowship are dependent upon the local churches." They could not act, change, or progress, without the approval, theoretically, of all the local churches in the denomination. Indeed, the denomination itself was something very unlike other American denominations according to this scheme, for it referred to the local churches alone. All other agencies of fellowship were servants of the Congregational Christian churches. The General Council, therefore, as one of these agencies, "must abide by the direction of its 5,700 masters."[6]

In contrast, Congregationalism B stood for "freedom" (to maintain the parallels to the Cold War rhetoric). An organization like the General Council was not controlled by the churches; rather, it was controlled by its own members. The General Council functioned as a local church in relation to the rest of the fellowship. Horton gathered a number of "denominational units" into his argument — the Association, the Conference, and the General Council, along with the American Board of Commissioners for Foreign Missions, the Board for Home Missions, and the affiliated colleges — and declared them all independent in their own spheres. Of course, the freedom these units enjoyed was Christian freedom, which meant "freedom to be Christianly responsible":

> Between the various bodies [within the denomination] . . .
> there is no master-servant relationship: it is that of friend to

[5]See Søren Kierkegaard, *Concluding Unscientific Postscript* (trans. David F. Swenson and Walter Lowrie; Princeton: Princeton University Press, 1941) 493–98. This book was very popular among theologians at the time. Consider, for example, the Kierkegaardian echoes in H. Richard Niebuhr's "Concluding Unscientific Postscript," the final chapter of his still-influential *Christ and Culture* (New York: Harper, 1951). See also the comment of Robert McAfee Brown comparing the "rediscovery" of Kierkegaard with that of P. T. Forsyth in n. 9 below.

[6]Horton, *Of Equability and Perseverance*, 3.

friend. The organs of fellowship serve the local churches not because they must, but because they may, and in the same spirit the local churches contribute to the organs of fellowship.[7]

Horton concluded that Congregationalism B was the actual polity of the Congregational Christian Churches and it was the polity that would be perpetuated in the new denomination through the *Basis of Union*.

The theological crux of Horton's argument was not presented orally in the Minister's Address to the General Council, but it was included in the written document distributed widely by the General Council after the Oberlin meeting. In this addendum, Horton developed the notion of local autonomy as it pertained to local churches; he then applied the theory to the General Council on the biblical principle that "where two or three are gathered in Christ's name, there is Christ in the midst of them": "this is the beginning of all authority in the Church, a worshipping company in one spot inquiring for the will of God with Christ in its midst."[8] Thus the Council in its biannual meetings, as well as the bureaucracy that executed its will *inter regnum*, became a kind of local congregation, with the same rights and responsibilities as all "churches" to the fellowship and to God. Calling upon the ghost of P. T. Forsyth, who was enjoying a second career at the time among Congregationalists and Protestants in general (Forsyth's orthodoxy led some of his disciples to call him "a Barthian before Barth"),[9] Horton reminded his readers that the local church was an "outcrop" of the Church Catholic in a particular place. This vision of catholicity informed Horton's interpretation of congregationalism and, for that matter, ecumenism in general.

At the conclusion of his address, Horton called for calm during the time of the court appeal. Reviewing the progress of union conversations since 1938, Horton recommended the example of equability demonstrated

[7]Ibid., 6.

[8]Ibid., 8.

[9]Indeed, Horton's nephew, Robert McAfee Brown, was gathering material for his Union Theological Seminary doctoral dissertation on P. T. Forsyth during 1950. The dissertation was subsequently published as *P. T. Forsyth: Prophet for Today* (Philadelphia: Westminster, 1952). In his introduction, Brown quotes Horton's colleague, Truman Douglass: "I would say that the rediscovery of P. T. Forsyth . . . may be as momentous for the quickening of Christian thought as the return of Kierkegaard after a century of obscurity" (p. 9). Horton first heard Forsyth preach in Mansfield College at Oxford in 1913.

by members of the Evangelical and Reformed Church. He noted that they had both given up their own polity to accept congregational polity[10] and they had spurned an overture for union from the Presbyterians, remaining true to their engagement to the Congregational Christian Churches. He alluded to the possibility of drawing up a constitution before the union was effected.[11] "Equability" meant bringing all the groups together to work their way together out of the crisis. "Perseverance in well doing" meant to continue the Church's missionary enterprise—to wage the battle against Satan, as Horton had said earlier in the address. But this required a mighty and large church. Only Congregationalism B, he concluded, was equipped to accomplish such a monumental task.[12]

Of Equability and Perseverance in Well Doing was Horton's key contribution to the union debate among Congregationalists. It served as a summary of the difficulties encountered thus far in the movement toward union and it foreshadowed (perhaps even initiated) conflicts yet to come. The greatest contradiction imaginable from an ecumenical point of view would be to create schism in pursuit of church union and unity. Fear of such an outcome—reflected in the injunction against extended discussions of the trial—explains Horton's cautious engagement of his opponents in the Congregational Christian "fissionable fellowship."

---

[10]This would not have played well to an Evangelical and Reformed audience. Indeed, on more than one occasion Horton emphasized to Congregationalists that they would not have to give up anything but would gain a great deal in the union. Evangelical and Reformed people tended to speak in terms of the mutual sacrifices necessary for the sake of greater union. In a 1985 interview, James Wagner, successor to Goebel as president of the Evangelical and Reformed Church, noted: "Doug Horton was the kind of chap who was so anxious to smooth things over and meet objections which were being raised by all sides, that without (I am sure) ever intending it to be this way, it amounted to the fact that he was talking out of both sides of his mouth and saying one thing to one group of people and another thing to another (group)." See George H. Bricker, "James E. Wagner Remembers: An Oral History Interview," *Historical Intelligencer* 3 (1985) 6.

[11]This initial openness to writing a constitution in advance underscored Wagner's critique, mentioned in the previous footnote. After further discussions with the Evangelical and Reformed people, Horton distanced himself from the constitution-before-union idea and this became a focal point for conflict among Congregational Christians in the ensuing years.

[12]Horton, *Of Equability and Perseverance*, 7–8.

Horton advanced three highly contestable arguments in favor of Congregationalism B. The argument from history claimed that Congregationalism B, though a twentieth-century development, was in direct continuity with Congregationalism since its arrival on the shores of New England in the early seventeenth century. Here Horton favored the arguments of the historians Champlin Burrage and, above all, Perry Miller, over against the reigning Congregationalist historians of the denomination: Gaius Glenn Atkins and Frederick L. Fagley, and the venerable Williston Walker.[13] Horton accepted the thesis that Congregationalism as it developed in America should trace its origin not to the Separatist tradition of Robert Browne but to the Puritans of the Massachusetts Bay Colony. John Robinson of the Leyden Church in Holland also figured prominently here, especially the developments in his theology before the departure of some of his members to the Plymouth Colony. Horton developed this argument more completely in his 1952 book, *Congregationalism: A Study in Polity*.

Horton's second argument was pragmatic: Congregationalism B enabled the denomination to act quickly and effectively in the ecumenical community, in mission to the world, and in the ongoing battle against the Devil. During the Cold War era, Horton felt the Church needed a united force to combat the Devil's agents. Although he did not supply specific examples of these agents, surely the threat of atomic annihilation and the likelihood of war in Korea provided evidence of their work. A corollary to this argument (not taken up specifically in the address, but articulated in numerous letters of the period) was the need for strong ministerial leadership in the denomination. Horton felt that a numerically and organizationally weak denomination would not attract excellent ministerial candidates from the seminaries; indeed, he anticipated

---

[13]Both Champlin Burrage in *The Early Church Dissenters* (Cambridge, England: Cambridge University Press, 1912) and Perry Miller in *Orthodoxy in Massachusetts* (Cambridge, Mass: Harvard, 1933) argued against the notion that the Separatist strain in Puritanism was the primary source of American Congregationalism. Gaius Glenn Atkins and Frederick L. Fagley, in *History of American Congregationalism* (Boston: Pilgrim, 1942), and Williston Walker, in *The Creeds and Platforms of Congregationalism* (New York: Scribner, 1893), took the opposing view. Frederick Fagley was a member of the executive council during the early years of the union controversy; he supplied Malcolm Burton with minutes from that committee's meetings. In his 1960 introduction to *Creeds and Platforms*, Horton offered a lengthy corrective to Walker's historiography.

"an exodus" of the denomination's most promising seminarians to other churches because "strong organizations attracted strong leaders."[14]

The third argument in favor of Congregationalism B was ecclesiastical. Here, Horton defined Congregationalism B's polity in terms of freedom and fellowship, with the bureaucracy designated as an autonomous unit, like a local congregation. Because, according to congregational principles, all that was necessary to be an outcropping of the "Church Catholic" was contained within the local congregation, Horton had to describe the bureaucracy as a congregation in order for it to be on an equal footing with all the other churches. He could not, as the Evangelical and Reformed Church could, describe the whole complex of relationships among synods, conferences, churches and denominational leaders as "the Church," since each individual church was sufficient unto itself as a church under the authority of Christ. Ironically, therefore, Horton had to assert the principle of local autonomy on behalf of the General Council, even though he described this principle in other contexts as an enemy to ecumenism.

It may be that this conception of the General Council as "Church" was behind Horton's insistence, already in 1938, that the title of his position include the word "minister" in addition to "secretary of the General Council." Horton argued that the General Council was like a church because worship, including preaching and the celebration of communion, occurred while the General Council was in session. But did these activities make it a church in the congregational sense of the word, therefore entitling it to the "rights" of local autonomy, or, as Horton preferred to say, "authority within its own sphere"? This matter of the bureaucracy's role and power became the focus of debate within the Congregational Christian Churches throughout the union controversy. As an unresolved matter, then, Congregationalism B became one of Douglas Horton's enduring contributions to the United Church of Christ.[15]

[14]Horton further stated in a letter to Harold Bruce, professor of government at Dartmouth College: "What will happen if we do not unite? There will be a general exodus of our leading thinkers and spiritual guides. This will begin in our seminaries, where most of our ecumenical pioneers are found. Our present ministerial shortage will be cruelly augmented by the departure of seminary students and young ministers into other denominations." Horton to Harold Bruce, 13 January 1949, BGC.

[15]In addition to C. Conrad Wright's "The Growth of Denominational Bureaucracies," see the articles by two United Church of Christ seminary presidents: Benjamin

William Scott, a Horton ally, explored the implications of Horton's position in a letter that may have been intended humorously. Scott put forward a request that certain ordination candidates from Union Seminary in New York receive their ordination in the so-called "Church of Christ in the General Council" so that their loyalty to the denomination might be duly recognized. Horton dismissed Scott's suggestion, noting that the Church of Christ in the General Council was intended simply for those "who cannot unite with any ordinary local church." Horton recommended instead that the young men in question unite with the Riverside Church, the Broadway Tabernacle, "or some other regular church." But the point remained: if the General Council was indeed a church, did it ordain ministers? For that matter, did it baptize new members? The difficulty of seeing how it could perform such basic church tasks led many of Douglas Horton's detractors to reject the concept of polity embodied in Congregationalism B.[16]

One final aspect of Horton's address was significant: the suggestion to establish a constitution as a preliminary step toward union. For reasons that will be explored presently, a constitution might appease those in the Congregational Christian Churches who wanted guarantees in advance of the merger, but the very idea was contrary to the "ecumenical spirit" of the Evangelical and Reformed Church.

Of Equability and Perseverance in Well Doing was the first volley in the protracted match over twentieth-century American Congregationalism. By resolution of the General Council at the 1950 meeting, a committee was established to study issues of polity and unity, then report back to the General Council with findings that would clarify for the denomination the true nature of Congregationalism. Called, initially, the "Committee on Congregational Polity and Church Union," it included representatives of both pro- and antiunion camps. The committee was chaired by L. Wendell Fifield, whose brother James was pastor of the denomination's largest church, First Congregational Church in Los Angeles. James was also the West Coast leader of the opposition group

---

Griffin, "A Movement in Search of Church: Some Unfinished Business for the United Church of Christ," *Prism* 7 no. 2 (1992) 52–60; Peter Schmiechen, "The Church as an Image of Reconciliation: An Analysis of the Crisis in the United Church of Christ," *Prism* 9 no. 1 (1994) 7–26.

[16]William T. Scott to Horton, 31 December 1953, BGC; Horton to William T. Scott, 4 January 1954, BGC.

called "Anti-Merger." Wendell Fifield, meanwhile, was pastor of the Plymouth Church of the Pilgrims in Brooklyn, among whose members was Mr. Kenneth Greenawalt, another leader in the antimerger movement and the lawyer for the Cadman Church. Wendell Fifield was deemed by all to be a fair and reasonable man whose mildly partisan position in favor of the union cause was tempered by the significant opposition to union within his own family and congregation. Other members of the committee included Roland Bainton, church historian at Yale; Liston Pope, biblical scholar and dean of Yale Divinity School; Henry David Gray, self-described "mediator" in the merger controversies and pastor of the Oneonta Congregational Church in Pasadena, California; and Malcolm Burton.

Within days of Horton's address, the Committee for the Continuation of Congregational Christian Churches of the United States, a group headquartered in Chicago, published a significant pamphlet in opposition to Congregationalism B. The pamphlet was offered as part of the ongoing conversation that the Committee on Congregational Polity would need to take into account in its assessment of true congregationalism. *Congregationalism B: Replies to the Address "Of Equability and Perseverance in Well Doing"* ridiculed Horton and praised the Steinbrink decision.[17] The guiding hand behind the pamphlet was Malcolm Burton. The pastor of Second Congregational Church in New London, Connecticut, Burton had been present at the Cadman trial (at Mr. Greenawalt's side) from the third day of deliberations onward. Early on, he launched his own pamphleteering campaign against the merger. Burton was the son of the previous secretary of the General Council and perhaps for this reason he took a particularly personal interest in the denomination's nature and destiny. He received copies of executive committee minutes through Frederick Fagley, associate secretary of the General Council—a practice begun in 1947 when debates about the merger from all sides were encouraged in *Advance*, the denomination's newspaper. The debates were cut off by editor Scotford after several months because of their divisive quality. But no one told Fagley to stop sending

---

[17]Marion Bradshaw, Malcolm Burton, T. M. Shipherd, et al., *Congregationalism B: Replies to the Address "Of Equability and Perseverance in Well Doing"* (Committee for the Continuation of the Congregational Christian Churches of the United States: circa August 1950; pamphlet).

minutes to Burton, so inside information found its way into Burton's numerous pamphlets and went out to Congregational Christian ministers and, on occasion, to Evangelical and Reformed Church leaders as well.[18]

Burton was ungenerous and prone to attribute the worst possible motives to his opponents. His vituperative rhetoric made him easier to dismiss than the quality of his arguments actually warranted. His extended essay in the *Congregationalism B* pamphlet, titled "In Reply to Dr. Horton," for example, made a strong case in favor of Congregationalism A, as Horton had labelled it. Against the charge that in Congregationalism A every single church must give approval before the General Council could act, Burton countered that it was only when the General Council "tried to do something contrary to its own nature" that the problem of the churches' collective approval arose. The General Council was free to initiate "all the inspirational programs it wants to without the consent of every church." But the real issue was whether or not the General Council had the power to create a new body, in this case the United Church. Burton insisted that it had no such power, neither on behalf of the churches nor "merely" for itself.[19]

The heart of Congregationalism B was the theory of "independent spheres of autonomy." Judge Steinbrink called this theory "a conglomeration of confusion and conflicting statements with a cacophony of ideas." The contradiction to which Burton was particularly drawn rested between the claims that the General Council spoke only for itself *and* that the General Council discerned and then spoke the mind of the whole denomination. Moreover, in arguing that the General Council spoke only for itself, Horton had claimed that the members of the Council were independent individuals. But as Burton pointed out with reference to Barton's *Law of Congregational Usage*, delegates to the National Council (and its successor, the General Council) were representatives of the churches. Again, the council and the bureaucracy that represented its interests *inter regnum* could not be powers unto themselves; their power came from and was returned to the churches. If this was so, then the idea that the General Council could effect an "organic union" and in

---

[18]Burton recounts these details in *Disorders in the Kingdom*, 40–41.
[19]Malcolm Burton, "In Reply to Dr. Horton," in *Congregationalism B*, 19, 21.

particular act "only for itself" was a denial of the nature of the fellowship that Burton maintained ought to prevail among the Congregational
Christian churches.[20]

Burton's sustained and reasoned objection to Congregationalism B
focused on the improvisational character of the denomination's polity
as Horton presented it. Burton admitted that this polity was preserved in
the *Basis of Union*; but that was precisely why Burton was against the
Basis of Union. According to Burton, Horton actually was proposing a
new kind of polity—one that enabled the executive committee to be
more "adventurous," particularly in the ecumenical realm. But these in-
novations, Burton claimed, were not traditional Congregationalism.

Marion Bradshaw, professor at Bangor Theological Seminary, also
cast the debate in relation to the "exciting ecumenical movement." He
pitted the movement toward "organic union" over against Protestant liberalism and argued that a loss of freedom resulted from the effort to
marshal the forces of Protestantism into one large and fixed religious
organization. More power than was necessary or appropriate was granted
to the leaders of the churches involved in the movement and this led
inevitably to power over the local congregations. Bradshaw pointed to
the irony in the assertion that the ability to fight social ills was only
effective if the church was a powerful, authoritarian force. The cause
and the ultimate goal were liberal, but the means, Bradshaw argued,
were totalitarian.[21]

Bradshaw also suggested that the source of Horton's Congregationalism B was traceable to Karl Barth and not to the liberal Protestant
tradition in which, Bradshaw claimed, American Congregationalism
stood. Despite the fact that the World Council of Churches in general
rejected the notion that the Council itself was in any way a church,
Bradshaw pointed to Barth's address to the First General Assembly at
Amsterdam entitled "The Church—The Living Congregation of the Living Lord Jesus Christ" as a key to Horton's alleged concern to sanctify

---

[20]Ibid., 21. What Evangelical and Reformed members would think of this notion of
"organic union" is never addressed directly in the papers under study, but the commitment of an autonomous church council and its bureaucracy to union was foreign to the
Evangelical and Reformed Church's understanding of "organic." Organic, for them,
meant that the entire denomination committed itself to union with another denomination; out of that union a new church body would emerge.

[21]Marion J. Bradshaw, "On the Denominational Divide," in *Congregationalism B*, 15.

denominational structures. Speaking of the relationship that pertained among local congregations, synods, and the free associations related to them for such purposes as mission and education, Barth was quoted as saying: "they also live by the grace given to the one Church, and in fulfilling their service to the one Church, *they too are churches in the full sense of the word*."[22]

Bradshaw's comments are particularly instructive in relation to the quality of the opposition to Congregationalism B. Bradshaw focused on the tendency of Congregationalism B toward centralized authority, which he rejected. He also rejected the ecumenical movement to the extent that it reflected this tendency. "Organic union" would result in a diminishment of the local church's authority, according to Bradshaw. Many others like him preferred the concept of "federated union" as a means of cooperating among churches without surrendering local autonomy. But this position was consistently cast as being antiecumenical by the pro-union partisans.

One final comment from the *Congregationalism B* pamphlet is worth noting for the insight it offers into the personal nature that the conflict had assumed since the Howard Conn affair. In his essay "Congregationalism 'Aye' or 'Nay'?," S. T. Roberts discussed the difference between "*Grade* A" and "*Grade* B" Congregationalism. The Philadelphia businessman's reference to the controversy about "Grade-A" lawyers was a subtext that ran through the eight paragraphs of Roberts's critique, resolving in an endorsement of the Steinbrink decision and a victory for the lawyers Horton had allegedly demeaned in his infamous letter to Conn.[23]

Friendlier opposition to Douglas Horton's Congregationalism B could be detected among various supporters of the proposed union. Frank M. Sheldon, pastor of the Center Congregational Church in Lynnfield, Massachusetts, expressed his fundamental support for the denomination's effort to appeal the Steinbrink decision. He understood the court's ruling concerning the essential nature of Congregationalism as "unwarranted" and an invasion of the state into a religious matter. Sheldon did take exception, though, to Congregationalism B and suggested, in one remarkably long sentence, that the very concept may have led to the

---

[22]Ibid., 15.
[23]S. T. Roberts, "Congregationalism 'Aye' or Nay'?," in *Congregationalism B*, 6–7. Emphasis added.

General Council's initial failure in the courts (a concern echoed frequently among the ecumenically inclined):

> May it not be that emphasis upon your position, which apparently was accepted by some of our defense witnesses, and possibly our attorney, turned attention in the trial from what should have been our main defense, namely, that free, independent, autonomous local Congregational Christian Churches, in all local church matters, have as part of that freedom, the right to send representatives to create and develop and *control* organizations which shall do certain things committed to them by these local churches, and that these churches may, through like representatives at times change and modify these organizations which they created.[24]

Sheldon also recalled his own work as a member and chair of the Commission on Inter-Church Relations and Christian Unity during the period when the Basis of Union was hammered out. He drew attention to the section of the document that dealt with government, which was "exercised through Congregations, Associations, Conferences and the General Synod in such wise that the autonomy of each is respected in its own sphere." Sheldon insisted that this provision had been intended to affirm the autonomy of the denomination's agencies only in the restricted spheres "granted them by the churches through the delegates who represented those churches." He also noted that members of the Evangelical and Reformed Church would not be likely to embrace the notion of "unrestricted autonomy."[25]

Horton was genuinely gratified to receive "friendly" criticism of his position and even noted on one occasion during his exchanges with Sheldon: "I don't know when I've had more fun (of this kind) than I'm having now in discussing the matter of Congregational polity with you."[26] Horton may have used this dialogue to develop a distinction that would find its full articulation in his book on Congregational polity, published in 1952 and dedicated to Fifield's "Committee on Free Church Polity and Church Union." In relation to the responsibility that prevailed among the churches and the General Council, Horton drew a distinction be-

---

[24]Frank Sheldon to Horton, 1 July 1950, BGC.
[25]Ibid.
[26]Horton to Frank Sheldon, 1 August 1950, BGC.

tween moral and spiritual responsibility, on the one hand, and legal (that is ecclesiastical or civil) compulsion on the other. He argued that the General Council had no legal responsibility to the churches; it was wholly independent of them ecclesiastically (as a church among churches). And yet "the very glory of Congregationalism lies in the fact that though the council is not bound legally to report to the churches, it devotes itself wholly to them." This moral and spiritual responsibility, according to Horton, was the basis of true Christian fellowship. Otherwise, as soon as the General Council became a "representative democracy[,] the denomination turned toward Presbyterianism."[27]

Another friendly critic of Congregationalism B was David Beach, pastor of the Center Church in New Haven, Connecticut. Although sympathetic to Douglas Horton's general view of a "connectional" congregationalism, Beach, like Sheldon, objected to the idea that the General Council and its interim bureaucracy somehow constituted a wholly autonomous "congregation." Lack of clarity on this point, Beach feared, would lead to further losses in the courtroom. He proposed, therefore, that a committee meet with the General Council's lawyer, Loren Wood, to discuss the true nature of representative congregationalism. Unless a clear description of the denomination's true polity could be conveyed to its lawyer, Beach feared that subsequent presentations of a confused polity in court would only result in more failures:

> My diagnosis of Mr. Woods [sic] is that he has lost the true dimension of the woods, which provide both freedom for the local churches and representative power for the order of our fellowship, in the indubitable trees of our liberty.[28]

In his response, Horton encouraged Beach to contact Wood directly. Horton conveyed Wood's (and his own) enduring understanding that "the General Council is not representative of the churches in the sense generally understood in American law." This determination, presumably, resulted from a careful study of the General Council's constitution. Horton also noted that Wood would base his appeal on the assertion that Judge Steinbrink had no jurisdiction over spiritual matters; the only real

[27]Ibid.
[28]David Beach to Horton, 23 November 1950, BGC.

issue in the case should be over property rights—which, in any case, the *Basis of Union* guaranteed to the local churches.[29]

Mollified by the plan for the appeal, Beach still refused to accept the notion that Congregationalism B accurately described the relationship prevailing among the Congregational Christian churches. He stated the heart of the matter in a letter to Horton dated 11 November 1950: "In our double heritage—our separatism and the connectionalism—every argument, however accurate either from the point of view of law or of practice which emphasizes the freedom of the General Council, supports separatism."[30] In other words, Horton could point to a long historical tradition of fellowship and mutual recognition of churches (extending back to William Ames and the early days of Puritanism), which could be drawn upon in support of the ecumenical impulses of the whole denomination and, in particular, the General Council. Still, as long as the General Council insisted that it operated "legally" (that is "ecclesiastically") only on its own behalf—as an autonomous entity—the basic polity beneath this insistence was separatism. Ironically, from Beach's point of view, Horton effectively embraced the polity of his opponents to argue that they had no "control" over the General Council.

As an alternative to both Congregationalism A and B, Beach (perhaps inevitably) proposed "Congregationalism C." The "C" stood for "conciliar" (or "Connecticut") as the true form of American Congregationalism. Beach and the Board of Deacons at the Center Church devoted years of study to the concept in communication with the investigations undertaken by the Fifield Committee. According to Center Church, the basic tenet of Conciliar Congregationalism held "that each Congregational Christian Church has the power and the duty to act through councils."[31] Thus councils could act; they did have power, as the Cambridge Platform of 1648 and the Saybrook Platform of 1709 had established. Councils were not essential to the actual being of a church, but they were necessary for its well-being. On the other hand, councils were not "like churches," contrary to Horton's famous assertion. When the General Council met, the churches were being represented in that assembly, according to Beach.

---

[29]Horton to David Beach, 31 October 1950, BGC.

[30]David Beach to Horton, 11 November 1950, BGC.

[31]"Conciliar Congregationalism and the Center Church Amendment," n.d. [1954], 1, BGC.

Beach and his board of deacons circulated a number of pamphlets that put forward the case of Congregationalism C to the denomination. The most significant of these was a twenty-two-page document called *Three Constitutional Proposals: A Study of the Conciliar Tradition Among the Congregational Christian Churches in the United States*. The principle argument of *Three Constitutional Proposals* was that the Congregational Christian Churches had always been conciliar. This tradition was preserved in the merger of 1931 and, most significantly, enshrined in the General Council's "Constitution." Thus, when the Constitution stated, "The purpose of the General Council is to perform on behalf of the united churches," it meant that the council was a representative body of churches. But Center Church conceded that the statement could be confusing and was made so by advocates of Congregationalism B in particular. Therefore, they proposed three amendments to the Constitution that would spell out the precise nature of the denomination's polity once and for all.[32]

In a letter of appreciation and criticism, Horton attempted to persuade Beach of the imprecision of *Three Constitutional Proposals* and, therefore, of the inappropriateness of bringing the document before the 1954 meeting of the General Council in New Haven. Horton also wished to avoid a conflict with the report from the Committee on Congregational Polity and Church Union, already scheduled for presentation at the meeting. He encouraged a sharpening of the issues that then might be presented at a later General Council meeting.[33] Actually, Beach's

[32]*Three Constitutional Proposals: A Study of the Conciliar Tradition Among the Congregational Christian Churches in the United States* (New Haven: First Church, 1954) 22.

[33]Horton to David Beach, 30 March 1954, BGC. Beach and the Center Church did refine their arguments and shaped them into the "Center Church Amendment" for adoption by the General Council in 1956. They argued that the General Council's Constitution was flawed precisely because to the extent that no legal, i.e. ecclesiastical, responsibility was imposed upon the agencies, the sense of Church broke down. On "church" principles, the local congregation was the church. To be an equal and autonomous denominational unit, therefore, the bureaucracy had to be a church. On this point Horton was logical, but the theory had no historical precedent. Only in recent times had a perpetual bureaucracy come into being. True, agencies for cooperation and councils to attend to specific problems were formed, and there was an unbroken tradition of fellowship as opposed to Separatism. But, according to the Center Church Amendment, Congregationalism in America was a history of representation on behalf of churches — not individuals or self-perpetuating and autonomous agencies. By the time this pro-

position in the *Three Constitutional Proposals* was quite well formulated. Beach offered an articulate challenge to Horton's concept of Congregationalism B. Horton may have wished to keep the proposal out of the discussions at New Haven, in part because it favored a Congregationalism that would be familiar to the hometown crowd.

While the Beach proposal did not come to the fore in New Haven, the "Fifield Report" did. This was the report undertaken by the Committee on Congregational Polity and Church Union, constituted in 1950 to respond to issues concerning congregational identity and practice. The Fifield Report was a major disappointment insofar as it could not describe a definitive congregational polity. After four years of study, the Committee remained significantly divided on the issue. L. Wendell Fifield outlined the problem clearly in a letter to Beach: "The crux of the whole matter of unity on the polity level is the relationship of the General Council to the churches, or the proper powers of the General Council in view of its own nature and the principle of autonomy of the local church."[34] Convincingly persuaded by no particular viewpoint, the committee report offered no conclusive description of Congregational Christian polity. The opportunity Horton signaled as presenting itself in *Of Equability and Perseverance in Well Doing*, namely to define the true nature of "this fissionable fellowship's" polity, remained, after four years, unresolved; and Horton's description of Congregationalism B — one available, articulated alternative — did not, in fact, meet with general acceptance in the denomination.

Perhaps it was inevitable that no definitive statement could be made about the polity because there was no definitive polity, no clearly defined church order. This conclusion was drawn by James L. Gustafson, at the time a Yale doctoral student concerned with sociological method. In his report prepared for Fifield's committee, Gustafson traced the same history and came to many of the same conclusions about congregational polity as Horton, Beach, and Sheldon. Then he characterized the present situation in the denomination as one of paralysis or "anomie." The hope toward which Gustafson pointed but of which he saw no sign in the

---

posal was presented, the uniting synod with the Evangelical and Reformed Church was in sight and Center Church's insights seemed irrelevant. In fact, they were not, as the subsequent history of the United Church of Christ has revealed.

[34]L. Wendell Fifield to David Beach, 15 February 1954, BGC.

contemporary church was "a new synthesis of contemporary apprehensions of the faith and adequate sociological forms."[35]

The "anomie" problem was not resolved through the reestablishment of a strong theological platform upon which to order relationships within the denomination (or, at least, with Beach, constitutional language to define these relationships). The urgency to clarify church order associated with the Steinbrink decision was not, as it turned out, a central factor in the subsequent court appeals. The matter focused on whether the General Council had power to act on behalf of the churches. Once it was determined that it did, the problem became how to bring as many churches as possible into the union. This process led to the final crisis on the Congregational trail toward union and to Horton's eventual departure from the scene.

Victories for Unity and the Lingering Controversy

On 5 May 1952, the Appellate Division of the Supreme Court of New York handed down its ruling in *Cadman v Kenyon*. The ruling criticized the Steinbrink decision for, in effect, "interfering with ecclesiastical matters in which temporal rights are not involved." The court limited its focus to the matter of the General Council's right to use funds collected from the churches. It established that no "fiduciary obligations" were legally imposed upon the General Council. In other words, all funds given to the General Council were "absolute gifts" and the General Council had the right to use them as it saw fit. The court refused to discuss ecclesiastical or doctrinal questions, leaving those issues to be resolved by the denomination itself.[36]

The Cadman Church appealed the case next to the Court of Appeals, the highest court in the state of New York. In its decision of 3 December 1953, this court too ruled in favor of the General Council. Against the Cadman Church's argument that Congregationalism would be altered by the merger, the Court declared: "the proposed union will in no way change the historical and traditional pattern of the individual Congrega-

[35]James L. Gustafson, "A Study in the Problem of Authority in Congregational Church-Order" (circa 1953; mimeograph) 30, BGC. For further discussion of the "anomie" problem, see Keiling, *Die Entstehung*, 71-73.

[36]Decision of the Appellate Division of the Supreme Court, Second Judicial Department, State of New York, *Cadman v Kenyon*, 279 App. Div. 1074, 5 May 1952.

tional Christian church." Furthermore, the General Council had no power to compel any church to participate in the union. The traditional "freedom" of the churches was not threatened by the merger. Finally, the *Basis of Union*, which was a voluntary agreement in any case, did not interfere with the faith or worship of any congregations. Underlining the findings of the Appellate Court, the Court of Appeals determined that the funds given to the General Council were gifts and that, despite allegations to the contrary, it had not been demonstrated that General Council funds had been used for anything other than authorized purposes.[37]

Although these court decisions never addressed the matter of "true" congregational polity (because that was an ecclesiastical matter), they effectively legitimized Horton's Congregationalism B, at least insofar as the court dealt with the General Council as if it were some kind of legal entity. In other words, the court recognized the bureaucracy's power to act on its own behalf. Whether or not that meant that the bureaucracy was "a kind of church," the Court declined to comment. The General Council, meanwhile, directed its efforts to guarantee that the autonomy of the local church would prevail in the new church since retaining local autonomy was the grave concern of numerous dissenting churches. One way to ensure autonomy was to enshrine the principle in the new denomination's constitution.

Already in 1950, Horton appeared to advocate drafting a constitution in advance of union with the Evangelical and Reformed Church, as his address *Of Equability and Perseverance in Well Doing* suggested. Recognition of the general concern for a constitution was codified in a resolution adopted by General Council in 1952. The "Claremont Resolution," as it came to be called in the ensuing debates, instructed the executive committee on how union conversations should proceed if and when court restrictions were removed. Three points figured prominently in the subsequent controversy among the Congregational Christians. The "Claremont Resolution" 1) called for a joint meeting of Evangelical and Reformed and Congregational Christian delegates who would, "if both [groups] approve," assume responsibility for the preparation of a draft of a proposed constitution for the anticipated, united fellowship; 2) re-

---

[37]Decision of the Court of Appeals, State of New York, No. 388, *Cadman v Kenyon*, 306 N.Y. 151, 3 December 1953.

quested that the executive committee be in communication with the Committee on Free Church Polity and Unity throughout the drafting process; and 3) underscored the concern among Congregational Christians that the draft "preserve all the spiritual and temporal freedoms and rights" traditionally enjoyed by the Congregational Christian Churches.[38]

In numerous letters with members of his own denomination, Horton emphasized the need to develop a constitution.[39] But these exchanges occurred during a period when direct contact with the Evangelical and Reformed Church was prohibited by the unresolved Steinbrink decision. After the decision from the Court of Appeals in 1953, the churches were free to reenter into negotiations and Horton's position on the matter of a constitution changed, at least in part because much had changed in the Evangelical and Reformed Church between 1950 and 1953. For one, Louis Goebel, Horton's executive counterpart since 1938, went into retirement. He was replaced by James Wagner, once pastor of Saint Peter's Evangelical and Reformed Church in Lancaster, Pennsylvania, more recently vice-president of the denomination, and a longstanding member of the Evangelical and Reformed committee on church union. Wagner did not express the same enthusiasm for union as had his predecessor.

For the first time since the Steinbrink decision, on 8 February 1954, an informal meeting took place between advisory committees of the Evangelical and Reformed Church and the Congregational Christian Churches. Wagner was characterized in the official minutes of that meeting (probably written by Horton) as maintaining "it would be a relief to his Church if it were decided not to resume negotiations looking toward the proposed union."[40] For a time in early 1954, Horton was telling his

---

[38]Resolution 52 G 28, adopted by the General Council of the Congregational Christian Churches on 20 June 1952, *Minutes of the General Council, 1952* (New York: General Council of the Congregational Christian Churches, 1952) 23.

[39]For example, Horton to S. Reid Chatterton, 28 March 1950, BGC; Horton to John H. Alexander, 6 August 1952, BGC; Horton to David Beach, 30 March 1954, BGC.

[40]"Brief Minutes of the Joint Meeting of the Administrative Committee of the Evangelical and Reformed Church and the Advisory Committee of the Executive Committee of the General Council of the CC Churches," 9 February 1954, 1, BGC. Also quoted in the letter from Gerhard Grauer to Horton, 20 February 1954, BGC. Writing to correct the record, Grauer went on to say: "If such a statement was made, it must have been in connection with any additional concessions or new ideas which might be offered to hold up proceedings."

correspondents that the merger was dead.[41] This news was particularly well-received by Congregationalist opponents of the union with the Evangelical and Reformed Church. There was even talk of opening up conversations with the Disciples of Christ, who had expressed an interest in uniting with the Congregational Christians as far back as 1940.[42] This relationship was considered worth pursuing by many members of the executive committee, including Vere Loper, pastor of the First Congregational Church in Berkeley. He argued that the "best possibility" for the union idea, in light of the opposition gathered against the Evangelical and Reformed Church, was "with the Disciples."[43]

Given the prevailing mood of uncertainty about union in both the Congregational Christian and Evangelical and Reformed denominations, the formal meeting that had been scheduled for April between executive committees from the two groups was postponed until October. In the meantime two important meetings took place in the separate denominations. At a meeting of the Evangelical and Reformed General Council (that denomination's equivalent of the Congregational Christian executive committee), also held in February, great emphasis was placed on "the ecumenical Spirit of our Church" and the responsibility it levied upon the leadership to accomplish church union.[44] In the aftermath of that meeting, Robert Brodt, pastor of the Salem Evangelical and Reformed Church in Allentown, Pennsylvania, wrote to Horton to inform

[41]Horton to Alfred Rapp, telegram, 8 February 1954, BGC: "[Wagner] told us quite definitely that so far as he was concerned it would be a relief if negotiations were not taken up again"; see also the letter from Horton to Mrs. Jean Reed, 15 February 1954, BGC: "I don't think you need worry about the proposed union between the Evangelical and Reformed Church and the Congregational Christian Churches. From what I hear, the Evangelical and Reformed will be giving it up."

[42]Horton to Alfred Rapp, 8 February 1954, BGC: "The Disciples of Christ have now signified that they want to enter into negotiations with us."

[43]Vere Loper to Horton, 16 February 1954, BGC; see also Horton's reply of 18 February 1954, BGC. See also the exchange between Horton and Warren Wilder Towle, minister of the Congregational Christian Conference of Missouri, 25 and 27 March 1954, BGC. Towle argued that a "covenant plan" with the Disciples was far more likely to succeed than the "organic union" upon which the Evangelical and Reformed Church insisted. Horton replied that he intended to keep in close contact with the Disciples, whose polity, at least, posed no barrier to union (theologically, on the other hand, Horton anticipated "disagreements").

[44]Quoted in Keiling, *Die Entstehung*, 157, from the Minutes of the General Council of the Evangelical and Reformed Church, 16–18 February 1954, 5.

him that the hesitancy about union expressed by Wagner was not the general attitude of the Evangelical and Reformed Church. Brodt enclosed with his letter a copy of an article he had written for his denomination's magazine. The proponents of the merger merely needed a little time to rally their forces, according to Brodt, who argued that "[the] difficulties to be overcome in completing the merger are not too great a price to pay for loyalty to the ecumenical ideal."[45] This information, however, was not broadcast widely to the Congregational Christian Churches.

In the months preceding the second significant meeting, the biennial meeting of the Congregational Christian Churches at New Haven, the *Christian Century* featured several articles suggesting that the merger would not take place for a long time, if ever. The first of these, "Is Congregationalism Sectarian?," was written by Roland Bainton, a member of the Committee on Church Unity and Polity. Bainton spelled out the difficulties already encountered in the union effort. He noted the lingering fear of "totalitarianism" among many opponents of the union. And while he argued forcefully in favor of union, his lengthy article leaves the impression that the Congregational Christian Churches would need much more soul-searching before union could become possible.[46]

Three months later, the *Christian Century*'s 12 May 1954 editorial page raised the provocative question, "Congregationalists to Drop Merger?" The writer noted that the executive committee "does not anticipate that it will have any recommendations on the merger" for the upcoming General Council meeting in New Haven. Had all the court battles been pursued and won, the writer wondered, just so that the majority might surrender to the will of an obstinate minority at this late date? Somewhat sarcastically, the editorial concluded with the suggestion that the leadership of the denomination should be handed over to the merger's opponents, for they were the ones who were really setting the denomination's ecumenical agenda.[47]

In his 6 June 1954 article "A Communication," James Wagner responded to the earlier editorial. He noted that all members in the Evan-

[45]Robert D. Brodt to Horton, 30 March 1954, BGC. See also Robert D. Brodt, "This is Our Opportunity," *The Messenger of the Evangelical and Reformed Church*, 12 January 1954, 16–18.

[46]Roland Bainton, "Is Congregationalism Sectarian?," *Christian Century*, 24 February 1954, 234–38.

[47]"Congregationalists to Drop Merger?," *Christian Century*, 12 May 1954, 573.

gelical and Reformed Church were "deeply conscious of the continuing imperative resting upon the followers of Christ to persist in the efforts seeking to repair the rents in the garment of his Body, the church." The upcoming meeting of the General Council, he suggested, would indicate to the Evangelical and Reformed leadership how to go about accomplishing this task. Wagner wondered what the Fifield Committee would have to say about the nature of Congregational polity. He wondered, too, about the extent of dissident sentiment in the Congregational Christian Churches. Finally, he wondered what the Claremont Resolution meant when it called for a "constitution for the General Synod of the united fellowship." This phrasing sounded to Wagner, at least, like a merging of bureaucracies, not the organic union the Evangelical and Reformed Church desired. So he called for patience and understanding. "Rome was not built in a day," he concluded, suggesting that a long span of time would precede any union.[48]

No proposal toward union with the Evangelical and Reformed Church was presented by the executive committee of the Congregational Christian Churches at the General Council meeting of 23–30 June 1954, in New Haven; however, a resolution from the floor was passed to continue negotiations toward the merger. The Council also received the report of the Fifield Committee, with its multiple descriptions of Congregational Christian polity. In light of the turmoil over the church union problem in recent years, Wendell Fifield himself argued that a "covenant fellowship" should be the preferred approach to ecumenism among Congregational Christians, not the "organic union" sought by the Evangelical and Reformed Church. In another proposal passed by the delegates, the "New Haven Resolution" reaffirmed the commitment to union as it had been expressed already in the "Claremont Resolution" in 1952. The executive committee was entreated to proceed according to the earlier instructions "so far as they are still applicable."[49] In his summary of events for the *Christian Century*, Harold Fey noted: "Opinion here seemed to indicate that it will take some years to complete the process of union with the Evangelical and Reformed Church" but that such a union was not absolutely impossible.[50]

---

[48]James Wagner, "A Communication," *Christian Century*, 2 June 1954, 676.

[49]Minutes of the General Council of the Congregational Christian Churches, 23–30 June 1954, 21–22.

[50]Harold E. Fey, "Congregationalism—Plus?," *Christian Century*, 14 July 1954, 845–47.

Two conflicting ecumenical trajectories converged in Cleveland in October 1954 and led to what would become the final episode of Horton's official involvement in the effort to unite the Evangelical and Reformed Church with the Congregational Christian Churches. On the one hand, public opinion in general held that if the Evangelical and Reformed and Congregational Christian merger were to take place at all, the union would not be consummated for quite some time. From the Evangelical and Reformed side, serious questions had been raised, in particular by the denomination's new president, about the possible contours of any agreement between the two churches. From within the Congregational Christian Churches, it was assumed by many, in particular the opponents of the union, that negotiations would have to start all over again: a new constitution, at least, would have to be written and agreed upon by the churches before the union could go ahead. But in opposition to this gradual approach, there was another ecumenical trajectory, one that passed through Evanston—the site, it will be recalled, of the earliest organized opposition among Congregational Christians to the union—acquiring, in transit, a certain sense of urgency.

During August 1954 the World Council of Churches had convened its Second General Assembly in Evanston. Horton served as chair of the American Committee for the assembly. George Richards (Barth translator and president of the Reformed Church during its merger with the Evangelical Synod) was also a member of that committee. And many of the leaders of the two denominations had been actively involved in the gathering, including Horton's second wife, Mildred McAfee Horton, whom he had married in 1945 after the death of Carol Williams Horton. So when the representatives of the Evangelical and Reformed and Congregational Christian executive committees met in Cleveland to discuss future union possibilities, expectations for the proposed United Church of Christ were low even while hopes for the universal Christian Church were high.

The joint meeting began with presentations from the two denominational leaders. James Wagner expressed "major concerns, if . . . not profound misgivings" about the state of affairs as they existed between the two churches. Wagner caught the Congregational Christian leaders off guard: they had no prepared answers to his concerns and were in a state of confusion. In his improvised response, Horton suggested that the *Basis of Union* provided sufficient grounds for negotiations, were they to proceed.[51] This observation addressed, in part, Wagner's "misgivings." Still, in the joint committee meetings as well as the separate meetings that were interspersed between them, there seemed to be little hope of bringing the two churches closer together. Raymond Walker, minister of the First Congregational Church in Portland, Oregon, and chair of the Congregational Christian executive committee, noted at one point that "twelve years of efforts seemed to be ending in futility."[52] For their part, the Evangelical and Reformed people were prepared to put forward a resolution composed by Louis Goebel, calling for the end of negotiations should any deviation from the existing "Basis of Union" be introduced by the Congregational Christian Churches. The primary reason for the resolution—which, however, was never introduced into the joint discussions—was the perceived agitation for a constitution in advance of union.[53]

But contrary to the seemingly inevitable disappointment, a wholly unexpected change occurred. According to Raymond Walker's report, "the Spirit of a new Pentecost fell upon the baffled company."[54] The recent World Council General Assembly in June was recalled. With the watchwords of that assembly—"Christ calls us to mission and unity"—in mind, the joint committee returned to the concern that had inaugurated negotiations twelve years earlier: how to make unity in Christ a visible reality. The Congregational Christian group accepted the Evangelical and Reformed position, acknowledged earlier by Horton, that the *Basis of Union* already provided a sufficient framework for a new constitution. The leaders of both denominations unexpectedly brought this position back to their members:

> In accordance with actions of the General Council of the Congregational Christian Churches and the General Synod of the Evangelical and Reformed Church, we reassert the

[51]James Wagner, "Preliminary Statement on the CC-ER Merger Prepared for the Joint Meeting of the CC Executive Committee and the Evangelical and Reformed General Council," 12–13 October 1954, 5, BGC. This narrative follows the account of Keiling, *Die Entstehung*, 158–59.

[52]Raymond Walker, "Report and Reflections Concerning the Joint Meeting of the Executive Committee of the General Council of the Congregational Christian Churches and the General Council of the Evangelical and Reformed Church, held at Cleveland, October 12–13, 1954," BGC.

[53]See the important "Confidential Resolution on the Union," BGC.

[54]Walker, "Report and Reflections," 2.

validity of the Basis of Union with Interpretations as the basis for this merger. We feel that the matter of the drafting of a constitution is adequately provided for in this instrument.[55]

While this statement generally satisfied supporters of union in both churches, it came as a shock to those within the Congregational Christian Churches who assumed that efforts with the Evangelical and Reformed Church had been totally thwarted or at least severely restricted by the "Claremont Resolution."

Many voices were raised in protest against the executive committee's proposed course of action. In addition to longstanding opponents of merger such as Malcolm Burton and the Committee for the Continuation of Congregational Christian Churches, certain heretofore "moderates" entered the fray, among them L. Wendell Fifield. Fifield's "balanced view" of the union issue prior to the events of October 1954, "despite many pressures to which he had personally been subjected," had long been a source of admiration and respect among proponents of the union.[56] But in an open letter to the executive committee that was published in the Congregational Christian magazine, *Advance*, Fifield registered his objections to the "new plan of procedure" devised by the executive committee to promote the cause of union with the Evangelical and Reformed Church.

Fifield's numerous complaints are reducible to a few key points. Most remarkable is the sense he conveyed of calculated betrayal on the part of the denomination's leaders. He accused them not only of completely ignoring the report that he and his committee had worked four years to produce, but he also alleged that the executive committee advanced a new plan of union "in direct contradiction to the definite instructions" contained in the "Claremont Resolution." In contrast to the careful procedure developed in light of the Cadman case and resulting in the recommendation to produce a constitution, the executive committee had responded "overnight" under the alleged "guidance of God's spirit" with a proposal that effectively mocked the sacrificial work of countless "consecrated people" over a long period of time. Moreover, the plan to rein-

---

[55]Statement attached to "Minutes of the Joint Meeting of the Congregational Christian Executive Committee and the Evangelical and Reformed General Council, October 12–13, 1954," 5, BGC.

[56]"An Official Reply to Dr. Fifield's Letter," *Advance*, 12 January 1955, 3–4.

troduce the *Basis of Union* and "Interpretations" was a response to the wishes of the Evangelical and Reformed Church; it did not reflect the general concerns of the Congregational Christian Churches as Fifield understood them. Finally, nothing less was at stake for Fifield than the very nature of the Congregational Christian fellowship. "There is no middle ground," he concluded. "Many who have been pro-merger will be anti-usurpation."[57]

The executive committee's response was printed next to Fifield's "Open Letter" in the 12 January 1955 issue of *Advance*. With specific reference to the full text of the "Claremont Resolution" (which accompanied the two letters), the executive committee noted that the provision for a constitution was contingent on the approval of the Evangelical and Reformed and Congregational Christian leaders. Already in his memo of 22 November 1954, Raymond Walker (in consultation with Horton) explained that the *Basis of Union* represented the only established legal grounds upon which negotiations could proceed. In addition, the loyalty of the Evangelical and Reformed people through years of litigation needed to be honored.[58] Since neither group, ultimately, approved of the preparation of a constitution, the executive committee felt that it was operating in the spirit of the "Claremont Resolution" to forego this option.[59] As for the allegation that the "new plan" emerged overnight, the committee pointed out that the *Basis of Union* had been the focus of the union process "overwhelmingly sustained by the General Council" since 1942. Fifield's major theological reference was to the Holy Spirit. He had written: "The assumption that a program worked out in a few short hours, based upon the wish-thinking of a preponderant majority, expressed the guidance of God's spirit, seems to me the greatest tragedy of this whole tragic business." Although the committee reiterated that many more than "a few short hours" were required to arrive at the proposed program, they refrained from commenting upon "the theological implications of Dr. Fifield's denial of the power of the Holy Spirit to illumine minds 'in a few short hours.' " As for the implication that the leaders had usurped power, the committee called upon all

[57]L. Wendell Fifield, "An Open Letter," *Advance*, 12 January 1955, 2–4.

[58]Raymond Walker, "Why Didn't the Executive Committee at its October 1954 Meeting Initiate the Drafting of a Constitution for the United Church?," 22 November 1953, BGC.

[59]"An Official Reply," 3.

Congregational Christians, the minority as well as the majority, "to address their arguments to the issues at hand and to refrain from the impugning of motives and threats of schism and lawsuits."[60]

The Oneonta Controversy

The opponents of union frequently leveled the accusation that a radical authoritarian strain had been interjected into Congregationalism since the appearance of Douglas Horton, an authoritarianism that threatened the centuries-long tradition of freedom within and among the churches. This refrain was most often sounded in the writings of Malcolm Burton, for whom Horton always represented a deviation from the standard of leadership set by Burton's father. What Horton saw as the need for effective organization, leadership, and denominational strength was often equated with the larger demons of the American psyche during the extended period of union negotiations. Thus, in the early phases of the process, the perceived authoritarian impulses of the prounion forces were linked to the fascist values of America's mortal enemies (and the cultural forbears of the Evangelical and Reformed Church): the Germans. Later the Communists were alleged to lurk behind the ecumenical impulse toward union. Indeed, a careful study of the rhetoric employed against Horton from the time of the Cadman case onward would probably reveal close affinities to the tactics of Joseph McCarthy, who was also active during this period. If this is so, then the story of these descendants of Plymouth might supply an interesting contemporary supplement to Arthur Miller's theatrical commentary on the era, *The Crucible*, which made its debut in January 1953.

In a report submitted to the executive committee shortly after the resolve was made to continue to pursue union, Raymond Walker characterized a large portion of the union opponents as "more fundamentally opposed to Horton and other denominational officials" than the union per se.[61] Indeed, Burton wrote a lengthy letter to Horton and Wagner, questioning the authenticity and authority of statements made by Horton. The tone of the letter, written by Burton in his capacity as

---

[60]Ibid.

[61]"Report from Raymond Walker regarding an appearance before a meeting called by the 'Committee for the Continuation of Congregational Christian Churches in the USA,' " 4 November 1954, 2, BGC.

director of the Committee for the Continuation of the Congregational Christian Churches, is remarkable for its vehemence. Without explicitly calling Horton a liar or deceiver, Burton came close:

> The fact that Dr. Horton cites no authority for the definite statements he has made would seem to indicate that he cannot readily and convincingly do so. The fact that Dr. Wagner does not confirm Dr. Horton's statements would suggest that they do not conform to the understandings which Dr. Wagner sought to arrive at in the Cleveland meeting when, to use his words, "We tried to our utmost to make sure that we were no longer dealing in ambiguities."[62]

Horton refused to respond directly to Burton's letter, suggesting that it was composed "in a manner which is not customary in letters written by gentlemen." Instead, he wrote a letter to the executive secretary of the Continuation Committee, Howell Davies, in which Horton declined "to enter into a quarrel with the son of [his] distinguished predecessor."[63] But "quarreling" had long been a feature of the merger controversy among Congregational Christians. It is interesting to note the letterhead of the Committee for the Continuation of Congregational Christian Churches of the United States in this regard. Among the illustrious opponents of the proposed United Church of Christ were listed Joseph Fackenthal and Raymond Fiero, both of whom figured prominently in the "grade-A Lawyer" conflict of the late 1940s, which also centered more on personalities than theology or ecclesiology.

The dominance of personalities over issues was particularly evident in the events leading up to the "Oneonta controversy." The Oneonta Congregational Church in Pasadena, California, invited Horton to speak about the proposed union with particular reference to the decision not to compose a constitution prior to union. Because Oneonta was a relatively friendly church situated in close proximity to numerous antimerger churches, Horton was initially anxious to bring the union case to the region. Then too, the church's well-respected pastor, Henry David Gray, had been an advocate of a certain kind of moderation throughout the union discussions. But as events unfolded, the Oneonta controversy

---

[62]Malcolm Burton to Horton and James Wagner, 4 December 1954, BGC.
[63]Horton to Howell Davies, 6 December 1954, BGC.

served as a paradigm for the distrust and miscommunication that perpetuated ill will within the Congregational Christian fold.

Gray, pastor of the Oneonta congregation, was a frequent and early correspondent with Horton, having led a youth delegation to the meeting of the International Council of Congregational Churches in 1949. Horton had presided at that meeting, which took place on the campus of Wellesley College in the final year of Mildred McAfee Horton's tenure as president there. The cross-country trip taken by Gray's group afforded him the opportunity to visit numerous congregations and to speak with many ministers during the summer of travel. In a letter to Horton shortly after he returned to California from his twenty-four state "odyssey," Gray reported "a very unhappy Congregationalism, not just because some are for or against [the merger], but more basically because there is a central deficit—lack of trust." A "united church," under the conditions Gray witnessed, could only be "a farce." Gray articulated his own basic fear in relation to the proposed merger: "that the spiritual shall be lost in mere size and that the basic need in our churches for real revival shall be covered up in growing organization."[64]

In Gray's opinion, the fellowship needed to be guaranteed protection from centralized leadership and excessive organization in a constitution as a prerequisite to merger. This was the position he advocated during the church-by-church voting process in 1949 that resulted in the controversy over the 75 percent vote figure. In fact, the Oneonta Church refused to vote either for or against the proposed union to avoid aligning itself with either of the contending parties. In a letter to Goebel, Gray characterized the position of his congregation as "unequivocally ecumenical" and "unequivocally free-minded." The Oneonta Church refused to "go into a united church which is centralized in authority or credo or which infringes upon the autonomy of the local church." On the other hand, with a constitution to spell out what the relationships in the new church would be, the Oneonta Church could make a concrete decision about its own future in relation to the proposed union.[65]

In a paper he wrote in the fall of 1951, Gray presented his own vision of how the union might best be effected. Titled "Free Church and the Ecumenical Movement," the paper discussed the theology, polity, and "churchmanship [sic]" of the Congregational Christian Churches and

[64]Henry David [H. D.] Gray to Horton, 11 August 1949, BGC.
[65]H. D. Gray to Lewis Goebel, 2 June 1949, BGC.

concluded with certain recommendations concerning the merger. As an alternative to the currently suspended plan of "organic union," Gray recommended gatherings at the local, state, and national level to bring the members of the two denominations together to talk with and learn about each other. The two denominations should also officially enter into a "covenant-relationship" for two or more years, during which time a "true common spirit" would be nurtured between the covenanting partners. Gray argued that the union that would result from this process was preferable to the "process of attrition of the opposition [and] shrewd organizational arrangements" that characterized the current state of affairs in the two churches.[66] During this period, Gray served as a member on the Free Church Polity and Unity Committee. His position on the "covenant-relationship" approach to church union, with slight alterations, found its way into the committee's final report and, as noted above, was advocated by Fifield.

Interestingly, Horton found himself in complete agreement with Gray's statement of the Congregational Christian theological stance. After pointing out the impossibility of beginning any kind of "covenant-relationship" with the Evangelical and Reformed Church until the court case was finally settled, Horton advocated the approach. He then embellished it with a return to the suggestion made in his *Of Equability and Perseverance in Well Doing* speech: "My own thought is that during this [covenant-relationship] time a duly appointed joint committee might be working on a constitution. The beauty of having a constitution in hand . . . seems to me sufficiently obvious."[67] In a letter sent to Gray four months later, after the first appeal of the Cadman case had been won, Horton reiterated his concern to Gray that a constitution should be written "before any union is effected."[68] Gray later advocated this position at the Claremont meeting, in his role as a member of the Committee on Free Church Polity and Unity, and in his letters to Horton after 1952.

---

[66]H. D. Gray, "Free Church and Ecumenical Movement," n.d. [circa 1951], typescript, BGC. Gray offered perhaps the most sustained discussion from an opposing Congregational Christian viewpoint concerning the relationship between polity and theology in the merger dispute. His important book *The Mediators* (Pasadena, Calif.: American Congregational Center, 1984) differs from this earlier version concerning Gray's call for a constitution. On the other hand, his extended discussion of the "Fifield Report" is an important contribution to the story of the merger.

[67]Horton to H. D. Gray, 4 January 1952, BGC.

[68]Horton to H. D. Gray, 28 April 1952, BGC.

Horton's position on the merger changed after the meeting with the Evangelical and Reformed executive committee in October 1954. Up until then, however, Henry David Gray and others like him had no reason to believe that the union would go ahead without a written constitution to spell out the polity of the new church and to guarantee the freedom of the churches. Thus the "shock" that Gray expressed in relation to the course of action put forward by the executive committee in its "Letter Missive" of October was not unjustified.[69] Indeed, for Gray the action of the executive committee confirmed his earlier fears that there was a general lack of trust in the denomination, that an "overhead authority" possessed of "self-assumed powers" was "pushing the business [of merger] through" without regard to "all viewpoints."[70]

It is clear from his letters and actions that Horton did not want to alienate Gray from the union cause. So while he acknowledged that no constitution could be ratified before the union was consummated, Horton left open the door for working on a constitution that would be ratified shortly after the union went into effect. In a letter dated 26 November 1954, Horton proposed to Gray that he should be a member of the select, six-person joint committee appointed to work on the constitution.[71] On 20 December, Gray conveyed his appreciation for the confidence Horton had extended in recommending him for a position on the committee. He also expressed the need to produce a "provisional Constitution" as quickly as possible.[72] And so a commodious cordiality had been reached between the two men as Christmas drew near. But this goodwill would be severely tested in the new year.

On 27 January 1955, Horton received a telegram from Gray and Otto Knudsen, the minister of the Southern California Conference. Horton

---

[69]H. D. Gray to the Executive Committee, 22 October 1954, BGC.

[70]H. D. Gray to Raymond Walker, 6 December 1954, BGC.

[71]Horton to H. D. Gray, 26 November 1954, BGC.

[72]H. D. Gray to Horton, 29 December 1954, BGC. In his various attacks on the church bureaucracy's assumption of power, Gray never mentioned Horton specifically and tended to focus on leaders at the local and state level as examples of what he opposed. A friendship, or at least a mutual respect seems to have existed between Gray and Horton. In any case, during the fall of 1954 and the spring of 1955, Horton was helping Gray to locate his next church appointment. Of the options presented to him, three seemed most compelling: a short-term assignment in a Congregational church in Australia; the senior minister position at Plymouth Church of the Pilgrims (replacing L. Wendell Fifield) in Brooklyn; and the senior minister position at Center Church in Hartford, Connecticut, to which Gray ultimately repaired.

was asked to "present the pro merger position" to a mass gathering at the Oneonta Church in Pasadena on 28 February 1955. Although he had planned to be in Chicago on that particular day, Horton immediately canceled his prior commitment and accepted what he thought was a personal invitation from a friend as well as an official invitation from the Southern California Conference. A week later, Horton received a phone call from Gray. Gray handed the conversation over to the Rev. Harry Butman, senior minister at the Church of the Messiah in Los Angeles, and a prominent antimerger activist. Butman asked if Horton would be willing to come to Pasadena under the sponsorship of the local Committee for the Continuation of Congregational Christian Churches of the United States—the group directed nationally by Malcolm Burton and committed to resisting all denominational merger efforts.

Horton affirmed his willingness to appear before any Congregational Christian churches in good standing, while noting that the Continuation Committee had received no official recognition from the General Council. On the next day, 9 February, Butman sent a letter to Horton, confirming their conversation and thanking him for his willingness to "debate" Malcolm Burton in the public forum.[73] Horton immediately sent a telegram canceling the arrangement:

> Word just reached me from Harry Butman that affair on the 28th is designed to be a debate. This is first intimation I have had of that fact. As officer of General Council it is impossible for me to regard as debatable a matter which has been voted by Council. Must therefore regretfully cancel the engagement. Please tell Harry. Am sorry that misunderstanding has occurred. Shall be happy to come to you any time possible under original arrangements.[74]

This communication ended the first round of the controversy. Horton likened his situation to that of a minister in a local church whose congregation had voted to alter the sanctuary's architecture. It would be wholly inappropriate for the minister of that church to continue to debate the matter publicly.[75]

---

[73]Horton to Jesse Perrin, 11 February 1955, BGC. See also the draft of Horton's undelivered speech, "Is This the Congregationalism We Want to Continue?," n.d. (circa 20 February 1955), BGC, and the letter from Harry R. Butman to Horton, 9 February 1955, BGC.

[74]Telegram from Horton to H. D. Gray, 10 February 1955, BGC.

[75]Horton to Jesse Perrin, 11 February 1955, BGC.

On 11 February, Gray sent a letter to Horton, noting that the complexion of the meeting had changed "radically" and that Gray was "not at all happy about the way it was rearranged." Gray left open the offer to sponsor a "fair presentation" by both Burton and Horton without the emotionally charged atmosphere that would likely transpire were a debate held.[76] On 15 February, Butman sent a telegram to Horton, blaming the deceptive wording of the initial telegram (alleged to have been sent by Gray and Knudsen) on Gray's wife. Butman claimed that his use of the word "debate" was "unfortunate and inaccurate." He reiterated his request that Horton present his views on the same platform with Burton but not in the "spirit of debate." Butman also noted, somewhat ominously, that with publicity for the event already in circulation, Horton's failure to appear might be misunderstood. Butman concluded by promising Horton "a most cordial welcome" and hailing the event as "an opportunity for fellowship in the best congregational tradition."[77] In the spirit of fellowship (though deploring the "methods of controversy" employed by Burton[78]), Horton consented to the original arrangement. The meeting would occur according to plan.

But by 17 February, Horton had received two more pieces of information that brought the proposed meeting to its second and final cancellation. First came a letter from Knudsen, whose name had appeared on the telegram that initiated this episode. Knudsen noted that he was merely asked by Mrs. Henry David Gray to introduce Horton at the proposed Oneonta meeting. "I want to believe that there has been a misunderstanding," Knudsen wrote, "though it is difficult to see how willingness to introduce could be construed as consent to extend an invitation on the part of the Conference Moderator."[79]

The last straw was a handbill distributed by four southern California ministers to publicize the Oneonta event. Under the heading "Let's Save Congregationalism," the handbill began: "some of us believe our fellowship is in genuine danger." Assiduously avoiding the word "debate," it promised that both sides of the union issue would be presented:

> Mr. Douglas Horton . . . will present the point of view of those who, by merging with the Evangelical and Reformed

[76]Letter from H. D. Gray to Horton, 11 February 1955, BGC.

[77]Telegram from Harry Butman to Horton, 15 February 1955, BGC.

[78]See Horton, "Is This the Congregationalism," 2.

[79]Otto Knudsen to Horton, 14 February 1955, BGC.

Church, would become the United Church of Christ and Mr. Malcolm K. Burton will present the point of view of those who wish to save the Congregational Christian Churches from becoming the United Church of Christ.

Accompanying the handbill was a copy of L. Wendell Fifield's "Open Letter to the Executive Committee," though, as Horton noted later, the "Official Reply" to that letter was not included in the publicity materials. The handbill was signed by Gray, Butman, James Fifield, and another longtime merger detractor, the Rev. Raymond Waser of the Pilgrim Congregational Church in Pomona, California.[80] In his 18 February telegram to Gray, Horton noted that the handbill—released without his knowledge or consent—"makes debate practically inevitable." It also appeared "antagonistic to the Executive Committee" and seemed to suggest to Horton, at least, that he would not really be a guest among those gathered at Oneonta Church in Pasadena on 28 February. He therefore canceled the engagement once and for all.[81]

Shortly after the scheduled event fell apart, Horton announced his resignation from the position of minister and secretary of the General Council and accepted a new position as dean of Harvard Divinity School. Responsibility for nurturing the United Church into being was thereby handed over to persons who enjoyed some distance from the long history of personality conflicts and whose energies might better serve to advance the cause of church union.

The Oneonta episode confirms the thesis, put forward by Raymond Walker, that Douglas Horton had become the personal target of much of the opposition and that forthright discussion of issues had become impossible among certain entrenched antiunionists. Indeed, at one moment of particular exasperation, Walker noted that some of the antimerger people had "found careers in the program of opposition and they have jobs to protect." He even labeled certain of the movement's leaders "psycho-neurotics."[82] This language was not the kind Horton ever used, at least not publicly, and certainly not in official correspondence. By all

[80]H. D. Gray, et al., "Let's Save Congregationalism," n.d. (circa 14 February 1955), BGC.

[81]Telegram from Horton to H. D. Gray, 18 February 1955, BGC.

[82]Raymond Walker to Horton, 27 October 1954, BGC.

accounts, Horton remained diplomatic in dealing with his opponents. Even Burton admitted that, with one mild exception in 1947, he never saw Horton "lose his cool."[83]

On the other hand, the cumulative animosity toward Horton among his detractors was not wholly unjustified. Horton had advocated the introduction of "Interpretations" to the *Basis of Union* after the initial failure of the *Basis* to receive the necessary votes from the Congregational Christian churches. While this move may have been politically necessary to advance the cause of union, it also imported unresolved Congregational Christian conflicts into the founding document of the emerging United Church of Christ. Horton played a significant—if not the central—role in the subsequent decision, in 1949, to proceed with the union plan even after the obvious failure of the plan to receive a majority vote of 75 percent. And from 1950 to 1954, Horton had certainly advocated that a constitution be drafted before any attempt at union. So it was not unreasonable for men like L. Wendell Fifield and Gray to suspect Horton of slight and major deceptions.

Still, the sentiment in favor of union was overwhelming in the Congregational Christian Churches. Despite outrageous assertions to the contrary from, in particular, L. Wendell Fifield's brother James, Horton knew that more than 90 percent of the churches would participate in the union, whether or not they would go on record as favoring it. The debate over union had exposed a great deal of rancor within the Congregational Christian denomination. The more sensational aspects of the debate, as the present account has demonstrated, centered on personalities and were related to power struggles within the Congregational Christian denomination, as an emerging bureaucracy endeavored to act on behalf of the entire denomination. The more significant aspects of the debate concerned the nature of American Congregationalism: its history, polity, and ecumenical possibility. In the end, the latter, crucial debate was left unresolved and the matter of church union was determined by a simple vote for or against merger.

The strongest argument against depicting Horton as an authoritarian with an incurable desire for power is the action he took shortly after the Oneonta controversy. In March, Horton visited the office of Nathan Pusey, president of Harvard University. He also visited the Houghton

[83]Burton, *Disorders in the Kingdom*, 206.

Library on that school's campus in the hope of acquiring an original Latin version of John Norton's book *Response to Apollonius*.[84] By April he had announced his resignation from the General Council in order to become the new dean of the Harvard Divinity School. The deanship at Harvard was by no means a step down for Horton. But if he had been driven by ego merely, he most likely would have stayed on in his position with the General Council in order to preside over the church he had worked for over fifteen years to bring into being. Instead, he handed that responsibility over to others. With the personality issue out of the way, the matter of unifying the new church could take center stage.[85]

As dean of the Harvard Divinity School, Horton could continue his work for union, but his future efforts on behalf of the United Church of Christ would be made behind the scenes, more or less. New leaders in the Congregational Christian Churches pursued the course of action Horton had set in motion sixteen years earlier. Two years after Horton's departure for Harvard, the union between Horton's denomination and the Evangelical and Reformed Church was consummated.

[84]Horton to William Jackson, 9 March 1955, BGC.

[85]This interpretation of Horton's motives in relation to the merger is developed in Daniel Novotny's baccalaureate address, "Under Obligation," presented to the University of New Hampshire in 1969. See "UNH Graduates 'Fighting 69th,' " *Portsmouth (N.H.) Herald*, 9 June 1969.

CHAPTER FIVE

Douglas Horton's Deanship at Harvard Divinity School

In retrospect, at least, Horton linked his own rise to national prominence with the Harvard Divinity School. In his 1957 revised foreword to Karl Barth's *The Word of God and the Word of Man*, Horton told of how he "ran across" Barth's book on the "new books" shelf in the Andover-Harvard Theological Library a generation before.[1] His reference to that earlier era may have been merely coincidental; nevertheless, certain persons who were present in the Harvard community at the time and certain events that occurred then would have a significant bearing on Horton's return, as it were, to the Divinity School during the summer of 1955 as its dean.

The hyphenated name of the library in which Horton found Barth's book, the "Andover-Harvard Theological Library," announced the wedded status of two theological schools. Harvard Divinity School had been an explicitly "nondenominational" institution since 1880; before that it was, for more than sixty years, the center for the training of Unitarian clergy in America. This Unitarianism, in turn, was anchored in over 150 years of Puritan tradition, dating back to the founding of Harvard Col-

---

[1] Karl Barth, *The Word of God and the Word of Man* (trans. Douglas Horton, 1928; repr., with a revised foreword by Douglas Horton; New York: Harper and Row, 1957) 1. Although the exact date of Horton's providential encounter is not known, it doubtless occurred sometime after February 1926 and before February 1928. According to Dennis Voskuil, the book was acquired by the library in February 1926. See Voskuil, "From Liberalism to Neo-Orthodoxy," 78.

lege in 1636 for the purpose of ensuring an educated ministry in the New World. For its part, Andover Theological Seminary (located in Andover, Massachusetts, some twenty miles north of Cambridge) was a Congregational institution, established in the early nineteenth century to train ministers in the "orthodox" Calvinist tradition that Harvard had so earnestly abandoned in the embrace of a "rational Christianity" that was subsequently called Unitarianism. Ironically, Andover Theological Seminary itself became a bastion of liberal Protestant thinking in the late nineteenth century through exposure to continental theology, in particular to the work of German theologian Isaac Dorner.[2] By the twentieth century, the Calvinist doctrine of election—which had been a central issue leading to the removal of the "orthodox" faculty from Cambridge to Andover—seemed no longer a matter of contention among New England liberals. In 1910, the Andover Seminary relocated to Cambridge and soon thereafter took up residence in the newly erected Andover Hall. In 1922, the faculty, students, and facilities of Harvard and Andover were united.

For a brief period during the postwar Jazz Age, the combined resources of both theology schools were focused on the twin tasks of training an educated ministry for the liberal Protestant churches of New England and preparing scholars to teach religion in the nation's seminaries and colleges. Unfortunately for Harvard, a court order in 1925 effectively annulled the wedding of the faculties. The conflict that provoked the court order, as Harold S. Davis, lawyer for the Harvard Divinity School, expressed it in a letter to the school's dean, Willard Sperry, was grounded in doctrine. Andover faculty members adhered to the "Shorter Catechism" of the Westminster Confession of Faith (1646) and were required to subscribe—if not always in writing—to the "Andover Creed," a statement of doctrine derived from the Westminster Confession. The Andover Seminary's board of visitors argued that exposure to the teachings of Harvard Divinity School instructors, who were not required to

---

[2]For the Harvard history, see Levering Reynolds Jr., "The Later Years (1880–1953)," in *The Harvard Divinity School: Its Place in Harvard University and in American Culture* (ed. George H. Williams; Boston: Beacon, 1954) 187–210. For the Andover story, see Daniel Day Williams, *The Andover Liberals* (1941; New York: Octagon Books, 1970). For the importance of Dorner, see Hutchison, ed., *The Modernist Impulse*, 84–88. Philip Schaff, who had been Dorner's pupil in Germany, taught briefly at Andover during the Civil War prior to his move to Hartford Seminary. For Schaff's pioneering role in exposing Americans to Dorner, see Penzel, ed., *Philip Schaff*, xl–xli.

subscribe to the "Andover Creed," essentially "corrupts Andover students." As a result of the decree, most of Andover's faculty and students and all of its endowment withdrew to Newton Centre, some twelve miles west of Cambridge, to form the Andover Newton Theological School. In Cambridge, meanwhile, the Harvard Divinity School retained Andover Hall and the library.[3]

The divorce of the Andover Theological Seminary from the Harvard Divinity School marked the beginning of a decline at the Divinity School, a decline Douglas Horton would eventually be called upon to help reverse.

Harvard Divinity School: The Years of Isolation, 1925–1955

Horton's predecessor at Harvard Divinity School was Dean Willard Sperry. As the minister of Central Congregational Church in Boston, Sperry had taught practical theology part-time at Andover beginning in 1918. When the faculties were combined in Cambridge in 1922, Sperry was appointed dean and professor of homiletics—a gesture promoted by Harvard's president, A. Lawrence Lowell, to help accommodate the Andover faculty members to their new surroundings. Horton may have known Sperry prior to the latter's assumption of the deanship; in any case, when he learned that Sperry would be visiting the campus of Wesleyan University during the spring of 1923, Horton invited the new dean to stay with the Horton family at the parsonage in Middletown.[4] On another occasion in 1928, Sperry accepted Horton's invitation to meet with neoorthodox theologian Emil Brunner at the Harvard Club in Boston. Brunner was then on a tour of various seminaries in the United States, including Harvard Divinity School.[5] By the 1940s, Sperry

[3]Harold S. Davis to Willard Sperry, 26 January 1923, CWS. This brief account of the Andover controversy and its resolution has two points of intersection with Horton's past and future careers. Newton Centre, the retreat of the Andover faculty, was already home to the Baptist Newton Theological Institute, where Horton himself had taught a course in Congregational polity during the 1920s. And Harold S. Davis, the Harvard Divinity School's lawyer, played a role in the "grade-A lawyer" controversy that would encumber Horton in 1947.

[4]Horton to Willard Sperry, 10 November 1922, CDH.

[5]Horton to Willard Sperry, 5 October 1928, and reply from Willard Sperry to Horton, 9 October 1928, CDH. For a brief discussion of Brunner, see Voskuil, "From Liberal-

and Horton were well acquainted through their work in the Faith and Order movement. They corresponded occasionally during these years, discussing the relationship between Congregationalists and Unitarians who shared, according to Horton, "a bond made sacred by long association."[6]

The Harvard Divinity School fell on hard times in the 1920s and 1930s. This decline was aggravated by economic depression and, in the 1940s, the war emergency. Year after year the university covered the Divinity School's debts, which ranged from $15,000 to $30,000 per annum between the years 1926 and 1953. Dean Sperry's annual reports to the president of Harvard University reflected the Divinity School's predicament. His refrain in the report for the academic year 1936–1937 is typical: "our deficit cuts deeply into the University's income from undesignated funds. We are grateful that the University is so generous in its dealings with us."[7] The Divinity School's financial difficulties stemmed in part from the disinterest of the university's president, James Conant, a chemist, who "was inclined to regard theology (in contrast to science) as a divisive rather than a unitive principle in education." In addition, Divinity School enrolment was down compared with that of other leading theology schools such as Yale, Union, and Chicago, because the liberal theological tradition that the Divinity School had always exemplified seemed outmoded by the 1930s. Prospective students who were interested in the "neo-orthodox" theologies of Barth, Brunner, and the Niebuhrs simply did not apply to Harvard.[8]

Sperry remained a defender of the school's teachers and its liberal, neoorthodoxy-resistant curriculum, arguing that the "historical method breeds a fair-mindedness which is often sorely wanted in Protestant pulpits."[9] But despite his rhetorical efforts, Sperry had a difficult time coun-

---

ism to Neo-Orthodoxy," 118, and George H. Richards, "With Theologians in Germany and Switzerland," *Bulletin of the Theological Seminary of the Reformed Church in the United States*, October 1931, 6–9.

[6]Horton to Willard Sperry, 4 January [*sic*, for February] 1948, BGC.

[7]Willard Sperry, "Annual Report to the President (1936–37)," 6, Dean's Office: Annual Reports to the President (1936–1952), CWS. The deficit figure is from "Report of the Committee to Visit the Divinity School," in *Reports of the Visiting Committees of the Board of Overseers of Harvard College for the Academic Year 1943–1944* (Cambridge, Mass.: 1944) 166, CHU.

[8]See Reynolds, "The Later Years (1880–1953)," 212–14.

[9]Sperry, "Annual Report to the President (1936–1937)," 5.

tering the prevailing notion that the Harvard Divinity School "was a way out of the parish ministry rather than into it."[10] Although the Divinity School did maintain a bachelor's degree program leading to the parish ministry, the number of students in that program was never great. In 1942, for example—when registration in the Divinity School peaked prior to the end of World War II—fewer than half of the Divinity School's ninety-nine students were actually enroled in the bachelor's degree program.[11]

By the 1943–1944 academic year, the future of the Harvard Divinity School looked bleak. In its report to the Overseers of Harvard College, the Committee to Visit the Divinity School noted that within six years all but one member of the current faculty would be retired. Financially, the School was not prepared to replace those faculty members; the preferred course was one of inaction that would allow one or two of the positions to remain unfilled as a preventive measure against increasing debt. Realistically, according to the report, there was little hope of expanding the faculty in order to give it any kind of standing comparable with that of Harvard's other schools, in particular the Law School and the Medical School. Meanwhile, when ranked against other major university-related theology schools, Harvard was hopelessly outclassed. The Committee to Visit the Divinity School cited a report authored by Sperry to underscore this fact. With five professors and two part-time lecturers, Harvard's faculty was significantly smaller than that of the other nationally renowned schools: Yale had 27 faculty members; Chicago, 30; and Union, 38. Harvard's annual budget, at $62,216, was also by far the lowest of the four schools (Yale, $225,570; Chicago, $229,000; Union, $583,543). And so the Harvard Divinity School seemed destined to become "merely a place for research by graduate students and productive scholarship on the part of three or four professors."[12]

But the Committee to Visit the Divinity School ultimately resisted this destiny:

---

[10]Willard Sperry, "Annual Report to the President (1945–1946)," 3, Dean's Office: Annual Reports to the President (1936–1952), CWS.

[11]"Report of the Committee to Visit the Divinity School," 167. This situation also holds true for the present-day Divinity School, but today there is a master of theological studies (MTS) program that offers an alternative to ministerial training.

[12]Ibid., 166.

> [S]hould the School be compelled to operate on its present income, this will mean that Harvard has abandoned all sense of obligation to raise up a "literate ministry" for the churches of America. In view of the history of the College and the University . . . it is difficult to see how we could justify to ourselves and to the general public a neglect of the historical discipline of theology or of concern for the moral and spiritual life of the country.[13]

Citing the ongoing war and its attendant evils, the committee argued that the need for organized religion in the nation had never been greater. If the Divinity School were allowed to "dwindle away," the university would be left "with no source of ethical teaching at the highest level other than literature and philosophy," both of which the report argued were "insufficient for the needs of humanity." As its motto, *Veritas*, demanded, Harvard's commitment was to "Truth," and religious truth deserved "at least equal rank in the hierarchy of knowledge." What the university, the culture, and the churches needed was a task for which the Harvard Divinity School was "uniquely fitted," namely, "to revive a living theology for free, individual [people]." Emphasizing the unitive forces—the ecumenical movement, interfaith and interchurch councils, and the uniting of denominations—that were bringing a new vitality to organized Christianity, the committee recommended that the Harvard Corporation, the governing body of the university, appoint a commission of theologians, ministers, and seminary leaders to study and make recommendations concerning the future of the Divinity School.[14]

Although the visiting committee seemed to favor the expansion of the Divinity School's role in the life of the university, the members of the subsequently formed commission did not perceive their mission to be predetermined by the earlier report. The "Commission to Study and Make Recommendations with Respect to the Harvard Divinity School"— also known as the "O'Brian Commission" after its chair, John Lord O'Brian—produced a report dated 15 July 1947. In its report, the commission stated bluntly that it was confonted with two questions: 1) "Whether the School should be abolished or continued"; and 2) "If continued, what changes would be necessary to make it an adequate institu-

---

[13]Ibid., 168.
[14]Ibid., 169.

tion and one of permanent value."[15] In a "Confidential Appendix" to his annual report for the year 1946–47, Dean Sperry noted that the stark phrasing of the first question had done the Divinity School "no little disservice," as it conjured rumors of the Divinity School's impending demise.[16] It was even suggested that the library, faculty, and students might relocate to more commodious environs such as the campus of Oberlin College and Seminary in Ohio.[17]

But instead of advocating an ignominious exile for the Divinity School, or even suggesting a modest repair of the depleted faculty, the O'Brian Commission argued that the age demanded "a new center of religious learning" and that Harvard ought to provide that center.[18] The scope of the commission's proposal was astounding. The faculty would have to be expanded from its present number of four to between fifteen and twenty-five professors — with particular emphasis in the fields of systematic theology, philosophy of religion, Christian ethics, and practical theology. The student population would have to increase threefold. While Sperry's responsibilities were divided between the Divinity School and the Memorial Church, the office of the dean would in the future be located exclusively in the Divinity School. In addition to administrative responsibilities, the dean would be expected to devote time to scholarship and teaching. Renewed emphasis would be placed on training well-educated ministers, of whom the nation was in short supply. But the nation and the world also needed first-rate scholars, teachers, and professors of religion — especially given the demise of European universities in the aftermath of war — and Harvard had a historical commitment and a moral obligation to provide them. All of this would cost a great deal of money. The O'Brian Commission assumed that an endowment of between four and five million dollars would have to be secured in order to bring the Harvard Divinity School to a preeminent position among the world's university-related theological schools.[19]

---

[15]*Confidential Report of the Commission to Study and Make Recommendations with Respect to the Harvard Divinity School* (Cambridge, Mass., 1947; pamphlet) 4–5, CHU.

[16]Willard Sperry, "Confidential Appendix to the Annual Report to the President (1945–1946)," 1, CHU.

[17]According to George H. Williams, "Divinings: Religion at Harvard College from its Origins in New England Ecclesiastical History, 1636–1992" (unpublished manuscript, 1998), chapter 8, Harvard Divinity School Archives.

[18]"Confidential Report of the Commission to Study and Make Recommendations," 6.

[19]Ibid., 45.

In 1949, Harvard University circulated an inquiry among the alumni and friends of Harvard Divinity School. Called *A New Center of Religious Learning at Harvard*, the sixteen-page booklet reported the findings of the commission and sought opinions concerning the viability of the commission's plan. Three years later, the Harvard Divinity School Endowment Fund produced another booklet soliciting financial commitments to the program.[20] On the opening page of both booklets appeared Harvard's "Matherean Seal" with its motto, *Christo et Ecclesiae* — "to Christ and Church." This motto displaced, or at least complemented, the reference to another Harvard motto, *Veritas*, alluded to in the 1943 report from the Board of Visitors. *Christo et Ecclesiae* underscored the hope placed in Christianity itself during the postwar era: "with its peculiar sense of values, [the Christian tradition] does provide strong ties of common loyalty and understanding that transcend the boundaries of Nation, race, and class."[21] Meanwhile the need to transcend these boundaries was brought home at the very end of the 1949 booklet in a quotation from General Douglas MacArthur:

> We have had our last chance. If we do not now devise some greater and more equitable system, Armageddon will be at our door. The problem is basically theological and involves a spiritual recrudescence and improvement of human character that will synchronize with our almost matchless advance in science, art, literature and all material and cultural developments of the past two thousand years. It must be of the spirit if we are to save the flesh.[22]

The significance of this theological problem was not lost on Harvard's alumni and friends. With the generous assistance of John D. Rockefeller Jr., by 1955 the Divinity School was within reach of its revised goal of securing seven million dollars in the endowment fund. The school was finally in a position to call a permanent successor to Willard Sperry, who retired from the deanship in 1953.

---

[20]See *A New Center of Religious Learning at Harvard: Prepared and Issued at the Request and with the Authorization of the President and Fellows of Harvard College,* 1949, and *A New Center of Religious Learning at Harvard: Prepared by the Harvard Divinity School Endowment Fund,* 1952, CHU.

[21]*Confidential Report of the Commission to Study and Make Recommendations,* 3.

[22]"A New Center of Religious Learning at Harvard," 15.

But before turning to that story, let us set the stage by returning briefly to Horton's discovery of Karl Barth's book in the Andover-Harvard Library sometime between 1926 and 1928. During the same period, but in another corner of the university campus, a young bookworm read the great books while remaining unknown to most of his classmates. Nathan Pusey was not religiously inclined in those youthful years. "Many of us took the position," he recalled in a 1957 *Newsweek* article, "that religion was of no consequence. . . . Life seemed to be better understood on the Left Bank of Paris." Pusey was graduated from Harvard in 1928. During the ensuing year abroad, while momentum was building toward an economic crash back home, he well may have spent some time among the sages on the Left Bank. Eventually, however, a teaching career led him to consider the "role of the spiritual" in academic life. His sensibilities were sharpened while teaching at Wesleyan University in the early 1940s. In 1944 he became the president of Lawrence College in Appleton, Wisconsin—coincidentally the school that had granted Horton his first honorary doctorate degree several years earlier—and it was there that Pusey "came actively to grips with the place of religion in the college curriculum."[23] By the time he returned to Harvard in 1953 as president of the University, Nathan Pusey was a prominent lay leader in the Episcopal Church with well-known ecumenical sensibilities.

Rejuvenation: The (Protestant) Ecumenical Vision of Pusey and Horton

Significantly, Pusey delivered his first major public address as Harvard's president at the opening convocation of the Harvard Divinity School in Andover Chapel on 30 September 1953. No president had ventured over to the Divinity School—peripherally located in the northeast corner of Harvard's campus—to give a major address since Charles Eliot, in 1909, and Pusey made this fact the centerpiece of his speech. Pusey contrasted his own sense of the religious needs of the time with what Eliot—imbued with the same optimism of the pre–World War I era that had made the *Lusitania* a symbol of hope for Horton's mentor, S. Parkes Cadman[24]—had envisioned as "the religion of the future." Whereas

[23]"Religion in our Colleges," *Newsweek*, 10 April 1957, 118.
[24]See the discussion of Cadman's speech "A New Day for Missions" (1908) in chapter 1.

Eliot had believed that "the truth will progressively make men free, so that the coming generations will be freer, and therefore more productive and stronger than the preceding [ones]," Pusey judged such a faith inadequate for the present age of uncertainty. Eliot's religion left creeds, clerics, and churches behind; he looked to trained surgeons as "ministers of the new religion." Pusey, on the other hand, argued for the importance of the sacramental, the metaphysical, and the insights passed down from one generation to another through "old forms" such as creeds. He looked to the Divinity School to train professional ministers who, "with a firm grasp on the spiritual treasure that had been transmitted to them," would help shape "a new and more effective Christian society."[25]

Despite his frequent references to "Christianity," it should be noted that Pusey had mainline Protestantism in mind. Ecumenism at Harvard Divinity School in 1953 did not yet extend to Roman Catholicism, even if acceptable religiosity in America during the 1950s encompassed Protestant, Catholic, and Jew, as Will Herberg famously argued in his 1955 book.[26] Also noteworthy in this regard was Pusey's insistence on the use of the term "Christian" to include that denomination with which Harvard had maintained its closest ties for over 125 years: the Unitarians. Indeed, it was the liberal Unitarian philosophy advocated by Eliot—particularly as it developed beyond the bend in the road that turned toward humanism—which Pusey deemed insufficient for the religious needs of the Cold War era.

If Pusey's immediate predecessor as president, James Conant, had been leery of religion, preferring instead to regard science as the unifying force within the university and the world at large, the opposite was true for Pusey. The fact that science was not a uniting force in human society seemed self-evident in the aftermath of World War II. In his convocation address, Pusey signaled the importance of a "revitalized school of religious learning" whose unitive influence, he hoped, would be "increasingly felt throughout the whole University."[27] Pusey argued

[25]"An Address delivered by President Nathan M. Pusey at the opening convocation of the Harvard Divinity School," 30 September 1953, CHU.

[26]Will Herberg, *Protestant-Catholic-Jew* (New York: Doubleday, 1955). It is debatable, however, whether Herberg's portrayal of the American religious landscape was descriptive or prescriptive.

[27]"An Address delivered by President Nathan M. Pusey," 10.

that the Divinity School was not meant to be on the periphery of the university, but at its heart. He repeated this theme for many years in his annual baccalaureate addresses, sending new graduates out into the world with the suggestion that the Memorial Church, centrally located in Harvard Yard and the site where Pusey delivered those addresses, was the physical and symbolic center "from which all the rest of Harvard has grown."[28] Horton could not have wished for a more ecumenical colleague with whom he might share the final years of his professional career.

In a 1955 Valentine's Day letter to Pusey, Horton apologized for his inability to come up with the name of a suitable candidate for the deanship of the revitalized Divinity School. Horton had intended to recommend the Rev. Robert Luccock for the position, but it appeared likely that Luccock would become the senior minister at Madison Avenue Presbyterian Church in New York. That church's former senior minister, George Buttrick, had been called to Harvard in 1954 to assume the duties that Sperry had performed in his capacity as minister to the university's Memorial Church. Horton advised Pusey that he did have one or two other candidates in mind, should the president be interested; however, suspecting that a selection had already been made, he had no wish to press the matter further unless invited to do so.[29]

The invitation to do so came one Sunday in early March 1955. Horton was in Cambridge to preside at the baptism of his grandson. The service took place in Christ Church, the historic Episcopal church sandwiched between the Unitarian First Parish and the Congregational First Church on Garden Street. Horton read from the *Book of Common Prayer* and included a special prayer from a Congregational order of worship. Perhaps Pusey, a member of Christ Church, was among the congregants that morning. In any case, after a leisurely lunch with family and friends, Horton walked across campus to meet with Pusey in the president's home. Horton assumed that the meeting would focus on the several persons

---

[28]"Baccalaureate Address of President Nathan M. Pusey to the Harvard College Class of 1954," 13 June 1954, 8, CHU. See also the addresses of 1955 and 1956. The baccalaureate addresses of 1957 and 1958 were published subsequently in the *Christian Century*. Pusey's point was conveyed visually on the cover of the 22 April 1957 issue of *Newsweek* magazine. Above the title "Harvard's President Pusey: 'We Stand in Need of Faith' " is a photograph that contains the face of Pusey and the Memorial Church steeple.

[29]Horton to Nathan M. Pusey, 14 February 1955, BGC.

Horton wished to propose for the deanship at the Divinity School. But when Horton returned to his family later in the day, he "quietly said that the upshot of the conversation was that Dr. Pusey had asked him (D. H.) to become the Dean." The appointment, as Horton understood it, was to be for two years. Remarking on the attractiveness of the offer to her husband, Mildred McAfee Horton recorded:

> It is gratifying that Harvard should turn to a man in [Horton's] position, for it certainly indicates an interest in having the Divinity School re-associated with Congregationalism. It appeals to his interest in history to be party to such a move at Harvard.[30]

For his part, Pusey appreciated in particular not only Horton's "long service to Congregationalism . . . which more than any other is Harvard's historic faith" but also "his custom to take thought of the whole Christian church" as qualities Horton would bring to the deanship. Pusey was certain that Horton would continue to advance the cause of ecumenism from Harvard and that he would still be "working along with [his colleagues in the Congregational Christian Churches] for Christ."[31]

Pusey's choice of Horton was no minor matter. The crucial ingredient in the plan for the revitalization of the Harvard Divinity School was the deanship. The plan required a dean who would gather together a faculty and establish the direction of the school for years to come. Horton interpreted his responsibilities as twofold: he was called to the Divinity School to return Harvard theologically to "its early tradition" and to establish for Harvard "its place at the center of the ecumenical movement."[32]

Horton unrolled the blueprint for his administration in his convocation address at the beginning of the academic year in 1955. Published in the *Harvard Alumni Bulletin* under the title "The Desk and the Altar," the address serves as a marvelous compendium of the themes and chal-

---

[30]Mildred McAfee Horton to the Horton family, 13 March 1955, RHF.

[31]Nathan M. Pusey to "Friends and Associates of Douglas Horton," 20 September 1955, RHF.

[32]Horton to Truman Douglass, 8 April 1955, CGO. Accordingly, the first course Horton taught at Harvard, "Theology 10—The Nature and Function of the Church: Issues and Problems in the Contemporary Ecumenical Discussion," focused on the basic documents of the Commission on Faith and Order of the World Council of Churches. See the letter from George Williams to Horton, 26 May 1955, CGO.

lenges that would occupy the Divinity School during the next four years of Horton's tenure and for many years after that. He began his remarks with a deft juxtaposition of old and new. Noting that women were attending the Divinity School for the first time in the fall of 1955,[33] Horton recalled the name of Anna Maria Schurman, a woman who attended the Frisian University at Franeker (Holland) during the seventeenth century. "There was headshaking and mumbling among many when she applied," Horton pointed out—with perhaps a nod to the contemporary situation—but since the spirit of the Reformation still lingered at the university, "the administration capitulated and let her in." Schurman was "something of a religious genius." Separated from her male classmates by a curtain, she nevertheless (or perhaps consequently) excelled at the university. Her dissertation developed the thesis "The Study of Letters Is Becoming to a Christian Woman," a thesis, Horton pointed out, that the Divinity School now was adopting as its own.[34]

Horton then turned to the motto that had played a significant role in the campaign to rejuvenate the Divinity School. *Christo et Ecclesiae*, he suggested, reached Harvard by way of Franeker, where it had been carved in stone above the university's ancient gate. Horton might have mentioned that he, too, had taken this route to Harvard. For during the summer of 1955, he and his wife visited the museum on the grounds of the old university—closed since the age of Napoleon—in the Netherlands. There Horton obtained a photograph of the motto, a photograph that accompanied his address in the *Alumni Bulletin*.[35] The historical importance of the motto, by Horton's reckoning, was its affirmation of Harvard's Christian identity—an identity with which the school had been "endowed from its beginnings."

[33]Although Horton is often credited with this innovation, the change was planned during the interim deanship of George Williams. Throughout his tenure, Willard Sperry had opposed the admission of women to the Divinity School. "We may, perhaps, be fairly charged with stubborn antifeminism," Sperry noted in his "Annual Report to the President," 1949, CWS.

[34]Douglas Horton, "The Desk and the Altar," *Harvard Alumni Bulletin*, 22 October 1955, 116. The women attending Harvard Divinity School in 1955 were Joyce Mann, Emily Gage, Letty Russell, Constance F. Parvey, and Marianka Fousek.

[35]The Hortons subsequently decided to use the photograph for their Christmas card in 1955. In a letter to Dr. G. Van Wageninger, curator of the Franeker Museum, Horton discussed the significance of the photograph. See Horton to G. I. Van Wageninger, 29 December 1955, CGO.

Another endowment reached Harvard through one of Franeker's leading professors, William Ames. Horton noted that for close to a century after its publication in 1623, Ames's *Marrow of Sacred Divinity* served as the major—and for a time at least, the exclusive—book of dogmatics for Harvard's divinity students.[36] After his death, Ames's library was sent to Harvard. Appropriately, a portrait of Ames still hung in the Houghton Library, where Ames continued to assert his significance as a symbol "of the scholarly interest which has characterized Harvard from its inception." Horton's personal interest in Ames was longstanding. In the debates leading up to the formation of the United Church of Christ, Horton had used Ames as the primary exemplar of a nonseparatist Congregationalism. For Horton, Ames had represented the tradition of openness that made twentieth-century ecumenism a possibility for Congregationalists.[37] Ames's deep interest in scholarship and his unquestioned dedication to the Church were the twin pillars upon which Horton hoped to rebuild the Divinity School.

Although the immediate audience for his address was the Harvard Divinity School community, Horton's words were intended for a much wider audience. To the university, Horton wished to affirm the importance of scholarly work at the Divinity School. The Divinity School was not a simple trade school, Horton argued, nor was its academic freedom in any way restricted by the motto *Christo et Ecclesiae*. It sought students and teachers in the tradition of Ames—and therefore of Harvard itself. But for the churches to whom the Divinity School would send its graduates, Horton wanted to allay the fear "that unrestricted thought will eliminate in the Divinity School the factor of commitment to Christ and to Church." Against this notion, Horton argued that the search for "truth"—the *Veritas* of the Harvard motto—involved an act of faith. True Christian faith, Horton claimed, "feeds the life of enquiry."[38]

---

[36]The first English edition appeared in 1638.

[37]Objections to the United Church of Christ merger were articulated by some members of the Congregational Christian Churches on the grounds that Congregationalism since the days of Plymouth had been a Separatist movement, compelled to come out from the decadent Church of England. There was no ecumenical imperative, so these thinkers argued, to join together churches that God had set apart. For further discussion, see chapters 3 and 4. See also Horton, *Congregationalism: A Study in Polity.*

[38]Horton, "The Desk and the Altar," 117–118.

Finally, Horton insisted on the ecumenical nature of the Divinity School's Christian character. Indeed, he claimed that the Divinity School was more ecumenical than national and international ecumenical organizations; after all, the Divinity School did not shut out any group because of theological differences. Instead, the Harvard Divinity School "holds the Church to be the entire movement set into motion by Jesus Christ, and it leaves to every person and group the judgement as to whether . . . they are members of it or not." This may have reassured the many Unitarians in his audience, some of whom were skeptical about non-Unitarian Horton's assumption of the deanship.[39] For although Horton had opposed the decision, Unitarians were barred from participation in the National Council of Churches and World Council of Churches for their refusal to confess faith in a triune God. Now, during the "ecumenical" rejuvenation effort at the Divinity School, their historical relationship to the school received rare mention.[40] Horton's speech may have been of interest as well to Roman Catholics, who refrained from sending official delegates to any of the Protestant "ecumenical" gatherings. Pushing beyond the literal limit of the word "ecumenical," Horton also noted that the Divinity School maintained a "Christian attitude" toward non-Christian religions. There was a place for the forthright exchange of beliefs and practices at the Divinity School. Christianity "has its own saving insights to share," Horton counseled; "it amicably covets the insights of others, in the basic belief that all men are brothers."[41]

[39]Frederick M. Eliot to Horton, 28 May 1955, CWS. Concerning a recent speech of his that received press attention, Eliot noted: "I was urging the Unitarians to have confidence in the School under your leadership . . . I hope you will realize that my hearers included a few skeptical souls who needed to be told that they needn't worry!" Eliot, a long-time friend of Horton, was the president of the American Unitarian Association.

[40]Indeed, the Commission to Study and Make Recommendations noted that "the historic relationship of the School to the Unitarian Churches requires some institutional recognition, but we are persuaded that the future of the Divinity School at Harvard requires that it be a school completely under university control without particular denominational affiliation." Although the Commission recommended the establishment of a Unitarian Divinity House as a "deserved pied-à-terre within the school," this abode never materialized. See "Confidential Report of the Commission to Study and Make Recommendations," 29.

[41]Horton, "The Desk and the Altar," 118–19.

Roman Catholic and Interfaith Dimensions of "Ecumenism"

With the arrival of Horton as dean in 1955, the Divinity School entered a period of rapid growth and change. While the school's enrolment figure had reached a peak of 141 students during the 1954–1955 academic year, that figure increased by more than 50 percent in the first year of Horton's deanship, to 216. Horton remarked confidently to the *Harvard Alumni Bulletin* in October 1955 that "he must—and therefore will—raise $650,000 before Christmas" in order to secure major matching donations. The Divinity School's rejuvenation also received national media coverage. In October 1955 *Life* magazine sent reporter Claude Stanush and photographer Alfred Eisenstaedt to record developments on the Divinity School campus for the magazine's special Christmas edition. In a letter to Horton, Stanush considered the significance of the Divinity School's rejuvenation to the nation at large: "It is upon a well-trained and intellectually alert ministry that the future of Christianity in this country depends." He went on to praise the new vision and energy of Pusey and Horton. These men were generating an excitement at the Harvard Divinity School that made it more attractive to *Life*'s editors and readers "than any other theological school in the country." And in November, the *Christian Century* marveled that the admission of women to the Divinity School was "only the beginning of the metamorphosis that is taking place in this long-neglected member of the university family."[42] The influx of money, students, and faculty suggested that the vision of the Commission to Study and Make Recommendations was being made real. On account of the "sacred duty" announced in its earliest charters, Harvard Divinity School was developing into a new center of religious learning for the entire nation.[43]

---

[42]Horton's remark is recorded in the *Harvard Alumni Bulletin*, 8 October 1955, 63. In a report to the faculty, Horton identified the donors as "the Rockefeller brothers and the James Foundation." See CFM, 16 September 1955. The enrolment figures are from William Bentnick-Smith, "Memorandum to Dean Francis Keppel," 28 October 1955, CGO. Reference to the *Life* article is recorded in CFM, 16 September 1955. See also the letter from Claude Stanush to Horton, 6 September 1955, CGO. The "metamorphosis" reference is found in "Harvard Divinity School Opens with a New Look," *Christian Century,* 16 November 1955, 1344.

[43]Harvard's perceived moral and civil duties are described in detail throughout the "Confidential Report of the Commission to Study and Make Recommendations." See in particular 7–9 and 44.

Protestant hymns that "drip[ped] with sentimentality and should be banished." But his main point was that one could not accept one art form and reject another. It was at the very core a Protestant principle never to set up "a law . . . against anything in the realm of art."[48]

The crucifix received scant mention in the monthly faculty minutes before November 1956. At the meeting of 4 May, for example, Horton "spoke of redecorating the Andover Chapel" and showed the crucifix to the gathered faculty members. To theology professor John Dillenberger's inquiry concerning a prior discussion about the crucifix in the faculty's worship committee, Horton responded that the discussion had been wholly noncontroversial and "along traditional lines." New Testament professor Krister Stendahl, a member of the worship committee, said that the group had refrained from substantive discussion, and he suggested addressing the whole controversy theologically in a general debate throughout the school. As the university year ended, the matter was dropped.[49]

It was picked up again in the next semester when a four-foot long replica of the Larson crucifix greeted worshipers in the Andover Chapel one fall afternoon in 1956. Apparently, Horton himself had overseen the installation. He reported to the faculty in their meeting of 16 November that a group of students had requested to meet with him to discuss the crucifix. Horton expressed his hope that the Divinity School community would seize this newly revived controversy as an educational opportunity and explore together the relationship of Protestantism and the arts. Church historian and registrar C. Conrad Wright spurred a lively discussion when he motioned to establish a committee to investigate the nature of the community's views on the crucifix and report back to the faculty. Wright described the crucifix as a source of "great tension" and "grave concern" throughout the Divinity School; he considered it as "potentially one of the most divisive issues to come before the faculty."[50]

As the discussion unfolded within the faculty, it became clear that the controversy was not primarily theological: it was, rather, a controversy over procedure. Some faculty members were concerned about what they considered a unilateral action on the part of the dean. Others argued that the dean, as minister to the Divinity School and the person

[48]Tillich, "Opening Remarks," 1–3; emphasis in the original.
[49]CFM, 4 May 1956.
[50]Ibid., 16 November 1956.

responsible for worship in the Andover Chapel, had every right to arrange his domain as he saw fit. Horton said he was glad that the objections were out in the open. Indeed, he felt it had been necessary to confront the whole community with the actual work of art, rather than to have a theoretical debate about the use of a crucifix in a place of worship. His dramatic action had achieved its intended pedagogical effect.[51]

When the dust settled a month or so later, Professor Wright's "special committee to ascertain student and faculty sentiment concerning the crucifix" reported that widespread discussion throughout the community had appreciably relaxed the accumulated tensions. In general the student body maintained a degree of open-mindedness toward the crucifix, but such open-mindedness did not qualify as acceptance of the sculpture. The committee recommended, therefore, that the Larson crucifix be removed from the chapel until the question of worship had been engaged and discussed fully throughout the school and among the faculty.[52]

And so this early and highly abstract foreshadowing of a Roman Catholic presence at the Divinity School disappeared for a time. The incident served to expose a boundary that ecumenism at the Harvard Divinity School could not easily cross. The presence of an ostensibly Roman Catholic symbol in the chapel of this "non-denominational" school was an offense to a number of students. Meanwhile, the "sociological fact"[53] of this offense captured the faculty's attention and focused their objections on the actions of the dean. At least, this was how the crucifix controversy presented itself in faculty meetings. Clearly, Horton was enthusiastic about the ecumenically bold implications of the crucifix. But, at this early juncture in his deanship, he did not wish to challenge the faculty too aggressively on the matter. Nonetheless, the Larson crucifix reappeared in the Andover Chapel in the fall of 1957. In time it was accompanied by a wooden, hand-carved chalice, matching paten, and candlesticks. Horton had commissioned the artist Leroy Setziol, of Portland, Oregon, to create these items for the chapel. But on this occasion, no student protest ensued. Perhaps the calm was related

---

[51]Ibid., 16 November and 14 December 1956.

[52]Ibid., 14 December 1956.

[53]The phrase was C. Conrad Wright's. It referred to the unilateral installation of the crucifix in the chapel and the sociological meaning of that—from a certain point of view—undemocratic act. CFM, 16 November 1956.

to the fact that *The Scribe* had been discontinued, mysteriously, shortly after its editors raised the question "Do We Want a Crucifix in Andover Chapel?" But the calm may also have foreshadowed another metamorphosis the Divinity School was about to experience, one that enabled the faculty to consider the Roman Catholic presence directly.[54]

The Stillman Guest Professorship

Douglas Horton introduced the Larson crucifix to the Divinity School community on 29 February 1956. Two weeks earlier he had announced to the faculty his plan to reinstate to the annual rotation the third "Dudleian Lecture," which was eliminated unceremoniously after 1904, probably on account of its contentious and illiberal focus.[55] According to the terms set forth in the mid-eighteenth century, the third lecture was meant

> for the detecting and convicting and exposing the Idolatry of the Romish Church, their tyranny, usurpations, damnable heresies, and other crying wickednesses in their high places, and finally [for exposing] that the church of Rome is that mystical Babylon, that man of sin, that apostate church spoken of in the New Testament.

Horton suggested to his colleagues that a more positive approach to Catholic and Protestant relations should be advanced through the lectureship. Creatively, he insisted that such a change was an effective way to honor both the wishes of the donor and "the demands of the modern day."[56]

Two months later, in May 1956, while the crucifix controversy was astir among the Divinity School students, President Pusey was present at the monthly Divinity School faculty meeting. There he mentioned an inquiry brought to him from a member of the Harvard Catholic Club. Pusey's correspondent sought guidance in the effort to establish a chair

[54]Horton discussed the need for the new tableware as well as its design. See the letters between Horton and Leroy Setziol, 18 July 1957 to 6 February 1958, CSM.

[55]The Dudleian Lectures were established by the will of Paul Dudley, who died in 1751. The lecture topics, to appear in four-year rotation, were "natural religion, revealed religion, the errors of Popery, and the validity of non-episcopal ordination." See Williams, *The Harvard Divinity School*, 39, 270.

[56] The terms for the third lecture and Horton's comments both appear in CFM, 17 February 1956.

in Roman Catholic studies at the university. Several Divinity School faculty members expressed their concerns about who would be responsible for making such an appointment: would it be the Roman Catholic hierarchy, or would the university exercise authority over the decision? Pusey assured the faculty that the Harvard Corporation would have the final say in this appointment, were such a chair to be created. He also noted the advantage to Catholic students generally and to the Divinity School as well of having a "more established Catholic representation" at Harvard.[57]

Pusey and Horton had corresponded about the appointment prior to the faculty meeting. At the end of April, Pusey had forwarded to Horton the letter he had received from David Horgan, president of the Harvard Catholic Club. Pusey asked for Horton's comments and "help in formulating a reply," which Horton quickly supplied. In his cover letter to Pusey, Horton strongly advised against establishing the chair in the university under the auspices of the Faculty of Arts and Sciences. He felt that such a move would undermine all the work Pusey had accomplished in reestablishing the religious—that is, the Protestant—character of Harvard. To have a chair for Roman Catholic studies in the university, Horton wrote, "would take us back into the futile days of noncommitment—as if it were a matter of indifference to Harvard whether the university moved in a Protestant or a Catholic direction."[58]

In his attached "Memorandum on the Proposal of the Harvard Catholic Club," Horton spelled out the advantages of locating the chair in the Divinity School. While there would be "maximum contact between Catholic and Protestant scholars," there would not be competition among separate faculties leading to tensions and inevitable lawsuits. Within the Divinity School, Horton felt it would be better to keep the position from becoming "entrenched"; he therefore recommended that a regular—though untenured—faculty position be established. Horton envisioned an endowed chair that would rotate approximately every three years; the incumbent might be a theologian, then a historian, then a liturgist, and so on.[59] Satisfied with Horton's memorandum, Pusey incor-

[57]Ibid., 4 May 1956.

[58]Nathan M. Pusey to Horton, 30 April 1956, CSM; Horton to Nathan M. Pusey (with attached "Memorandum on the Proposal of the Harvard Catholic Club"), 4 May 1956, CSM.

[59]Ibid.

porated it into his reply to Horgan in mid-June, along with an advisory that the cost of an endowed chair would be around $400,000.[60]

Word about the possibility of a Catholic chair spread through Harvard circles during the summer and fall. In January 1957, Chauncey Stillman, an alumnus of the university, presented a proposal to Pusey for the establishment of a chair in memory of his father: the Charles Chauncey Stillman Chair of Catholic Theological Studies. Later that month Pusey set the proposal before the Divinity School faculty. Immediately, theology professor Paul Lehmann raised a caution that would be central to the debates about the chair during the ensuing months. Lehmann wondered if the Divinity School had established itself sufficiently in the eyes of the mainline Protestant churches to warrant this innovation. He was concerned that the Divinity School might be perceived as a graduate school of religion, merely—an image the school had acquired in the past but which it had been struggling nobly to overcome during this period of revitalization.[61]

With both Lehmann and Paul Tillich advising caution, the matter rested for a couple of months. Then on 17 April 1957, Horton proposed that the Divinity School accept the Stillman gift with the understanding that 1) the title "Chair of Roman Catholic Theological Studies" referred to the subject matter and not necessarily the confessional identity of the holder of the chair; 2) the appointment was for a specified period of time, and thus a "visiting," not a permanent, position; and 3) the Divinity School would determine the appointee. This last point was made because Horton wished to secure the Divinity School's enduring claim to the chair even though the chair holder would be expected to teach undergraduates in the Faculty of Arts and Sciences in addition to Divinity School students.

Significant debate ensued among faculty members who felt that the establishment of a chair of Roman Catholic studies might compromise the Protestant character of the Divinity School. President Pusey argued that the faculty's "prime responsibility [was] training scholars for the Protestant ministry." He did not think this mission was incompatible with the proposed chair. But others felt that the Protestant character of the school would be unnecessarily qualified. When the dust settled, Horton assured his colleagues that training for the Protestant ministry

[60]Nathan M. Pusey to David Horgan, 20 June 1956, CSM.
[61]CFM, 16 January 1957.

would be enhanced if Harvard's students could "see their own Protestantism in the light of critical eyes." He also announced that he had contacted the leaders of seven different Protestant denominations. They told him that they looked to Harvard for "a new step in Protestant-Catholic relations, carefully guarding Protestantism on the one hand and characterized by a certain *agape* toward other religions," on the other.[62]

On that note, the faculty voted twelve to six in favor of Horton's proposal on 17 April 1957. The following day, professor of theology and faculty secretary Richard R. Niebuhr received letters from professors Tillich and Dillenberger, who had been absent from the faculty meeting, registering their opposition to the vote.[63] Given significant opposition to the plan for the Stillman chair, President Pusey decided to initiate a "cooling-off" period, during which time no official action would be taken.[64]

Horton, however, campaigned forthrightly for the Stillman chair in the ensuing months. Characteristic of his advocacy was a speech he delivered later in April to a gathering of Divinity School alumni. Horton significantly cast the ecumenical overture in terms of the Puritan tradition. "We are a Puritan institution and remain so," Horton announced. But Puritanism had changed, he continued. Once in danger of its life, Puritanism had been "fugitive, self-protective." Now, however, Puritanism could "afford to be itself in a large way and take the initiative in religious magnanimity and understanding." In the end, Horton argued, it was Puritanism that brought Harvard to this "new and better epoch in what are usually called Catholic-Protestant relations."[65]

This line of rhetoric appealed to the generosity of spirit and openness that Horton had always attributed to William Ames. On the basis of his "Amesian" concept of Puritanism, then, Horton was arguing against separatism both at Harvard and in the concurrent, ongoing debates over the formation of the United Church of Christ, whose union was to be inaugurated in June 1957. Horton's speech also displayed the "hermeneutic of trust" that enabled him to find ecumenical intention behind the literal words of the Dudley bequest, its reference to the Roman Catholic Church as "that mystical Babylon [and] apostate church" notwithstanding.

---

[62]Ibid., 17 April 1957. The Protestant leaders are not named.

[63]Ibid.

[64]George H. Williams, "Dawson Minute (Draft)," 8 October 1971, 3, CGO.

[65]Douglas Horton, "Close Akin and Distant: Harvard Divinity School and Religious Bodies," 30 April 1957, 11, CDH.

With arguments like these at his command, arguments that were based more on ideological presuppositions than self-evident facts (as was also the case concerning Congregationalism B), Horton was able to solidify support for the Stillman chair from virtually the entire faculty. On 6 February 1958, Horton sent a letter to Roman Catholic theologian Christopher Dawson in Oxford, England, suggesting that he would have a very important matter to discuss in person with Dawson when he arrived in England the following week. Dawson was a Roman Catholic lay theologian of international renown. His Gifford Lectures of 1947 and 1948 were published as the significant volumes *Religion and Culture* and *Religion and the Rise of Western Culture*. Although he functioned as an independent scholar, Dawson had taught during the middle 1930s at the University College, Exeter, and at the University of Liverpool. The fact that he was not a member of any Roman Catholic order far outweighed (positively) his lack of ongoing teaching experience in the eyes of Dawson's future Protestant colleagues. Before the end of February 1958, Horton delivered to Dawson an invitation to become the Divinity School's first Stillman guest professor of Roman Catholic theology, and Dawson officially accepted.[66]

Besides the appeal to a benign—and from Horton's point of view, inevitably ecumenical—Puritan tradition, the struggle over the Stillman chair reveals tensions that inhered in Catholic-Protestant relations during the 1950s. These tensions were manifested in the objections raised against the Roman Catholic presence in the Divinity School, even among students and faculty members who would characterize themselves as "ecumenical." But the tensions are also evident subtly and perhaps more significantly in Horton's insistence that the Stillman chair should be situated in the Divinity School in the first place, rather than in the Faculty of Arts and Sciences. At least in the Divinity School, Protestant control could be exercised over the Catholic voice. This concern for Protestant hegemony in matters of religion was characteristic of the Divinity School during the Horton era. Indeed, the effort to

---

[66]Horton's preliminary letter never reached Dawson. The envelope was stamped "Undelivered for Reason Stated: Return to Sender." The reason stated at the bottom of the envelope was "Deceased." See Horton to Christopher Dawson, 6 February 1958, CGO; "Dean Horton's Report to the Faculty of Harvard Divinity School," 21 February 1958, CGO.

establish a center for the study of the world's religions also centered on the benefit of such a center to the mainline Protestant churches and their future ministers.

The Center for the Study of World Religions

During the fall of 1956—shortly after the Larson crucifix appeared in the Andover Chapel and just before the Stillman Chair was proposed—another overture was brought to Horton's attention. The Divinity School received the offer of a significant endowment to be used "to encourage the sympathetic presentation of the religions of the world as they are seen by believers in each faith." The offer came from Genevieve Ludlow Griscom, the surviving member of a community called Chapel Farm. The community had undertaken the sympathetic study of the world's religions under the guiding conviction of a fundamental unity and reality behind all religions, a common root "in the spiritual world" from which the truth of the various religions had grown. In their own studies, the members of Chapel Farm had paid particular attention to the mystical and devotional writings of various religions. Genevieve Griscom wished to expose students of religion to devout practitioners of other faiths so that the students might attain "a deeper appreciation of the spiritual insights of their own faiths."[67]

In an effort to secure the endowment for the Divinity School, Horton met on numerous occasions with Griscom and her representatives in New York City and at Colgate University. Meanwhile, the Divinity School faculty's Committee on Educational Policy drafted a response to Griscom's "Statement of Intent." From the faculty's point of view, her proposal presented various potential dangers. It could be construed as advocating a syncretistic view of religion, for example, which might in turn "magnify identities and minimize differences" among religions. This philosophical predisposition to impose a position seemed contrary to the exercise of free academic inquiry in all encounters among practitioners of different faiths. But the optimism of the donor was not seen as a serious deterrent to accepting the endowment. Indeed, the committee was enthusiastic about the prospect of engaging living representatives of the world's religions in conversation.[68]

---

[67]Genevieve Ludlow Griscom, "Statement of Intent," n.d. (circa October 1956), CFS.

[68]"Comment on the Preliminary Statement by the Committee on Educational Policy of the Harvard Divinity School, November 26, 1956," CFS.

Central to the concerns of both the faculty and Genevieve Griscom was the selection of an appropriate director for a program in the study of the world's religions. The faculty sought someone who was familiar with the denominational scene in American Protestantism; they also wanted a person who was an acknowledged scholar of religions. Once again, the Divinity School needed to chart a course between the university's emphasis on academic excellence and the need of the Protestant mainline churches for ministerial graduates imbued with a practical—rather than an exotic—sense of religion. But finding a person who could respond to these twin concerns proved difficult. It would take over a year for a candidate to emerge with the credentials that would satisfy the Divinity School, Griscom, and the donors whom Griscom represented.

In the meantime, Horton campaigned for the idea of expanding the Divinity School's relations with other religious bodies. In the same speech in which he introduced the idea of the Stillman Chair to Harvard Divinity School alumni, Horton contrasted the "literary" approach to the study of the world's religions with the approach he hoped to see inaugurated at the Divinity School in the near future. If students simply read the sacred writings of other religions and "corresponded" with practitioners of the systems under study, something useful could be learned. This, however, would prove unsatisfactory in the long run. Horton likened such an approach to learning about the human body from cadavers. "Medicine came alive when it began to deal with live bodies," he proclaimed. By analogy, conversations with the world's great religions needed to occur "at the point where they are most alive, namely, in the person of their devotees." Although Harvard University contained numerous "Christian experts" on a variety of faiths, Horton emphasized the importance of face-to-face encounters with "commanding representatives" of the world's religions.[69]

Horton reassured his audience that Christianity had nothing to fear from such encounters with people of other faiths. Echoing the Puritan minister John Robinson, Horton asserted, "Ours is a faith that enquires, that is never so much itself as when it is open to all the light that God has for it." Expanding on Robinson's famous insight (that "more light would break forth from the Word of God"), Horton extended an invitation to leaders of other religions to come to Harvard Divinity School:

[69]Horton, "Close Akin and Distant," 9–10.

"Let them exhibit to us and we to them our pearls of spiritual discernment until the school glows and corrusicates [sic] with new light on every truth to which we are committed."

For Horton, the purpose of the exchange was to prepare Divinity School graduates for ministry in the world of many religions. His own experience as a world traveler and as a trustee of the American University in Cairo undoubtedly informed this intention. Pan American World Airways inaugurated regularly scheduled transatlantic jet flights in 1958, and in the advent of the Jet Age, the distances that separated the world's various cultures were quickly shrinking. "Our graduates are going to encounter the religions of the world when they go out from these walls," Horton reasoned; "should they not make their adjustment to them here, where *agape* and *theologia* can meet under happy auspices?"

At the end of his speech, Horton framed the entire interest in world religions in the context of the mandate handed over to the school by the O'Brian Commission back in 1947: namely, to make the Divinity School a "center of religious learning." He again emphasized that this did not mean that the Divinity School was abandoning its Christian identity. On the contrary, he asserted that "We are Christians who want to know non-Christians better." He concluded with a powerful declaration of Christian faith that simultaneously expressed his faith that Christian hegemony had nothing to fear from other religions:

> We believe that the revelation of God in Jesus Christ is as ultimate as love can make it. This is our charter—and it seems to us to follow from this that contacts with other religions should be made and maintained in an aura of that very love which ruled the life of that same Jesus Christ.[70]

Throughout the year, Horton sought the names of candidates for the leadership of a center for the study of world religions. He brought the matter before his colleagues at the summer 1957 meeting of the Faith and Order Commission of the World Council of Churches and reported his findings to the faculty in the fall. Very few Americans appeared qualified for the position and it seemed as if it might be necessary to appoint a temporary director while looking for the right person for the post. Eventually, a tentative list of candidates was compiled and circulated to specialists around the world. In his response to the list, Wilfred Cantwell

[70]Ibid., 10–12.

Smith of the Islamic Institute at McGill University in Montreal, Quebec, introduced a new name to the pool: his colleague Robert Slater. Slater was an ordained priest in the Anglican Church. Though British, he had earned his Ph.D. degree at Columbia University in New York and taught there for a time before moving to Canada. He was also an expert on Theravada Buddhism, which he studied during six years as a lecturer at the Rangoon University in Burma. Smith called Slater's book *Paradox and Nirvana* (1948) "really brilliant" and cast Slater's attitude toward the comparative study of religion in terms that Horton could appreciate: "the significant matters of study in comparative religion are the points at which the religions most disagree, most searchingly challenge each other, rather than their similarities."[71]

Robert Slater proved to be the candidate for whom both Harvard and Genevieve Griscom were looking. In an agreement signed on Christmas Eve 1957, Griscom established an endowment called the "Fund for the Study of the Great Religions of the World" and transferred $400,000 to Harvard. Slater joined the Divinity School in the fall of 1958, the very term when Roman Catholic theologian Christopher Dawson first occupied the Stillman chair. It was Horton's final academic year as dean.[72]

The Horton Years at Harvard Divinity School

During the era of its revitalization (1953–1959), the Harvard Divinity School was transformed from a diminishing nondenominational school offering ministerial training and a doctoral program in the history of religions into a bastion of American mainline Protestantism and, indeed, a major ecumenical center for the world. Certainly Douglas Horton does not deserve all the credit for this metamorphosis. Forces were at work at Harvard and in the American culture generally that made Horton's tenure as dean so successful. At Harvard, plans for the revitalization of the Divinity School had been in place since before Dean Sperry's retirement. Vast sums of money had been pledged by the Rockefeller Foundation and many other agencies and individuals. New faculty members had appeared before Horton's arrival, including John Dillenberger in theology, Krister Stendahl in New Testament, and C. Conrad Wright

---

[71]Wilfred Cantwell Smith to Horton, 1 July 1957, CFS.
[72]Endowment Agreement, 24 December 1957, and the announcements of the Slater and Dawson appointments, 15 April 1958, CFS.

in New England church history. The appointment of Paul Tillich as University Professor was made without Horton's counsel, as was the decision to admit women to the Divinity School beginning in 1955. Of course, all of these advances occurred under the supportive wing of Nathan Pusey, whose enthusiasm for the Divinity School was unrivaled by that of other Harvard University presidents during the twentieth century.

Americans were also looking to religion during Horton's years as dean. American society experienced a "turn to religion" in the aftermath of World War II, the likes of which the nation had not experienced before. By 1957, church membership in the United States was at an all-time high of 67 percent of the population. In response to the demands of college students who were "on a great spontaneous quest [for] God" (according to *Newsweek* magazine), two thirds of the nation's state universities were offering courses in religion. Billy Graham's Madison Square Garden crusade attracted over a million participants, "breaking all records."[73] It is possible to conclude from such figures that Horton appeared at the Divinity School fortuitously in 1955 on the crest of a religious wave that he rode (albeit deftly) to the shores of retirement four years later.[74] Still, many of the advances made at the school during Horton's tenure were directly attributable to him.

When Horton began his deanship, 198 students were enroled at the Divinity School. Enrolment increased during each successive year of his tenure, and by his final academic year, 1958–1959, the total number of students had reached 256—more students than the school had ever before enroled. Horton was instrumental in generating good publicity about the Divinity School and its new mission. As mentioned above, *Life* magazine, the *Christian Century*, *Newsweek*, and the *Harvard Alumni Magazine* all offered extensive coverage of the Divinity School. In some cases, this coverage included profiles of Horton, in which he highlighted the needs and goals of the Harvard Divinity School.[75] During his

[73]Robert S. Ellwood, *The Fifties Spiritual Marketplace: American Religion in a Decade of Conflict* (New Brunswick: Rutgers, 1997) 177. Ellwood quotes from the article "Religion in Our Colleges," *Newsweek*, 22 April 1957, 115.

[74]Williams's account of the Horton years at Harvard tends to emphasize the momentum of forces already at work prior to Horton's arrival. See "Divinings," chapters 7 and 8.

[75]See the profiles of Horton in "Harvard Portraits—90," *Harvard Alumni Bulletin*, 8 October 1955, 63; "We at Harvard," *Newsweek*, 22 April 1957, 118; and "Divinity Dean Wins Harvard," *Christian Science Monitor*, 1 October 1955.

deanship, Horton also traveled extensively throughout the country to promote the Divinity School and to secure finances for its ambitious plans. By the spring of 1957, the value of the Harvard name in the field of theology was such that the Oxford University Press approached Horton with a proposal: Oxford wished to publish a series of carefully edited collections from the Reformation and post-Reformation era. The title for the series, it was hoped, would be "The Harvard Library of Protestant Thought." The name was intended to draw on Harvard's traditional and freshly minted reputations and to signal the involvement of Harvard's expanding theology faculty in the editorial process. John Dillenberger was to chair the editorial board. Although the Harvard Corporation did not allow the Harvard name to be used, the project did develop under Dillenberger's direction into the important series "A Library of Protestant Thought."[76]

The process of faculty selection was quite informal during this era and the dean's role in assembling new faculty was crucial. Potential candidates met with members of the faculty, or they were brought to campus to deliver a lecture at the Divinity School. If the appointments committee recommended the candidate to the dean, the dean would then decide whether or not to recommend the candidate to President Pusey. In cases involving tenure, an ad hoc committee of experts from outside Harvard would review the candidate's credentials and make its recommendation to the president.[77] Inevitably, friends and acquaintances of Horton ended up as candidates for faculty positions at Harvard Divinity School. Richard R. Niebuhr, for example, had served with Horton on their denomination's Joint Committee for the Preliminary Study of Theological Doctrine beginning in 1955, when Horton was still the minister to the General Council of the Congregational Christian Churches. In anticipation of Niebuhr's future significance, Horton suggested that the current Vassar College lecturer might well become "*the* thinker for the United Church [of Christ]."[78] Professor Robert Grant of Chicago was

[76]Correspondence between Horton and Wilber D. Ruggles, religious book editor at Oxford University Press, 8 April–6 August 1957, CSM.

[77]These procedures are spelled out by Horton in CFM, 16 September 1955. The constitution of ad hoc committees is identified in the Harvard Divinity School "Appointments Committee (1955–56)" and "Ad Hoc Committee (3/8/56)" files, CFS.

[78]See Horton to Vere Loper, 30 December 1954, BGC. Italics have been supplied, but Horton's emphasis is clear in the context of the original letter.

nominated for a position in New Testament, but he withdrew his name prior to review by President Pusey. Grant was the son of Horton's life-long friend, Frederick Grant, who served on the Episcopal committee that helped compose the *Basic Formula for Church Union* in 1938; he was also Horton's son-in-law. Amos Wilder, a longtime associate since Horton's ministerial days in Chicago, had been professor of New Testament at Harvard Divinity School since 1954. In 1956 he was promoted to the Hollis Professorship of Divinity, the oldest endowed chair in the nation.

The members of the ad hoc advisory committees, who were significantly involved in determining tenure decisions, were also generally well acquainted with Horton. Among those who served during Horton's tenure were Horton's former parishioner and longtime friend Wilhelm Pauck of the Chicago Divinity School and subsequently of Union Theological Seminary. Liston Pope and Roland Bainton of Yale University, both of whom had been Horton's allies in the effort to bring the United Church of Christ into existence, were also members of an ad hoc committee. So was Henry Pitney Van Dusen, president of Union Theological Seminary, who had, in his capacity as chair of Harvard University's External Committee during the mid-1950s, recommended Horton to President Pusey for the deanship. Van Dusen later reflected that his recommendation of Horton was "the best thing I ever did for Harvard."[79] As historian Heather A. Warren has demonstrated, Van Dusen was at the center of a network of Protestant leaders who exercised great influence over both the major theological schools in America and the worldwide ecumenical movement during the mid-twentieth century. Although Horton had been a lecturer in Congregational polity at Union between 1948 and 1955, he was not a member of Van Dusen's particular "Theological Discussion Group." Still, Horton's denominational and ecumenical activities brought him into contact with many of the members of that group, including Pauck, the Niebuhr brothers, and Walter Marshall Horton.[80]

In other words, Horton was a prominent member of the Protestant establishment. This network of church leaders exercised "custodianship" over Protestant religious institutions — and much else in American cul-

---

[79]H. P. Van Dusen, "I Knew Him When He Was a Trustee and Lecturer at Union Seminary," in "Douglas Horton, I Knew Him When: A Book of Reminiscences" (1966), RHF.

[80]See Heather A. Warren, *Theologians of a New World Order: Reinhold Niebuhr and the Christian Realists (1920–1948)* (New York: Oxford, 1997) 124–26.

ture—during the first half of the twentieth century.[81] Horton's network was pieced together over the many years of his career, beginning with his relationship to S. Parkes Cadman and Douglas Mackenzie. He also stayed in touch with important leaders in the Protestant establishment. The multiple contacts Horton made with Harvard Divinity School Dean Sperry, as described at the beginning of this chapter, illustrate Horton's ability to develop and maintain relationships with these leaders; his enduring friendship with fellow Barth student, Wilhelm Pauck, is another example. As part of this establishment, Horton served as a trustee on the boards of Princeton University and the American University in Cairo, as well as those of the theological seminaries of Hartford, Union, and Chicago.

This network also had significant ties to corporate America. One student at Harvard Divinity School during the Horton era recalled an eye-opening experience that took place during a meeting in Jewett House, the dean's home. On the mantel, apparently in a place of honor, rested a curious little box. The student asked what the object was, and Mildred McAfee Horton told him it was a radio. The student stared in disbelief as Mildred Horton demonstrated how the device functioned and informed him that it was put together with "transistors." The radio was not yet available generally, but she assured him that soon everyone would know about the transistor radio. Mildred Horton knew about it because she was a member of the board of directors of the corporation that manufactured it: the Radio Corporation of America.[82]

Contact with corporate America put Douglas Horton in touch with philanthropists and grant agencies that were enthusiastic about bolstering the Harvard Divinity School during its period of revitalization. Horton shepherded funds from the Rockefeller Foundation, for example, into the Divinity School's endowment.[83] He also maintained constant corre-

---

[81]Horton's familial ties to this network are discussed in chapter 1. See also William R. Hutchison, preface and "Protestantism as Establishment" in Hutchison, ed., *Between the Times.*

[82]This event occurred circa 1956. Related to the author by Richard Arthur, 16 June 1997.

[83]For Harvard's link to the philanthropic empire of John D. Rockefeller Jr., see Albert F. Schenkel, *The Rich Man and the Kingdom: John D. Rockefeller and the Protestant Establishment* (Minneapolis: Fortress Press, 1995). Although Horton is not mentioned in the book, he traversed the same American Protestant and ecumenical territory so dear to Rockefeller: the International World Missionary Conference, the National Council of Churches (Horton was on the planning committee for the NCC and

spondence with those predisposed to financially support the projects of various faculty members and visitors, not to mention the Divinity School's physical upkeep.[84] In fact, Horton oversaw significant physical changes at the Divinity School during his tenure as dean. Andover Hall was refurbished and the dean's office relocated from the second floor to a position on the first floor, near the entryway to the building. Significantly, Jewett House, directly across the street from Andover Hall, was established as the dean's residence. Not only was the Horton home an important symbol of the expanding Divinity School, but it also represented the developing Divinity School community. In an affectionate letter to the Hortons, sent after "another open-hearted" Christmas party at Jewett House, George Williams remarked on the house's unifying power. The Divinity School, according to Williams, "had been woven together now as one and . . . had under [the Hortons'] resourceful ministrations become one household of faith and common endeavor."[85]

In addition to refurbishing Andover Hall, Horton initiated two other projects that were completed during the tenure of Samuel Miller, Horton's successor as dean. The first was the construction of the new Center for the Study of World Religions, located on the property adjacent to Jewett House. The Center provided living quarters and study and worship spaces for scholars who were to come to Harvard from around the world. The second project was the addition of a much-needed wing to the Andover-Harvard Library. In 1957, Horton had envisioned an addition of five floors, but in the event of insufficient funds, he allowed that the fourth and fifth floors could be added later. After raising the necessary funds

---

Mildred McAfee Horton was the first female vice president of the NCC), and the World Council of Churches.

[84]For example, Horton maintained a lengthy correspondence with Geraldine Thompson of Brookdale Farm in Red Bank, New Jersey. Thompson provided significant underwriting for Richard McCann, who studied and taught about the problems of juvenile delinquency as a nontenured member of the Divinity School faculty. After McCann left Harvard for Andover-Newton, Horton secured funds from Mrs. Thompson for Professor Walter Leibrecht (who came to Harvard as an assistant to Paul Tillich) to continue McCann's work at the Divinity School. Expressing his appreciation of her previous generosity and soliciting future aid, Horton wrote to Mrs. Thompson, "I am afraid that the only contribution I have made to the campaign is to point out that we really need ten million dollars instead of just seven!" (Horton to Geraldine Thompson, 3 January 1956, CSM).

[85]George Williams to Douglas and Mildred Horton, 15 December 1958, CDH.

to ensure the project's success, Horton himself took delight in helping to design the new wing.[86] Later, in view of his significant role in orchestrating the construction of the new wing and because he had donated his personal rare book collection to the Divinity School, Horton's portrait was hung in the Rare Books Reading Room of the expanded library.

The Divinity School as a World Center for Religious Learning

The fame of the Divinity School during the Horton era made it a desirable destination for scholars from many nations. As the 1947 O'Brian Commission had hoped, Harvard truly had become a world center for religious learning, and the Divinity School attracted numerous international scholars. Three of these visitors in particular demonstrate Horton's decisive role in the Divinity School's metamorphosis and revitalization: Eberhard Bethge, Hoseki Shin-ichi Hisamatsu, and Georges Florovsky.

In the fall of 1957, Eberhard Bethge, on leave from his duties as pastor of the German-speaking Protestant parish in London, arrived at Harvard to spend a year collecting and editing the writings of his teacher and friend, the German theologian Dietrich Bonhoeffer, who had been martyred in the cause of resistance to the Nazis in 1945. The suggestion to invite Bethge was made by Paul Lehmann, who had known Bonhoeffer when they were both students of Reinhold Niebuhr at Union Theological Seminary in the early 1930s. (In 1939, Lehmann and Niebuhr tried jointly to arrange a speaking tour for Bonhoeffer in the United States, but Bonhoeffer was determined to return to Germany.) Horton heartily endorsed the invitation, in part because he had known Bonhoeffer personally through his work in both the Faith and Order and the Life and Works movements in the late 1920s. Horton worked tirelessly to obtain a grant for Bethge's stay. Eventually, the Danforth Foundation provided funds sufficient to bring Bethge and his family to Harvard.[87]

---

[86]See Horton's four-page memo, "Thoughts concerning additions to the Andover-Harvard Library: May 17, 1957," CGO. Horton's detailed memo even suggests how the furniture ought to be arranged on each floor. The "new wing" remained a three-story building until finances were secured to complete the fourth and fifth levels in 2001.

[87]Horton had first contacted the Rockefeller Foundation on Bethge's behalf, but he was turned down because the director had never heard of Bonhoeffer and considered him insignificant. See "Prospectus of the Bonhoeffer Research Project" and copies of the correspondence among Reinhold Niebuhr, Paul Lehmann, and Dietrich Bonhoeffer, CGO.

During the spring of 1958, Bethge taught a Harvard course on Bonhoeffer's theology using Bonhoeffer's book *The Cost of Discipleship*, whose English version, he was saddened to discover, lacked several key chapters.[88] In addition, he edited the first two volumes of Bonhoeffer's collected works and corresponded with hundreds of people who had known Bonhoeffer at different stages throughout the theologian's life. Eventually, Bethge prepared a 300-page manuscript which, after ten years and hundreds of more pages, became his seminal work, his Bonhoeffer biography.[89]

A second visitor to the campus during the fall of 1957 was the Zen master and professor of fine arts Hoseki Shin-ichi Hisamatsu of Kyoto, Japan. Professor Hisamatsu and his translator and colleague, Jikai Fujiyoshi, were brought to Cambridge by the Rockefeller Foundation. Horton played a significant role in arranging the itinerary for the two scholars. He helped set up meetings with the ministers of the Central Union Congregational Church in Honolulu; Zen interpreter Alan Watts in San Francisco; Stuart Anderson, president of the Pacific School of Religion in Berkeley; and Jerald Brauer of the Chicago Divinity School. Horton also arranged for Hisamatsu to meet with faculty from numerous departments and schools throughout the Harvard community.[90]

At Harvard, Hisamatsu gave five student seminars; three faculty lectures at Jewett House, the dean's residence; and numerous public lectures on such topics as Zen, art, and psychology. Horton conjectured that there was "no better place in the Western world to study Zen Buddhism" than at Harvard during that semester, particularly because Hisamatsu's friend D. T. Suzuki took up residence in Cambridge during Hisamatsu's stay.[91] Hisamatsu's presence at Harvard significantly advanced the cause of world religions at Harvard. Because of his contact with Hisamatsu, Paul Tillich undertook a journey to Japan in the sum-

---

[88]Eberhard Bethge to David Paton (of SCM Press), 2 February 1958, CGO.

[89]See Bethge's "Report," 27 November 1958 (sent from London), CGO. See also Eberhard Bethge, *Dietrich Bonhoeffer: Theologe, Christ, Zeitgenosse* (Munich: Chr. Kaiser Verlag, 1967). The English version appeared a few years later (*Dietrich Bonhoeffer: Theologian, Christian, Contemporary* [trans. Eric Mosbacher et al.; New York: Harper and Row, 1970]).

[90]See letters from Horton to Hoseki Shin-ichi Hisamatsu and others between July 1957 and February 1958, CGO, and the letter from Charles B. Fahs (of the Rockefeller Foundation) to Hisamatsu, 7 August 1957, CGO.

[91]Horton, "Close Akin and Distant," 12.

mer of 1960. During that pilgrimage, Tillich visited with Hisamatsu in a 700-year-old rock garden at a Kyoto temple and there "fell into a discussion . . . about the question of whether the rock garden and the universe are identical (the position of the Buddhists) or non-identical but united by participation ([Tillich's] position)." Tillich returned to the States shorn of his "western provincialism" and fascinated by the study of comparative religions.[92]

A third "visitor" to Harvard was the Russian Orthodox theologian Georges Florovsky. Father Florovsky was an Eastern Orthodox advocate of the ecumenical movement whom Horton had met through the Faith and Order movement. Florovsky intially came to the Divinity School as a guest lecturer in Eastern Church History in the fall of 1955.[93] He continued at Harvard during the ensuing years as professor of the history of Eastern Orthodoxy. In the spring of 1958, Florovsky delivered the "third" Dudleian Lecture on Catholicism, the first such lecture since 1904, now under the reformed focus promoted by Horton. The title of the lecture was "The Christian Dilemma."

The presence of these men and many other people like them showed a development in the life of the Divinity School that was very dear to Horton. In a letter to acting dean George Williams prior to his arrival on campus in 1955, Horton described in terms that approached the eschatological his vision for the Harvard Divinity School. "The Divinity School is a meeting place," he modestly began. He went on to consider the types of meetings that he thought could take place when the Divinity School functioned "like the meetinghouse of old New England." But in his concluding paragraph, Horton reached beyond the confines of the Puritan past and the Protestant present to articulate his vision for the future:

> In India it is said that the truly sacred places of the earth are those where two rivers meet. So Allahabad . . . lies at the confluence of the Ganges and the Jumna. In a somewhat similar way, it may be said that the Divinity School of Harvard University is a place of importance because it stands at the confluence of many streams. Here meet the precedents of the

[92]Tillich, "Informal Report on Lecture Trip to Japan—Summer 1960," 7, 15, CGO.
[93]Douglas Horton, "Annual Report of the Divinity School, 1955–1956," *Official Register of Harvard University*, 54/22, 363, CHU. See also "Horton Outlines General Expansion: Florovsky to Join Divinity Faculty," *Harvard Crimson*, 18 January 1956, 1.

past and the needs of the present, the insights of scholarship
and the eternal verities of faith, the grace of God and the
aspirations of all sorts and conditions of men.[94]

By the close of Horton's tenure at Harvard Divinity School in 1959,
his protoeschatological vision was at least partially realized.

The Horton Legacy at Harvard Divinity School

At the midpoint of Horton's Harvard career, in 1957, church affiliation
throughout the United States hit an all-time high. But within a year, religious participation decreased, at least among the mainline Protestant
churches. In 1958, for the first time since the end of World War II, Protestant church membership in general failed to increase in proportion to population growth. While Southern Baptists, Lutherans, and the Assemblies of
God, for example, actually experienced membership growth in 1958, the
United Church of Christ, the Presbyterian Church (U.S.A.), the Methodist Church, and the Episcopal Church all commenced a period of decline
that was to persist for the rest of the century.[95]

These four waning denominations, along with the Unitarians, made
up more than three-quarters of the Harvard Divinity School population
in 1958. This downturn did not affect the Harvard Divinity School population immediately. But in the year after Horton's retirement, his successor, Samuel Miller, reported a decrease in the total number of students to 217. Miller expected this number to stay relatively stable for
the next few years; still, he conceded that by 1960 the era of "spectacular growth" had passed.[96]

[94]Horton to George Williams, n.d. [circa July 1955], CGO.

[95]Ellwood, *The Fifties Spiritual Marketplace*, 176. Compare Wade Clark Roof and
William McKinney, *American Mainline Religion* (New Brunswick: Rutgers, 1987) 150,
and Douglas Horton, "Annual Report of the Divinity School, 1957–1958," *Official
Register of Harvard University*, 56/22 (21 December 1961) 295–96, CHU. In accord
with the general demographic assumptions made by the mainline churches, Peter L.
Halvorson and William M. Newman (*An Atlas of American Religions* [Atlanta: Glenmary,
1994] 126) claim that "between 1952 and 1971 the United Church of Christ gained
adherents at the same rate (14%) by which, in turn, it lost adherents between 1971 and
1990." Their figures, however, compare data collected in 1952 and 1971. They apparently neither account for the spectacular increases between 1952 and 1957, nor the
gradual decline that ensued thereafter.

[96]Samuel Miller, "Report of the Divinity School, 1959–1960," *Official Register of
Harvard University*, 58/26 (21 December 1961) 176, CHU.

In a sense, Horton had prepared the Harvard Divinity School for mainline Protestantism's numerical decline by expanding the school's client base. Horton promoted a kind of ecumenism that looked backwards to reclaim common traditions. His use of William Ames in the convocation address of 1955, for example, looked behind the veil of contemporary division between Congregationalists and Unitarians, to their common Puritan origin. Ames became so central to Horton's ecumenical vision that Horton taught and translated Ames's works for the rest of his life. Horton also introduced a daily "informal and brief dignified chapel service" soon after his arrival in Cambridge. His ecumenical sensibility was underscored by his choice of Edward VI's second prayer book for these community services. Horton preferred this order of worship because it was composed "before many of the divisions in Christendom had arisen."[97] Similarly, it could be argued that Horton's advocacy of the Larson crucifix represented an effort to affirm a symbol that preceded the division between Protestant and Roman Catholic.

Horton's ecumenism also looked forward. Specifically, he anticipated the ingathering of numerous Protestant bodies under the banner of organic church union. The first fruits of this effort appeared in 1957 with the establishment of the United Church of Christ. But as author and activist, Horton was also involved in a larger union effort. The "Greenwich Plan for a United Church" was composed in Greenwich, Connecticut, in 1953 and was circulated among the ecumenical committees of the mainline denominations for commentary and suggestions.[98] Horton, who had served on the Plan's drafting committee, drew attention to this effort in his Lyman Beecher Lectures at Yale in 1958:

> The so-called "Greenwich Plan" for a united church in the United States is the first one to be laid before American Christendom which avails itself of the principle that there may be, and let us say that in the completely united church there must be, a plurality of all the polities within the one order.

[97]CFM, 16 September 1955.

[98] Horton's early activities on the Greenwich Plan are not well documented (discussions with the Evangelical and Reformed Church were in full swing, again, by early 1954). But see the letter from Horton to John S. Neukom, 27 November 1953, BGC. See also chapter 6.

Although Horton did not believe the plan could be manifested for a hundred years, he expressed the hope that it would be "tried out on a small scale somewhere."[99]

The Harvard Divinity School presented a taste of the ecumenical future envisioned by the Greenwich Plan. With students and teachers from twenty-nine different American denominations plus ten foreign denominations assembled under one roof by 1957, the Harvard Divinity School had overcome its provincialism and become a model "ecumenical" institution not dependent on the fortunes of one particular denomination (Unitarian, Lutheran, Congregationalist) or one particular theological trend (neoorthodox, evangelical, liberal).[100] The Divinity School was indeed a meetinghouse, and according to Horton's ecclesiology, its function as a meetinghouse made it a kind of church. At the same time, through initiatives like the Stillman Professorship and the Center for the Study of World Religions, Horton, in good Protestant establishment fashion, opened the door to pluralism while keeping Roman Catholics as well as representatives of other world religions under Protestant custodial control. By the end of the 1960s that door to pluralism would swing wide open.[101]

[99]Douglas Horton, *The Meaning of Worship* (New York: Harper, 1959) 141–44.

[100]Douglas Horton, "Annual Report of the Divinity School, 1957–58," *Official Register of Harvard University*, 57/22, 295, CHU.

[101]A different version of the Horton Era story could be told in terms of conflicts between the Divinity School and the University, and between non-Protestants and the Protestant establishment within the University. Robert S. Ellwood explores some of these tensions in *The Fifties Spiritual Marketplace*, 195–97. See also William Warren Bartley III, "Religion at Harvard: The Philosopher, the Pundit, the Priest, and the President," *Harvard Crimson*, 28 March 1958, 1. Beginning with Pusey's correction of Eliot (in the "Convocation Address"), Bartley argues that Pusey took religion at Harvard in precisely the wrong (i.e., an ungenerous and antiliberal) direction. Horton manages to escape Bartley's wrath, but few others on the Divinity faculty are left unscathed.

CHAPTER SIX

The Institutionalization of the Ecumenical Impulse

Horton's metamorphosis from denominational executive to academic dean enabled him to play a new role in the ongoing effort to bring the United Church of Christ into being. No longer a high priest obligated to defend himself with respect to past or planned actions of the General Council, Horton could assume the prophet's mantle and prepare the way for the new church. Once the United Church of Christ was formed, Horton worked to further develop the "ecumenical impulse" within the UCC. Horton wanted to ensure that, as an institution, the United Church of Christ would be a "uniting church," first and foremost. The union of the Evangelical and Reformed Church and the Congregational Christian Churches was a sign of the future Church, a foretaste of the kingdom of heaven as Horton had anticipated it since the early 1920s. But the UCC represented only the beginning of a response to what was taken for a divine command in Horton's circle: to make the Church one, and thus a visible sign of union through Christ.[1]

Horton tried to build a denomination that was flexible and open to the future while, at the same time, carefully preserving the legacies of the past. The analogy he found most useful to describe the arrangement

---

[1]The watchwords of the United Church of Christ were taken from Jesus' "high priestly prayer" in the gospel of John: "That they may all be one" (17:21). Pope John XXIII appealed to the same passage to promote Christian unity during the Vatican II era. For further discussion see chapter 7.

he sought was marriage, and Horton himself worked tirelessly to make the marriage work. There is a certain symmetry in this analogy, for it unites the institutional and the personal in Horton's life. In 1944, after twenty-nine years of marriage, four children, and a long struggle with cancer, Horton's first wife, Carol Williams Horton, died. In the following year, Horton began to court Mildred McAfee, the president of Wellesley College and, during World War II, the commander of the Navy WAVES. Douglas and Mildred were married in September 1945. Their correspondence during the period of courtship made self-conscious and frequent reference to Douglas Horton's parallel efforts in the cause of union.[2]

This chapter considers Horton's continuing crusade to establish the United Church of Christ as a viable mainline Protestant denomination in the context of his lifelong commitment to ecumenism.

Establishing the Ecumenical Impulse for the Future

Horton expressed his vision for the future of the United Church of Christ in a sermon he delivered at Franklin and Marshall College in Lancaster, Pennsylvania, in September 1956. From the pulpit on the fifty-yard line of Williamson Field, Horton addressed the tenth General Synod of the Evangelical and Reformed Church—its final gathering before the anticipated uniting synod with the Congregational Christian Churches in 1957.[3] Horton's theme was "Christian meeting," a concept that was central to his understanding of divinity school education. Likening "Christian meeting" to marriage, Horton argued that "each

---

[2] In early August 1942, Mildred McAfee was sworn in as a Naval Reserve Lieutenant Commander, the first female commissioned officer in U.S. Navy history, and the first Director of the WAVES, or "Women Accepted for Volunteer Emergency Service." For an introduction to Mildred McAfee Horton, see Virginia Lieson Brereton, "United and Slighted: Women as Subordinated Insiders," in Hutchison, ed., *Between the Times*, 143–67. See also the unsorted Douglas Horton–Mildred McAfee Horton Correspondence (circa 1945–1968), RHF. A full discussion of the significant influence that Horton's two wives exerted on his ecumenical sensibilities is, regrettably, beyond the scope of this examination.

[3] An account of the Synod with a lengthy discussion of Horton's sermon appeared in the local newspaper. See "Spiritual Value of Church Union Delineated for Synod," *The (Lancaster, Pa.) Intelligencer Journal*, 3 September 1956.

person brings to a marriage his (or her) [sic] entire past," and if either person were to feel that "a great area of his life" were lost upon the partner, the marriage would be considered "a cheap and superficial thing."[4]

The meeting—and the proposed marriage—of the Evangelical and Reformed Church and the Congregational Christian Churches was not a superficial thing; it was, according to Horton, a "meeting in depth." Such a meeting involved the entire pasts of the two communities as they endeavored to "channel a new breadth for the Church in America." Pariticipants in the proposed union would include not merely the multitude gathered on the football field in the early fall of 1956 or their constituents in other parts of the country. Participants would also include "Luther, Calvin, and Zwingli [as well as] Cotton, Mather, and Hooker." The union would incorporate the liturgical practices of the two communities: the practices of Switzerland and Germany as well as "the very Puritan Prayer Book of Edward VI," itself the order of worship that Horton favored for services at the Harvard Divinity School. And this union would honor the polity and educational practices of each community.[5]

For Horton, this meeting among people was shaped "in its ultimate dimensions" by a meeting with Christ. Horton contrasted what he understood to be the individualistic experiences of other religions—the experience of transcendence in Buddhism, for example—with the "coalescence" of an entire congregation in the act of Christian worship. (Significantly, Horton emphasized Christ's presence through "fellowship"; his Evangelical and Reformed friends might have looked to the Lord's Supper for a sign of their unity in Christ, thereby affirming the primacy of the sacramental reality over the social one.) For Horton, meeting, friendship, marriage, and church union were all anchored in the activity of Christ, who was "reconciling the world to Himself." Ecumenism, then, and in particular the church union movement, was part of God's ongoing mission of reconciliation in the world.[6]

Horton reiterated some of the themes of his Lancaster sermon and expanded upon others during the year leading up to the uniting synod in

---

[4]Douglas Horton, "Meeting," manuscript of sermon delivered 2 September 1956, CDH.

[5]Ibid. This assertion about polity, however, contradicts Horton's assurances to his Congregational Christian colleagues that the polity of the UCC would be congregational. See the discussion on the "Interpretations" of the *Basis of Union* in chapter 4.

[6]Ibid.

June 1957. One particularly thorough discussion appeared in the pages of the *Christian Century*. In "Now the United Church of Christ," Horton retraced the histories of the two denominations, their similarities and differences in polity, the obstacles in procedures and cultures that had already been overcome on the way to unity, and the hopes each denomination held for the new one. After rehearsing these stories, Horton returned to his theme of "meeting" and also to the metaphor of marriage, carrying them to their logical conclusion: "It is by meetings and minglings that God continues to create the human race. So this meeting of two Christian denominations will be a point at which the entire past of those who meet will be fructified to create a new future."[7]

The offspring United Church of Christ would serve as a model of the "pluralism" that already existed within the different American denominations. All American denominations, Horton asserted, had spawned a variety of polities under the banner of particularity. "There is no great presbyterian, or even episcopal, system," Horton declared, "which does not contain congregational elements." Furthermore, he stated, there was no congregational system that did not have characteristics of other church polities. The difference with the newborn United Church of Christ was that the variations in its commingled polity would not be exceptions to a general rule; rather, variety was built into its system. Those practices that worked best, regardless of their ecclesiological origins, would be "declare[d] . . . *de jure* from the beginning."[8]

Although Horton envisioned numerous practical advantages to be gained by the united church, his sense of its significance was ultimately theological, as, to his mind, the United Church of Christ foreshadowed the ecumenical church of the future. Horton suggested that the two denominations were uniting because "the voice of God, the existential moment, compel[led] them." Whether or not the United Church of Christ as constituted in 1957 would survive in the long run, Horton felt that a significant step was being made "away from the scandal of denominationalism toward that one world which the Church should at once prophesy and demonstrate." Echoing the language of the Social Gospel movement, Horton placed his remark in the context of a task to be carried out on behalf of the kingdom of God:

[7]Douglas Horton, "Now the United Church of Christ," *Christian Century*, 12 June 1957, 735.
[8]Ibid., 734.

> The uniting groups do not expect the beams of the millennial
> sun to break out through the new relationship; but neither
> do they expect to be separated from that light which illu-
> mines every achievement planned for God's glory and car-
> ried out with devotion.[9]

Horton's balanced view of the gifts that each denomination brought
to the United Church of Christ stood in surprising contrast to the views
of Reinhold Niebuhr—perhaps the best-known member of the Evangelical and Reformed Church at the time of the union. Writing in his
denomination's magazine, *The Messenger*, one week after Horton's
Christian Century article appeared, Niebuhr evaluated the contributions
his own denomination brought into the new church and found them want-
ing. In particular, Niebuhr praised the cultural superiority of the "Congregationalists." He traced a direct line from Puritan Thomas Hooker to
principles of religious freedom, to democracy, and ultimately to religious pluralism. In contrast to Germany, the unity of the American nation was not established on "the old basis of religious uniformity,"
Niebuhr noted; rather, freedom for all religious groups made America
possible. And this principle of "freedom," according to Niebuhr, had its
origin in Congregationalism.[10]

Niebuhr pursued his argument concerning "the supremacy of the
Congregationalists in the cultural history of our nation" with reference
to the colleges, universities, and seminaries that they established. After
surveying a variety of institutions (Oberlin, Beloit, Grinnell, and Yale
among the colleges; Yale, Hartford, and Andover Newton—though not
Harvard—among the theology schools) and leaving unmentioned the
institutions of the Evangelical and Reformed Church, Niebuhr concluded:
"We come into this union . . . as poor relations." Still, Niebuhr looked to

---

[9]Ibid., 735.

[10]Reinhold Niebuhr, "A Landmark in American Religious History," *The Messenger*,
18 June 1957, 11–13. Although Niebuhr's favorable impressions of Congregationalism
were likely appreciated by Horton, Niebuhr's narration of Congregational history ironically followed the contested pattern established by Williston Walker (linking the denomination to Independency and the Separatists) and espoused by Horton's opponents
during the protracted merger debates. For an examination of an earlier negative assessment by Niebuhr of his own denomination, see Theodore Louis Trost, "Confessional
Identity: An Early Exchange," in *In Essentials Unity: Reflections on the Nature and
Purpose of the Church* (ed. M. Douglas Meeks and Robert D. Mutton; Minneapolis: Kirk
House, 2001), 108–12.

the new denomination as "a vivid example of the kind of mutual invigo-
ration which is proceeding in the whole range of American Protestant
pluralism," an example that offered "some hope of order out of what is
chaotic in that pluralism."[11] While Niebuhr was slow to elevate the Evangelical and Reformed tradition in the new church, Horton came to its
defense on numerous occasions (as illustrated later in this chaper). Horton
truly felt that the gifts of each denomination were needed by the new
church and he fought to have both traditions acknowledged and affirmed.

When the United Church of Christ finally did come into existence in
Cleveland on 25 June 1957, Horton's most obvious contribution to the
proceedings was the prayer he offered for the newly constituted church.[12]
But Horton also had a hand in the behind-the-scenes preparations for
the uniting synod. He wished to show that the United Church of Christ
was not the product of an obscure or extreme ecumenism; rather, the
"scandal of denominationalism" was being overcome through the ecumenical movement. Horton looked to the uniting synod as an opportunity to demonstrate this fact. Thus, when the consummation took place
there were present on the stage, at Horton's suggestion, representatives
from the United Church of Canada, a union of Congregational, Methodist, and Presbyterian churches created in 1925, as well as from the Church
of South India, a union of Congregational, Episcopal, and Presbyterian
churches created in 1947. Furthermore, Horton's Faith and Order colleague Bishop Lesslie Newbigin gave the keynote address to the uniting
synod. The symbolic significance was clear: while the UCC marked an
ecumenical advance in the United States, it was only part of a worldwide movement of uniting and united churches.[13]

Horton had long argued that there was a common faith—and even a
creedal tradition—within Congregationalism;[14] nevertheless, the Con-

---

[11]Niebuhr, "A Landmark," 12–13.

[12]Douglas Horton, "The Uniting Prayer," in *Growing Toward Unity*, 743–44.

[13]Horton recommended Newbigin and the two churches specifically in a letter to
James Wagner, 13 March 1956, CSM. Horton went on to suggest that the UCC keep in
"constant touch" with the Church of South India, as he foresaw that the "church of the
future" would have both "bishops in the historic line and also synodical presidents of
equal standing, but not in the historical line." This was the established arrangement in
South India.

[14]His first address to the General Council as minister discussed the themes of faith,
freedom, and order (that is, church order, or ecclesiology). Horton's favorite summary
of Congregationalism's corporate faith was the Cambridge Platform (1648), about which

gregational Christian Churches never adopted a common doctrinal statement. As a matter of fact, the Congregational Churches' Kansas City Statement of Faith (1913) had been kept out of the negotiations leading up to the 1931 merger of the Congregational Churches and the Christian Church, lest it undermine the Christian Church's conviction that for all believers there could be "no creed but Christ."[15] The Evangelical and Reformed Church, on the other hand, had an unambiguous confessional tradition. Members of the Evangelical and Reformed Church claimed Luther's Small Catechism (1529), the Augsburg Confession (1530), and the Heidelberg Catechism (1563) as their own, while allowing freedom of conscience in areas where these three disagreed. The second article of the *Basis of Union* had summarized the "faith" that united the Evangelical and Reformed Church and the Congregational Christian Churches. Article IV, Section F, of the *Basis of Union* called for a statement of faith to be written by a commission composed of members from the uniting communions. It also stipulated that any ensuing doctrinal statement would be "regarded as a testimony, and not a test, of faith."[16]

In the aftermath of the uniting synod, Horton served as vice chair on the Commission to Prepare a Statement of Faith. The commission's chair was Elmer Arndt, professor of theology at Eden Seminary in Saint Louis. After two years of careful work, the statement was presented to, and approved by, the General Synod in 1959 as a testimony to what was generally believed in the United Church of Christ.[17]

The Statement of Faith bore the marks of what might be called a late-1950s neoorthodox theological consensus. Trinitarian in structure and doxological in mode, it spoke of God's effort to save humanity from "aimlessness and sin," of God's justice, of reconciliation through Christ, of the sacraments' centrality in church life, and of the church's ongoing

---

he spoke at First Church in Cambridge, Massachusetts, during the Tercentenary Commemoration, 27 October 1948. See Henry Wilder Foote, ed., *The Cambridge Platform of 1648* (Boston: Beacon and Pilgrim, 1949) 51–53.

[15]John Von Rohr, *The Shaping of American Congregationalism, 1620–1957* (Cleveland: Pilgrim, 1992) 393.

[16]"The Basis of Union," cited in Keiling, *Die Entstehung*, 240.

[17]See Gunnemann, *The Shaping of the United Church of Christ*, 64–73. In addition to Horton and Arndt, other members of the commission included John C. Bennett, Nels Ferré, Walter M. Horton, Richard R. Niebuhr, and Daniel Day Williams from the Congregational Christian Churches; and Louis Gunnemann, Frederick Herzog, Roger Shinn, and Bela Vassady from the Evangelical and Reformed Church.

struggle to bring about peace and justice. The Barmen Declaration of the German Confessing Church (1934), written in opposition to the Nazi regime, figured centrally in the commission's deliberations.[18] The Barmen Declaration had been composed primarily by Karl Barth, who was enjoying a resurgence of popularity in the late 1950s, thanks in part to Horton's recently reprinted translation of *The Word of God and the Word of Man*.[19] The importance of another Confessing Church leader, Dietrich Bonhoeffer, was also inscribed in the Statement with reference to God's invitation to all church people "to accept the cost and joy of discipleship." The complete text of Bonhoeffer's book *The Cost of Discipleship* appeared in English for the first time in 1959, owing to the insistence of Horton's Harvard colleague, Eberhard Bethge.[20] Meanwhile, Bonhoeffer and the Confessing Church had been in close contact with the Evangelical and Reformed Church since the 1930s.[21]

For Horton, the Statement of Faith stood in a long line of Congregational creeds and platforms. However, he asserted, it "broke new ground" in its "form of an outpouring of gratitude to God for his mighty acts."[22] Meanwhile, Gerhard Grauer, pastor of the influential Saint Paul's Evan-

---

[18]See the letter from Horton to J. Douglas Northey, 7 January 1959, CDH.

[19]Horton's translation of Barth's *The Word of God and the Word of Man* appeared again in 1957 in the Harper Torchbook series after Horton obtained the rights to the translation from Zondervan, which had purchased them from Pilgrim Press. Barth's Volume IV.1 of the *Church Dogmatics* on the "Doctrine of Reconciliation" appeared in English in 1956.

[20]See the discussion in Chapter 5 concerning the use of Bonhoeffer's writings in Bethge's course at Harvard Divinity School. The phrase "the cost of discipleship" in the Statement of Faith came from the expansive English translation of the title of Bonhoeffer's work: *Nachfolge*, literally "discipleship."

[21]Bonhoeffer was a student of Reinhold Niebuhr and a friend of Paul Lehmann, both of whom were leaders in the Evangelical and Reformed Church during the 1930s. (Lehmann later became a Presbyterian.) In his "Report of Eden Theological Seminary" for 1940, Samuel Press drew attention to the faithful Christian witness of the Confessing Church's theological school "under the direction of Professor Bonhoeffer." In the face of Nazi opposition, the seminary continued to instruct pastors. Press suggested (prophetically, as it turned out) that Bonhoeffer's noble effort amounted to "training men for martyrdom." See *The Acts and Proceedings of the Fourth Meeting of the General Synod of the Evangelical and Reformed Church, June 19–26, 1940* (Saint Louis: Eden, 1940) 210.

[22]Douglas Horton, introduction to *Creeds and Platforms of Congregationalism* (ed. Williston Walker; Boston: Pilgrim Press, 1960) xiii.

gelical and Reformed Church in Chicago and chair of the Commission to Prepare a Constitution, suggested that the Statement of Faith was the true symbol of the new denomination's unity. He speculated that future historians of the United Church of Christ would always point out that the Statement "was adopted before a constitution was adopted," thereby suggesting that a common faith bound the two communities together prior to any polity arrangements.[23]

Horton's first retirement project after teaching a course on polity at Chicago Theological Seminary during the spring semester, 1960, was to write a book about the United Church of Christ. Significantly, Horton chose to discuss the UCC in relation to its constitution. As we have already seen in chapter 4, the matter of a constitution had been a source of enduring conflict throughout Horton's tenure as secretary and minister of the General Council of the Congregational Christian Churches. Horton's focus on the constitution of the new church and his involvement in the preparation of a Statement of Faith demonstrated his willingness to embrace the union effort at precisely those places that had produced the most conflict in his fellow Congregationalists before the merger. His role was to build bridges to the prevailing ethos in the Evangelical and Reformed Church around issues of confession and constitution.

Horton's book, *The United Church of Christ: Its Origins, Organization and Role in the World Today*, offered a paragraph-by-paragraph commentary on the Constitution of the United Church of Christ. In his discussions, he carefully reconstructed the various positions that informed the received text. Inevitably, then, the book explored a multitude of "road blocks and detours"—both within and between denominations—that had to be traversed in order to arrive at agreement. Horton advocated this process. In contrast to Archbishop Nathan Söderblom's famous assertion that "practical needs unite while theology separates," Horton insisted that "when theologians make a common enquiry . . . though their several points of departure may be poles apart they tend in a manner really spectacular to achieve a community of thought." This commu-

---

[23]Cited in Gunnemann, *The Shaping of the United Church of Christ*, 69. Grauer's generous view contrasts significantly with that of Henry David Gray and others from the Congregational Christian Churches who demanded constitutional guarantees in advance of the merger. In a touch of linguistic irony, *Grauer* appears less gray than Gray here. See the discussion in chapter 4.

nity, enshrined through organic union, was the United Church of Christ's gift to the ecumenical community—or so Horton assumed.[24]

But "community of thought" never meant, for Horton, uniformity of thought. This fact is made clear in Horton's discussion of a problem that had manifested itself in a variety of guises since his first address to the General Council of Congregational Christian Churches in 1940: namely, the autonomy of the local church. Throughout his career, Horton spoke about the delicate balance between freedom and fellowship in the life of the church. Three paragraphs of the Constitution addressed this matter from different angles. Paragraph 20 noted the "fellowship" responsibilities that obtain☐ reciprocally between the local congregations and the United Church of Christ as a whole. Paragraph 20 stated: "In mutual Christian concern and in dedication to Jesus Christ, the Head of the Church, the one [the local congregation] and the many [the denomination as a whole] share in common Christian experience and responsibility." Here the centrality of Christ favors fellowship; mutual responsibility and a connectional understanding of Church are the dominant values. In his commentary, Horton called attention to the "joint and individual responsibility meeting and mingling in every part of the church"—the dual nature of the covenant that drew the churches and the larger Church together.[25]

But Paragraph 21 of the Constitution asserts that "the autonomy of the local church is inherent and modifiable only by its own actions." The paragraph goes on at length to insist that no general synod, conference, or association of the denomination has any "power to abridge or impair the autonomy of any local church in the management of its own affairs." Thus, a noticeable shift in language occurs between Paragraphs 20 and 21. Whereas the former paragraph spoke of covenanted responsibilities entered into through the grace of God, the latter paragraph

[24]Douglas Horton, *The United Church of Christ: Its Origins, Organization and Role in the World Today* (New York: Nelson, 1962) 20. Horton based his assertion on experience gained in the Faith and Order movement and thus exposed a difference between his own presuppositions about ecumenism and those of Nathan Söderblom, whose vision shaped the Life and Work movement. On Söderblom, see Paul Abrecht, "Life and Work," in Lossky, et al., *Dictionary of the Ecumenical Movement*, 612–14.

[25]Horton, *The United Church of Christ*, 135–36. This discussion refers to the original version of the Constitution and Horton's references to that version in his book. In subsequent revisions, some paragraph numbers were altered (though the basic contents of the paragraphs have been retained in the Constitution to the present).

speaks of rights to be protected from infringement by the larger organization. The fear of hierarchy pervaded Congregational Christian critiques of the proposed church, and this paragraph spells out, in no uncertain terms, that no one could exercise authority over the local congregation. Of course, theologically, according to the Constitution, Christ exercised authority over all.

Horton noted that this extended paragraph, with its recitation of the rights of the local churches, was included "because some of the Congregational Christian Churches feared that in the United Church of Christ there would be less liberty in Christ than they had enjoyed in the past."[26] Certainly the paragraph harks back to issues confronted in the Cadman legal case. But by way of the "Interpretations" of the *Basis of Union*, the emphasis on local autonomy also enshrines Horton's own concept of Congregationalism B in the constitution. Paragraph D of the "Interpretations" declared, "Churches, associations, conferences, and the General Synod, being self-governing fellowships, possess autonomy in their own spheres, which autonomy is acknowledged and will be respected."[27] Congregationalism B, it will be remembered, argued that the General Council had authority to advance union negotiations because the General Council possessed the qualities—and, by implication, the rights—of a local congregation. In Paragraph 21, the principle of freedom seems to take precedence over the principle of fellowship. In any case, these two qualities are not presented in conversation with each other; they are related by juxtaposition more than anything else.

Uneasiness with this juxtaposition, perhaps, led the writers to incorporate Paragraph 22 into the Constitution. It reads: "Actions by, or decisions or advice emanating from the General Synod, a Conference or an Association, should be held in the highest regard by every local church." Horton understood this stipulation to balance the previous paragraph with something like the reciprocal property of equality. He wrote, "Always the whole must be protected against the parts and the parts against the whole; always the parts must succor the whole, always the whole [must] succor the parts." Although the privileges of the local church needed to be spelled out in Paragraph 21 in light of past conflicts among the Congregational Christian Churches, Horton looked to the future for

---

[26]Ibid., 136.
[27]Cited in Keiling, *Die Entstehung*, 253.

the guarantees of freedom and fellowship that these paragraphs intended to present and protect.[28]

In a later section of Horton's book on the UCC, the principles of Paragraph 21 — the principles, at least in part, of Horton's Congregationalism B — are carried over into other regions of the United Church. Thus, under the heading "Establishment or Recognition," the Constitution discusses the establishment of "boards, commissions, councils, offices, or other instrumentalities." The Constitution specifically states: "Such instrumentalities shall perform all their acts in accordance with the Constitution . . . and instructions given them from time to time by the General Synod." In his commentary on this paragraph, Horton noted that these instrumentalities "are not mere puppets of the Synod"; rather, "they are expected to take the initiative in Christian enterprise, making their own decisions within the general context of the fellowship of the whole church."[29] Just as the characteristic freedom of the local church was to be cherished in the broader context of fellowship, so was the freedom of the instrumentality to be respected by the General Synod.

Enshrining the Past

To construct the ecumenical future, Horton used the building blocks of the past. Horton's use of William Ames in his efforts to reconceive the Harvard Divinity School and to reinterpret Congregationalism has been discussed in previous chapters. In his thinking about Congregational Christian identity, as well as in his later reflections on the identity of the United Church of Christ, Horton turned time and again to the early Puritan writers. But he was not a Puritan chauvinist when it came to the United Church of Christ. He felt that the history and traditions of the Evangelical and Reformed Church were of equal importance to the new denomination; therefore, he worked to encourage Evangelical and Reformed historians and to enlist them in projects that would fortify the foundations upon which the new church could be built.

In a letter of 3 August 1956 to J. Robert Nelson of the World Council of Churches, Horton noted that a "half dozen basic books in history, liturgies, and the like" would be needed by the United Church of Christ

---

[28]Horton, *The United Church of Christ*, 138.
[29]Ibid., 194–95.

and that he intended to help bring these books into being.[30] Horton's own books on worship and the UCC constitution exemplify this conviction. In addition, from the time of his arrival at the Harvard Divinity School, Horton had undertaken the task of making available to a wider audience various works that he considered important for the edification of the contemporary church and its leaders. In the fall of 1958, for example, he translated the Latin text of William Ames's "An Exhortation to the Students of Theology" for distribution to the students at the Divinity School. In the "Exhortation," written in 1623, Ames endeavored to put aside doctrinal rivalry and address the question "What [ought] to be the purpose of the minister?" For Ames, the answer was to devote oneself wholly "to the glory of God and the edification of the church."[31] To do this, a proper theological education consisting of three elements — doctrine, method, and practice — was required. Ames felt the latter two had been set aside in preference for controversies surrounding the former. His tract argued for the importance of continued study of the scriptures in their original languages and continual practice in areas such as preaching and prayer. Horton reproduced the tract for what he considered its contemporary significance in the life of the ecumenical Church.

Also while at Harvard, Horton translated the Latin text of John Norton's *Responsio*. Norton had been the pastor of the church at Ipswich in the Massachusetts Bay Colony from 1635 until 1652; he succeeded John Cotton as minister in Boston and remained there until his death in 1663. Norton wrote the *Responsio* in 1645 as an answer to a series of questions posed by William Apollonius, the minister of the church in Middelburg in the Netherlands. Apollonius interrogated the position held by those Puritans who were called "Independents" in England but who associated themselves in New England with "The Way" — later called Congregationalism.

Horton argued that Norton's book was of enduring importance for several reasons: 1) it situated the practices of New England, particularly with regard to the issue of church government, in the context of the Continental reformation; 2) it made a systematic presentation of New England ecclesiology; and 3) it provided a substantial system of glosses

---

[30]Horton to J. Robert Nelson, 3 August 1956, CSM.

[31]William Ames, "An Exhortation to the Students of Theology Delivered at Franeker, 1623" (trans. Douglas Horton; Cambridge: Harvard Divinity School, 1958) 3.

that demonstrated the community of theological inquiry in which the New England church leaders had participated. Horton prized Norton's work in particular because of the breadth of the theological discussion it entertained. Beyond the vast treasure of Protestant scholarship from the New World, England, and the European continent, Norton made frequent reference to such Catholic writers as Aquinas, Gregory of Valencia, and Bellarmine. Horton also detected in Norton's text an openness to non-Congregational churches and the beginnings of a principle of tolerance. Although Norton did not apply this principle during his lifetime, Horton nevertheless suggested that Norton's essential understanding of the church "would one day involve the recognition of the Society of Friends (whom [Norton] greatly feared), the Baptists, and even (save the mark!) the Papists, as [Norton] would have called them."[32]

Finally, Horton appreciated Norton's book because its most frequently quoted author was William Ames. Norton therefore offered further evidence for Horton's thesis that Ames's theology "rule[d] the theological mind of New England" from its beginnings and for over a century thereafter.[33] Because of this belief, Horton insisted on the significance of Ames for the new United Church of Christ and for the ecumenical movement generally. Translating and promoting Ames occupied Horton for the rest of his life, and he would ultimately argue that Ames provided a key for opening up relationships between the Roman Catholic and the Protestant worlds.[34]

After his retirement from Harvard Divinity School, Horton continued his efforts to bring early Puritan writings to the attention of the general public. In 1960, he entered into an agreement with Pilgrim Press, the UCC's autonomous publishing unit, to serve as an "educational consultant for a publishing program of 'Congregational Classics.' "[35] The first

---

[32]Douglas Horton, introduction to *The Answer to the Whole Set of Questions of the Celebrated Mr. William Apollonius, Pastor of the Church of Middleburg. Looking Toward the Resolution of Certain Controversies Concerning Church Government Now Being Agitated in England*, by John Norton (trans. Douglas Horton; Cambridge: Harvard University Press, 1958) xvi-xviii.

[33]Ibid., xvii.

[34]Douglas Horton, "Let Us Not Forget the Mighty William Ames," *Religion in Life* 30 (1960) 434–42. The argument for Ames's ecumenical acumen is developed throughout Horton's *Toward an Undivided Church*.

[35]This relationship began on 1 July 1960. Horton received a fee of $200 per month for his services. See the letter from Charles Butts, general manager of Pilgrim Press,

of these to appear was a reprint of Williston Walker's *The Creeds and Platforms of Congregationalism*. Horton wrote the introduction to the edition and used that occasion to correct the former Hartford Seminary professor's historiography in light of recent scholarship. In particular, Horton disputed the notion that Robert Browne, the Separatist, "must be accounted the father of modern Congregationalism." Horton pointed to a document that Walker had omitted from his collection, the *Apologeticall Narration* composed by Congregationalists from the Westminster Assembly. Horton argued that the *Narration* demonstrated the *koinonia*—the "fellowship" or community orientation—of Congregationalism over against the centrality of Independency. He also argued for a historical understanding of Congregationalism that took into account the difference between an earlier Erastian relationship in New England that permitted the state to exercise authority in church affairs and the present circumstance of separation from the state. Any appeal to the ways of the earlier era, Horton argued, had to be corrected in light of the difference disestablishment made. Horton offered as an example of the new circumstance the role of synods. "[R]egularly meeting synods with authority over themselves are as good Congregationalism today as they were bad Congregationalism in the days of the theocracy," he posited, in words that echoed the controversies of the United Church of Christ merger debates.[36]

Horton offered his own translations of three theses by European scholars on William Ames for possible inclusion in the "Congregational Classics" series, but he later determined that the works were not of a sufficiently popular nature for a general readership.[37] At least two other volumes did appear in the series during Horton's tenure as consultant. One of these was the aforementioned *Apologeticall Narration*, written in 1643 by Thomas Goodwin, Philip Nye, Sidrach Simpson, Jeremiah Burrows, and William Bridge, and edited by Hartford Seminary's Robert Paul in 1963. The other was William Ames's *Medulla theologica* (1623), trans-

---

to Horton, 23 December 1960, CDH. The Eden Publishing House, which had published the books of the Evangelical and Reformed Church, was slowly absorbed into Pilgrim Press.

[36]Walker, *The Creeds and Platforms of Congregationalism*, vii, xiv.

[37]Matthias Nethenus, Hugo Visscher, and Karl Reuter, *William Ames* (trans. Douglas Horton; Cambridge: Harvard Divinity School Library, 1965). The work was published by Horton himself and distributed to various libraries at his own expense.

lated in 1968 by John Eusden of Williams College. Horton himself undertook a translation of *Bellarminus enervatus*, Ames's second systematic theology. This translation was incomplete at the time of Horton's death in 1968.[38]

Another concern of the "Congregational Classics" project was to produce a new history of Congregationalism in light of recent scholarship. General dissatisfaction, at least among Horton's cohort and the editorial board of Pilgrim Press, characterized the attitude toward the volume *History of American Congregationalism*, by Gaius Glenn Atkins and Frederick L. Fagley. Such dissatisfaction had been kindled by opponents of the merger, who used the book to support the argument for strict autonomy and, by implication, antiecumenicity. Horton maintained that it would be impossible to "revise" the book. Thus, in his capacity as chair of an editorial committee that included church historians Roland Bainton and George H. Williams, Horton recommended that the Press engage Robert Paul to write a new history after he finished his edition of the *Narration*. But Paul never completed the new Congregational history, and the Atkins and Fagley volume remained the definitive work until the 1990s.[39]

Horton did revise another publication by Gaius Glenn Atkins, a booklet titled *An Adventure in Liberty*. Atkins wrote the booklet in 1947 as a short introduction to the history of the Congregational Christian Churches. Aimed at a lay readership, the book was reprinted many times. According to Malcolm Burton, Atkins had written *An Adventure in Liberty* in opposition to the proposed merger with the Evangelical and Reformed Church.[40] But in his 1961 revision, Horton inserted a statement of Congregationalism B into the text. Reflecting on the nature of councils, conferences and associations, Horton noted: "It was for the mid-twentieth century to realize that these bodies have a theological complexion similar to that of the local church. . . ." He further insisted that these bodies "enjoy an authority over themselves (though not over the

---

[38] Thomas Goodwin et al., *An Apologeticall Narration* (ed. Robert S. Paul; Boston: United Church Press, 1963); William Ames, *The Marrow of Theology* (trans. John Eusden; Boston: Pilgrim Press, 1968); and idem, *Bellarminus Disarmed* (trans. Douglas Horton; Cambridge: Harvard Divinity School, 1969), microfilm.

[39] John Von Rohr's *The Shaping of American Congregationalism, 1620–1957* appeared in 1992.

[40] Burton, *Disorders in the Kingdom*, 70.

churches from which their members come) which derives from Christ." In the book's final paragraph, Horton presented the United Church of Christ as the crowning achievement of Congregationalism's adventure in liberty. He suggested that the unique union offered "encouragement to other unions throughout the Christian world" and that it brought "new vitality to the uniting communions."[41]

As a result of his work with Pilgrim Press, Horton also participated in the planning of a volume to be written by numerous United Church of Christ church historians including, from the Evangelical and Reformed side, Carl Schneider, David Dunn, and Bard Thompson; and from the Congregational Christian side, Roland Bainton, Robert Paul, and Wilhelm Pauck.[42] The projected title of the volume was "Our Common Heritage." Horton had very particular ideas about what should go into such a volume, and around 1963 he presented these ideas in a paper entitled "The United Church of Christ: A Look Backwards."[43] As the proposed volume's title suggested, Horton sought to emphasize commonalities. So, for example, he saw the union of German and British descendants in the merger as the "last and crowning instance of the mutuality of the two racial groups, the last chapter of a story begun long ago." Horton pointed to the influx of Continental theologians to Oxford and Cambridge in the middle of the sixteenth century, particularly during the reign of Edward VI. He also recalled the stories of Puritans forced to the Continent from England during the reign of Mary. These people found refuge in places like Strasbourg, Zurich, and Frankfurt. "Those were times when [our] spiritual ancestors showed brotherly love toward each other," Horton noted. He went on to speculate, "I think they would be happy, as they look down from heaven, to see their spiritual descendants permanently united."[44]

Horton pointed to other characteristics shared by the two groups in their historical past. He mentioned an early effort at cooperation between two systems of polity, the 1801 "Plan of Union" devised by Con-

---

[41]Gaius Glenn Atkins, *An Adventure in Liberty* (rev. by Douglas Horton; Boston: Pilgrim Press, 1961) 28, 48.

[42]Horton to "Gentlemen," 6 February 1961, CDH.

[43]Douglas Horton, "The United Church: A Look Backwards," n.d. [circa 1963], CDH. An early outline of the paper accompanied the letter of 6 February 1961, cited in the previous note.

[44]Horton, "The United Church: A Look Backwards," 3–5.

gregationalists and Presbyterians. Though ultimately unsuccessful, the plan did produce Union College in New York, where Horton's father had been a student. He drew attention to the mutual theological inheritance from the ancient and medieval church. And noting commonalities in worship, he recommended in particular the treasury of written liturgical forms brought into the union through the Evangelical and Reformed tradition. He asked the historians for help in relating the history of co-operation and goodwill to present circumstances.[45]

The Pilgrim Press's publishing plans changed by the mid-1960s in response to the social turmoil of the time, and consequently many proposed "heritage" volumes from both sides of the merger were not published. For example, a projected series of six volumes dealing with the Mercersburg tradition of the Evangelical and Reformed Church was never completed. Called the "Lancaster Series" and edited by Bard Thompson and George Bricker of the Lancaster Theological Seminary, the series produced only Philip Schaff's *The Principle of Protestantism* and John Nevin's *The Mystical Presence* before it was discontinued.[46] Nevertheless, for a time the new denomination did encourage creative historical work and the republishing of important documents.

Horton was a strong supporter of this effort. He demanded that the Evangelical and Reformed position be presented with as much enthusiasm as the Congregational position. When, for example, James Hastings Nichols's important book about the Mercersburg theologians, *Romanticism in American Theology*,[47] received an unfavorable review in the *Christian Century*, Horton wrote a personal letter to the editor, Harold Fey. Complaining of the "shabby" treatment Nichols's book had received in the 2 August 1961, issue, Horton remarked:

> My suggestion is that you find a writer like Bard Thompson
> . . . who could give you an article on the Mercersburg Move-
> ment in the course of which he would not only set forth the

[45]Horton to "Gentlemen," 6 February 1961, CDH.

[46]Philip Schaff, *The Principle of Protestantism* (ed. Bard Thompson and George H. Bricker; Lancaster Series on the Mercersburg Theology 1; Philadelphia: United Church Press, 1965) and John W. Nevin, *The Mystical Presence and Other Writings on the Eucharist* (ed. Bard Thompson and George H. Bricker; Lancaster Series on the Mercersburg Theology 4; Philadelphia: United Church Press, 1965).

[47]James Hastings Nichols, *Romanticism in American Theology: Nevin and Schaff at Mercersburg* (Chicago: University of Chicago Press, 1961).

importance of the Movement for contemporary ecumenicity but also correct the iniquities of the review.[48]

Horton believed that for the two denominations to truly meet in the manner he had described in his sermon at the final Lancaster General Synod of the Evangelical and Reformed Church, the traditions of both groups deserved to be represented and, indeed, honored.

The Broader Ecumenical Context

While Horton endeavored to extract from a particular understanding of the past a useable future for the United Church of Christ, he was less concerned, initially, about the details of the organization and structure of the new church. He believed that issues such as polity or the role of the denominational seminaries, for example, should be entrusted to the future, as the individuals united by the merger cooperated in their resolution. This attitude of openness was attributable in part to Horton's understanding of "freedom" within the polity of the United Church of Christ. But more significantly, it had to do with the sense that the United Church of Christ was a provisional arrangement on the way to a larger, more inclusive ecumenical Church.

The phrase "united and uniting" was often applied to the United Church of Christ to designate the church's expectation of additional unions in the near future. With the consummation of the union in 1957, there was a general sense, both inside and outside of the denomination, that the United Church of Christ would be a "catalytic agent for bringing together" other denominations throughout the United States. In an article typical of the prevailing mood at the time—and certainly representative of Horton's feelings on the matter—John R. Scotford assumed that the united church movement would "snowball." He thought other churches would want to join the United Church of Christ because it alone among mainline churches was capable of maintaining the diversities in matters of belief and worship that made it "easy" for anyone to join the new denomination. He also pointed to the sense of providence that informed much of the thinking (at least within the new denomination) about the United Church of Christ's mission: "Circumstances which no

---

[48]Horton to Harold Fey, 6 October 1961, CDH.

man could order or control have brought us where we are. Those who
have been the most involved in creating this union are the most convinced that they have been led by God."[49]

The United Church of Christ represented itself as the early fruit of a
mission to draw churches together, resembling in this regard the Church
of South India and the United Church of Canada. In retrospect, however, the United Church of Christ appears but a part, although a noteworthy part, of a much larger movement toward church union. Indeed,
the United Church of Christ's distinctive "passion for ecumenicity," as
Horton—quoting Evangelical and Reformed Church leader George
Richards—often characterized it, arose in an atmosphere of intense ecumenical activity and great expectations.[50] Perhaps the world could not
be "won for Christ in this generation," to paraphrase the watchwords of
the Student Volunteer Movement at the beginning of the century; but at
least the church could be *one* for Christ in a very tangible, organic way.[51]
Horton's activities in the broader ecumenical movement during the last
decade of his life continued his life-long effort to actualize the "ecumenical impulse" and make the inclusive ecumenical Church a visible
reality.

---

[49]John R. Scotford, "Will the United Church Snowball?," *The Messenger*, 19 November 1957, 16–17. Of course, opponents of the merger would also agree with the
second of these sentences without assigning credibility to the merger on this account.
Scotford, the editor of the Congregational Christian Churches' journal *Advance*, was a
long-time supporter of the merger. His book *Church Union, Why Not?* (Boston: Pilgrim, 1948) developed an essentially pragmatic argument for the merger derived from
the observation: "The man on the street has always believed that 'the churches should
get together' " (p. 1).

[50]Horton, "The United Church of Christ: A Look Backward," 10.

[51]The Student Volunteer Movement's slogan was "The evangelization of the world
in this generation." Horton and his Chicago colleagues had promoted church union with
a similar sense of mission: "[It is] the manifest duty of the followers of Christ everywhere to exert themselves to the utmost in realizing their unity in him. *Deus vult!* It
is the will of God for this generation." See Horton, ed., *The Basic Formula for Church
Union*, 15.

CHAPTER SEVEN

The Ecumenical Impulse in Other Areas

S hortly after completing his first academic year as dean of Harvard
Divinity School in 1956, Horton received a letter from the secretary of the Commission on Faith and Order of the World Council of
Churches. Robert Nelson wrote from Herrenalb, West Germany, to
inform Horton of his nomination to chair the Faith and Order Commission. Nelson noted the "noble" succession Horton would inherit were
he to accept the nomination and be elected at the commission's next
meeting the following summer: previous chairmen included Bishop
Brent of the Philippines and Western New York who had spoken elo-
quently for the cause of church unity at the Edinburgh Conference of
1910; Archbishop Temple of York; and Archbishop Brilioth of Sweden. Nelson also informed Horton that the committee's candidate for
vice chairman, the office Horton himself held at the time, would be the
bishop from the United Church of South India and Horton's friend,
Lesslie Newbigin. In his reply to Nelson, Horton made it clear that he
intended to retire from Harvard in the near future, at the conclusion of
the 1958–1959 academic year. He did not wish to "weigh [the commis-
sion] down with the super-annuated," but if this retirement plan would
"cast no shadow" over his nomination, Horton indicated his willingness to consider the position.[1]

[1] J. Robert Nelson to Horton, 21 July 1956, CSM; Horton to J. Robert Nelson, 1
August 1956, CSM. For the importance of Brent's speech at Edinburgh, see Rouse and
Neill, eds., *A History of the Ecumenical Movement*, 406–7.

This chapter considers Horton's work beyond those institutions, such as Harvard Divinity School and the United Church of Christ, that he helped to establish. Already in the 1940s, for example, Horton's passion for church union led him to help formulate the Greenwich Plan for Union. He remained involved with the plan until it was absorbed into an even more ambitious Protestant plan for the establishment of a "truly catholic, evangelical, and reformed church," the Consultation on Church Union. Then, after assuming the chairmanship of the Commission on Faith and Order at its executive meeting in New Haven in July 1957, Horton worked to maintain the commission's focus on the goal of church union during that formative period in the life of the World Council of Churches. Finally, Horton observed the transformation of Roman Catholicism during the Second Vatican Council. He advocated new relationships between Protestants and Catholics globally, and he worked locally (in New Hampshire) to model new possibilities among Christians in the post-Vatican II era.

The Greenwich Plan for Union

Already in 1946, before opposition to the proposed union of the Congregational Christian Churches and the Evangelical and Reformed Church had coagulated, Horton was involved with a plan to "consider the possibility of immediate closer unity of American denominations." At the instigation of the Congregational Christian Churches and the Disciples of Christ, a conference on church union was convened in December 1949 at Seabury House in Greenwich, Connecticut. Participants at the conference included representatives from the Congregational Christian Churches, the Disciples of Christ, the Evangelical and Reformed Church, the Colored Methodist Episcopal Church, the Methodist Church, the National Council of Community Churches, and the African Methodist Episcopal Zion Church.[2] This diverse array of delegates drew up "A Plan for a United Church in the United States" which came to be called the "Greenwich Plan." The plan was then submitted to the members of the various participating denominations for suggestions and criticism.[3]

---

[2] Two Presbyterian denominations also participated during the early stages of the plan, but they withdrew before a revised draft appeared in 1953.

[3] "Christian Unity," in *Digest of Minutes of Meetings of the General Council of the*

In a speech delivered before the Ohio Council of Churches in the early 1950s, Horton pointed to the salient features of the plan. It called for a uniform structure in episcopate, presbytery, and congregation, along with multiform relationships or organizations within the structure. Horton offered this example:

> In any single Presbytery (the name given to the new "county" or district body), for instance, a Congregational group can see to it that on any particular matter the action of the presbytery does not apply to it. This feature protects it from the exercise of what it might regard as authoritarianism. However, in the case of Methodists and Presbyterians who are accustomed to more authority from above, the decision of the bishop or the superintendent or of the proper presbyterian committee will be taken as decisive.[4]

Significantly, the planners gave to the institution they hoped to establish the name "The United Church of Christ."

Horton was a member of the executive committee of the Conference on Church Union throughout its entire existence. The Greenwich Plan did not advance greatly during the mid-1950s while the Evangelical and Reformed and Congregational Christian merger was being actualized, and while Horton himself was adjusting to new surroundings at Harvard. By 1957, however, the plan was under consideration by an American subcommittee of Faith and Order.[5] The excitement generated by those conversations encouraged Horton to draw attention to the plan in his Lyman Beecher lectures at Yale University.[6] By December 1958, a revised Greenwich Plan was prepared by the executive committee, which then included Ivan Holt, a bishop in the Methodist Church, a colleague of Horton's since the *Basic Formula* of 1938, and an active participant in the Faith and Order movement; Charles Merrill, for many years a

---

Congregational Christian Churches of the United States, 1931–1965 (New York: Congregational Christian Churches, 1971) 198–201.

[4]Douglas Horton, "The Discomfort of Being Ecumenical," n.d. [circa 1953], 13, CDH.

[5]Douglas Horton, "Final Executive Committee Report to the Churches [of the Conference on Church Union] by whose Representatives it was Originally Constituted," 14 April 1959, CDH.

[6]See Horton, *The Meaning of Worship*, 142–45.

leading ecumenist among the Congregational Christians; and Charles Clayton Morrison, a leader of the Disciples of Christ, publisher of the *Christian Century*, and owner and first editor of the quarterly ecumenical publication *Christendom*.[7]

The introduction to the Greenwich Plan document discussed the "divine imperative" for union. Echoing themes that Horton had stressed throughout his life, the authors asserted that "in a world of fear, hatred, distress and division, God has given the churches a message of reconciliation and a oneness which will bind all men to Him and in Him to one another." A testimony to the unity of the participating churches followed, outlining commonalities in belief, convictions, spirit, and purpose. The body of the plan set out the organizational matrix of the new church: local congregation, presbytery, conference (presided over by bishops), and the General Council. An additional section discussed the nature of ministry, noting, among other things, that ordination in the proposed church was "ordination into the Church Universal," conferred by the presbytery on recommendation of the local church and under the presiding hands of the bishop. The concluding section of the plan anticipated the growing together of practices and traditions as a "more perfect union" unfolded in the future.[8]

Several months after the 1958 revised plan appeared, Horton wrote to the leaders of the involved churches. He noted that the Conference on Church Union had been the only organization in the United States made up of regularly elected representatives of many denominations whose goal was organic union. But the recent North American Conference of Faith and Order at Oberlin had also resolved to form its own study group, under the direction of the National Council of Churches and in collaboration with the U.S. conference of the World Council of Churches, to look deeply into the matter of organic union. Horton judged that to have two different organizations devoted to oneness would contravene the purposes of ecumenism. So he proposed to assemble all the Greenwich Plan files, arrange for their safe deposit in the "Ecumenical Library" at Union Seminary, advise the new group of the Conference's work, and bring the Conference on Church Union to an end.[9]

---

[7]The other members were Kenneth Bath, Gaines Cook, and Ronald Osborn.

[8]"Greenwich Plan for a United Church: Revised Draft, December 1958," CDH.

[9]Horton, "Final Executive Committee Report to the Churches [of the Conference on Church Union]," 2–3.

It is probably no mere coincidence that one year after the Greenwich Plan was shelved, Eugene Carson Blake preached a famous sermon in San Francisco's Grace Cathedral proposing the organic union of the major U.S. Protestant denominations. Blake, the Stated Clerk of the Presbyterian Church, had been the president of the National Council of Churches from 1954 to 1957, and he remained (along with Mildred McAfee Horton) on its board. He also had been a delegate to the 1932 Faith and Order conference in Lund, Sweden, and, more significantly, to the conference in Oberlin, where, as noted, the Greenwich Plan came under some scrutiny. Blake called for interdenominational discussions leading to a united Protestant Church. Given that he was preaching to a congregation at Grace Cathedral, part of the Episcopal Church, his comment on the role of bishops was of particular significance. Blake suggested that

> without adopting any particular theory of apostolic succession, the reunited church shall provide at its inception for the consecration of all its bishops by bishops and presbyters both in the apostolic succession and out of it from all over the world from all Christian churches which would authorize or permit them to take part.[10]

Essentially, Blake's proposal drew the Episcopal Church into the conversation that the Greenwich Plan began. The Conference on Church Union had included no Episcopal representatives. Consequently, the plan had discussed the bishop as an "advisor" to churches and ministers of the "congregational category," as a Synod or Presbytery "executive" to those of the "presbyterian category," and as a "bishop" in relation to historic American Methodism.[11] In other respects, however, the Blake proposal's lineage was easily traceable to Greenwich. Indeed, after the Presbyterians, the Episcopal Church, the United Church of Christ, and the Methodist Church joined together "to explore the establishment of a United Church truly Catholic, truly Reformed, and truly Evangelical," they organized themselves under the title of the "Consultation on Church Union"—thereby recycling most of the name and all of the initials from the Greenwich effort.[12]

[10]Hiley Ward, *Documents of Dialogue* (Englewood Cliffs, N.J.: Prentice-Hall, 1966) 161–66. Cited in Cavert, *The American Churches in the Ecumenical Movement*, 254.

[11]"Greenwich Plan For a United Church: Revised Draft, December 1958," 9.

[12]Before these initials belonged to the Greenwich Plan, they were used by the ecumenical division of the Disciples of Christ, the "Council on Christian Unity."

Certainly Douglas Horton favored the recognition of bishops in the ecumenical church of the future. In a 1956 letter to James Wagner anticipating Bishop Newbigin's appearance at the uniting synod of the UCC, Horton had already made this confidential ecumenical aside:

> I could be a member of a denomination in which there were ministers both episcopally ordained and not episcopally ordained, as in South India at the present moment. . . . I should go further. I should be willing to belong to a denomination in which there were bishops in the historic line and also synodical presidents of equal standing, but not in the historic line. I believe that the church of the future will look something like this.[13]

By 1966, the Consultation on Church Union, or COCU, had devised a preliminary "Outline for a Possible Plan of Union." From his position as a member of the United Church of Christ's ecumenical council, Horton was an active advocate of the COCU proposal. He even prepared a lengthy paper analyzing the proposal in relation to the distinctive ecclesiology of the UCC. He concluded that as long as the UCC's theory of local autonomy were preserved—as he claimed it would be in the COCU proposal—there was plenty of room for bishops in the planned fellowship.[14] Meanwhile, the United Church of Christ had been making plans since 1963 to unite with the Disciples of Christ in advance of the anticipated pan-Protestant union.[15]

Thus, by the mid-1960s, it seemed likely that the ideal of church union in the United States that Horton had advocated for his entire life would be realized. This new mood was not merely the product of American optimism; it was directly related to international developments in the Faith and Order movement among Protestant and Orthodox Christians, and especially to the significant changes that were occurring in the Roman Catholic Church during and after the Second Vatican Council, concerns with which Douglas Horton was also deeply involved.

[13]Horton to James Wagner, 12 March 1956, CSM.

[14]Douglas Horton, "The Autonomy of the Local Church," n.d., CDH.

[15]See, for example, "Disciples, UCC Groups Ask Authority to Draft Union Plan," *The United Church Herald*, 15 December 1963, 25. Of course, as the executive officer of the Congregational Christian Churches, Horton had been in touch with representatives of the Disciples of Christ prior to and throughout the negotiations toward union with the Evangelical and Reformed Church. See chapter 3.

The Commission on Faith and Order of the World Council of Churches

As vice chairman of the commission, Horton preached the closing sermon at the Third World Conference of Faith and Order in Lund in 1952. At the time, in the midst of the legal controversies that had engulfed the Congregational Christian Churches in the Cadman case back home, Horton spoke in apocalyptic terms about the judgment Christ would render upon the world's disunited churches. "When [Christ] calls for a living body in his Church and we give him an Ezekiel's valley of disjointed members, when He desires . . . a symbol of his oneness among us and we return weak fragments of mutual unsympathy," Horton intoned, "He will get Him a new people, leaving the parts of this false Church . . . to go the way of the devotees of Apollo and Diana, and slip into oblivion." The Faith and Order Commission, according to Horton, was the primary advocate for church union within the broader ecumenical movement.[16] Horton's zeal for unity, his organizational skill (he had been chosen to chair the American Committee to prepare for the Second General Assembly of the World Council of Churches at Evanston in 1954), and his practical ability in bringing about the United Church of Christ, made him the logical successor to Archbishop Brilioth, who resigned as chair of the Faith and Order Commission in 1957.

Horton served two three-year terms as chair. His activities in Faith and Order paralleled and informed his work at the Divinity School as well as his efforts to establish the UCC as a viable institution. On the one hand, he was focused on future church union efforts in and through the World Council of Churches. On the other hand, he was concerned to maintain the past and the traditions held dear by the member churches. He also helped to redefine the Faith and Order Commission's institutional role in relation to the World Council, ensuring its commitment to the church union enterprise for decades to come.

This chapter has thus far described a trajectory leading from Horton and the Greenwich Plan through the 1958 Faith and Order conference at Oberlin to Eugene Carson Blake and the Consultation on Church Union.

---

[16]Douglas Horton, "The Closing Sermon at Lund," in *The Third World Conference of Faith and Order Held at Lund, August 15–28, 1952* (ed. Oliver S. Tomkins; London: SCM, 1953) 316–17.

Yet this narrative may mislead by omission: the Greenwich Plan was but one ecumenical vision evaluated at the Oberlin conference. It must be stressed that "church union" was itself a term subject to exegesis. Indeed, the question, "What is the nature of the unity we seek?" had been central to Faith and Order's existence ever since Bishop Brent argued, at Edinburgh in 1910, that mere cooperation among churches was insufficient and that "organic union" was the ideal toward which all Christians should strive.[17] This question recurred over and over again because "organic union"—what St. Paul described to the Ephesians as the Church "joined and knit together by every joint with which it is supplied when each part is working properly" (4:16)—had always been a contested ideal, even within the Faith and Order movement itself. The concept came under particular scrutiny after the formation of the World Council of Churches because it had to compete, again, with the cooperative model of unity that was preferred by many in the Life and Work movement, the missionary enterprise, and among the Orthodox churches.

After the Oberlin meeting, the conversation on unity was continued by the working committee of Faith and Order. In July 1958, this committee delivered a report on "churchly unity" to the Central Committee of the World Council of Churches. Although he was not a member of the working committee, Horton commented on the report in an address to his colleagues later that summer. In particular, Horton noted the bold intention of the phrase "churchly unity." Horton suggested that the working committee "did not want the Faith and Order movement to halt at the *status quo*." He understood the word "churchly" to be an antonym of the word "cooperative"—which, he admitted, "describes our work today."[18]

Horton was frustrated. He was frustrated in part by the very successes the Faith and Order movement had achieved in such areas as "inter church aid and service to refugees [and] in international affairs." Against the notion that cooperation was all that Faith and Order needed to promote, Horton brought the emphasis back to the active task of unity:

> Churchly unity is what we want but do not have. It is the
> blue mountains in the distance on which we have to keep

---

[17]See Lesslie Newbigin, "Organic Union," in Lossky et al., eds., *Dictionary of the Ecumenical Movement*, 1028–29.

[18]Douglas Horton, "Churchly Unity" (an address to members of the Faith and Order Commission), n.d. (circa July 1958) 1–2, CDH.

our eyes if, in our Herculean choice, we are to resist the solicitations of the fair maid *Cooperatio*.[19]

Underlining the working committee's report, Horton looked toward future unity in "one baptism, one gospel, the breaking of one bread, a corporate life of witness and service, a ministry and members acknowledged by all, and the ability to act and speak together as occasion may require." Horton felt that church union should be built on this foundation and that it was Faith and Order's responsibility to engage the matter precisely at these points of frequent dispute. In other words, the real challenge was not simply to get along, it was to become one.

In his presentation, Horton modeled his great hopefulness for this project. Speaking of the Society of Friends, he noted: "It is against the rite of communion with forms fixed and absolute . . . that [Quakers] inveigh—but to believe that they have given up on communion with Christ and one another is to misunderstand their way of life."[20] The *power* of communion was present, if not the *form* of communion, among the Quakers. To understand this distinction was to advance toward closer union. And to promote this kind of understanding with the goal of "the unity of a living organism," said Horton (recalling the words of the 1937 Edinburgh Conference on Faith and Order) was the real purpose of Faith and Order.[21]

Eventually the spirit of the working committee's report found its way into the "Report of the Section on Unity" at the third assembly of the World Council of Churches in New Delhi in 1961. The New Delhi report was noteworthy for its definitive expression of "organic union"—the objective that guided Faith and Order throughout Douglas Horton's tenure as chair.[22] In its second and most famous paragraph, the report retained the phrases Horton had considered so crucial to the report's substance, including those referring to "one baptism, bread, and ministry."[23] In fact,

---

[19]Ibid., 2.

[20]Ibid., 8.

[21]Ibid., 10.

[22]"The Report of the Section on Unity," in *The Ecumenical Movement: An Anthology of Key Texts and Voices* (ed. Michael Kinnamon and Brian E. Cope; Grand Rapids: Eerdmans, 1997) 88–92.

[23]The document was famous for its statement of "organic union"; it was also notorious for containing one of the longest sentences in the history of the ecumenical movement. See "New Delhi 1961: Section III on Unity," paragraph 2 in *Documentary History of Faith and Order, 1963–1993* (ed. Günther Gassmann; Geneva: WCC, 1993) 3.

"baptism, eucharist, and ministry" would become the focus of much of Faith and Order's work over the ensuing decades.

Another aspect of the Faith and Order Commission's work during Horton's tenure as chair is worth brief mention. At the same time that Horton was translating William Ames and John Norton and offering their wisdom to the contemporary church, his colleagues in Faith and Order were wrestling with the matter of tradition and its role in ecumenical relations. A theological commission had been set up in the mid-1950s to explore the relationship between the many traditions of individual denominations and the Tradition that comprised the whole of Christian faith and practice as handed down through the Church. An interim report was delivered at the 1960 meeting of Faith and Order at Saint Andrews, Scotland. That meeting was most noteworthy for the presence of official representatives from the Roman Catholic Church, including Monsignor Willebrands, who would go on to work for the Secretariat for the Promotion of Christian Unity during the Second Vatican Council. The final report, "Scripture, Tradition, and Traditions," was delivered at the World Conference on Faith and Order at Montreal in 1963. The report raised the question: "Does not the ecumenical situation demand that we search for the Tradition by re-examining sincerely our own particular traditions?"[24] To a great extent this question had shaped Douglas Horton's ecumenical career thus far; it continued to determine his interests during the last years of his life.[25]

Throughout his tenure as chair of the Commission on Faith and Order, Horton was involved in a protracted debate about the relation of Faith and Order to the World Council of Churches. The sense of "frustration" that he conveyed to his Faith and Order colleagues in the "Churchly Unity" address stemmed from Horton's perception that Faith and Order's importance had diminished under the new ecumenical arrangement. In August 1959, Horton went before the Council's central committee to air his grievance. He noted that, structurally, Faith and

[24]"Scripture, Tradition, and the Traditions (1963)" in Gassmann, ed., *Documentary History*, 13.

[25]Kallistos Ware points out that an ecumenical approach that was both critical and affirming of distinct traditions "made the production of 'Baptism, Eucharist, and Ministry' possible," with its question to the churches: "How far can your church recognize in this text the faith of the church through the ages?" See Kallistos Ware, "Tradition and Traditions," in Lossky et al., eds., *Dictionary of the Ecumenical Movement*, 1016.

Order was designated a "commission," a small unit of the larger "Division of Study." Horton objected to this setup because, he argued, Faith and Order was "no matter of study, simply"; instead, it was an activist movement dedicated to visible church union. Under the existing arrangement, according to Horton, "the commission chiefly concerned with Christian unity [was] submerged in a vast structure devoted to cooperation as cooperation." This positioning, Horton felt, was a denial of Faith and Order's historical role in the ecumenical movement. He therefore urged the committee to make the necessary changes to the structure of the World Council of Churches at the upcoming Third World Assembly in New Delhi.[26]

The difficulties Horton encountered pointed to a shift that was taking place in the ecumenical movement internationally. While American Protestants responded positively to the unitary impulses of the Greenwich Plan and the Blake Proposal, the non-Western churches, especially the Orthodox, were unimpressed with what they called "ecumenism in space"—that is to say, the effort to reach agreements among the denominations as they currently existed. For the Orthodox, the way the denominations currently existed was precisely the problem. The name the Orthodox gave to this problem was "schism." They proposed to counter the problem with an "ecumenism in time": a recovery of the "common ancient and apostolic tradition from which all [of the denominations] derive their existence."[27] Perhaps the World Council of Churches had intentionally underplayed "union" and emphasized "cooperation" in deference to the increasing Orthodox presence in the organization. Or perhaps Faith and Order's apparent diminishment was an unintentional slight. In any case, Douglas Horton brought the focus of Faith and Order back to visible church union for a time at least. This emphasis would undergo further challenge and affirmation in its encounter with Rome.

Dean of the Ecumenical Observers at Vatican II

Horton's mission from 1962 until his death in 1968 was to foster closer ties between Catholics and Protestants. During the autumn of 1962 and for three successive autumns after that, he was an official observer at the Second Vatican Council. Horton made many friends in Rome; he

---

[26]Douglas Horton, "Speech Before the Central Committee," August 1959, CDH.

[27]"Orthodox Contribution to Section II, New Delhi, 1961," in Kinnamon and Cope, eds., *The Ecumenical Movement*, 92–93.

also transmitted his experiences to his fellow Protestants and others in lectures, articles, and books. Moreover, he worked in his home state of New Hampshire to promote the expanding ecumenical view. Horton insisted that the reordering of relationships now underway among the churches would have an inevitable effect on the world, for it established "a unity to serve as a pattern to nations, races and classes themselves desperately needing a unity."[28]

At the conclusion of a prayer service for Christian unity in January 1959, Pope John XXIII announced plans to hold an ecumenical council for the universal church. The task of the council was to renew the religious life of the Catholic Church and to "bring up to date" its teaching, discipline, and organization with the unity of all Christians as the ultimate goal. This process of drawing the church into closer relation with the needs of the world in the present day became known by the Italian word *aggiornamento*. The Vatican asked leaders of the Catholic Church for suggestions about what ought to be on the agenda. More than 9,300 proposals were received, resulting in twenty specific projects that focused on such topics as liturgy, ministry, laity, ecumenism, and the church in the modern world. In a later address, the Pope invited Christians belonging to churches "separated from Rome" to participate in the process "at close quarters," noting — with, perhaps, a nod to the ecumenical movement — a general desire "for a return of unity and peace, according to the teachings and the prayer of Christ to the Father."[29] This openness to the larger Christian world stood in sharp contrast (at least in the minds of many Protestants) to prior Catholic practice. It suggested that this Second Vatican Council would differ greatly from the First Vatican Council, which concluded in 1870 after promulgating, among other things, the doctrine of papal infallibility.

When the Second Vatican Council began on 11 October 1962, no one knew how long the assembly would continue. One indication that it might extend beyond the planned three-month session of 1962 came the next day, on 12 October, when the members voted to elect their own commissioners rather than accept the list of commissioners prepared by the

[28]Douglas Horton, "The Church in a New Dawn," n.d. [circa 1968], CDH.

[29]Pope John XXIII, "*Humanae Salutis*," 25 December 1961, in Walter M. Abbott, *The Documents of Vatican II* (New York: American Press, 1966) 709. The Pope's reference is to John 17:21, the watchword of the United Church of Christ. See the discussion in chapter 6.

Papal court and its bureaucracy, the Roman *curia*. As the commission would exercise a degree of control over the debate and other procedures of the council, this gesture demonstrated the independent spirit of the delegates. Pope John XXIII died in June 1963, before the beginning of the council's second session. His successor, Pope Paul VI, announced his intention to continue the council, and it met for a total of four sessions, concluding on 8 December 1965.

The Secretariat for Promoting Christian Unity, or SPCU as it was called for short, was created by Pope John XXIII to enable "those who bear the name of Christians, but are separated from [the] apostolic See to find more easily the path by which they may arrive at that unity for which Christ prayed."[30] Cardinal Augustine Bea was president of the SPCU; Johannes Willebrands, who had attended the Faith and Order meeting at Saint Andrews in 1960, was secretary; and Tom Stransky, a Paulist father and an American, served as assistant to the secretary. Father Stransky coordinated most of the activities for the observers at the Second Vatican Council, which included supplying accurate information on the work of the council; transmitting the insights of the observers to the various commissions (e.g., theological, missions, ecumenical) of the council; and finding areas of commonality in the interest of promoting Christian unity.[31] Various Protestant and Orthodox confessional groups were invited by the Secretariat to send delegate observers to the Second Vatican Council, and more than 180 observers participated during the four sessions of the council. Of these, only one was acknowledged to have faithfully attended each of the 168 plenary sessions and the ten public assemblies: Douglas Horton.

In a speech he routinely delivered around the country during the spring and summer of 1963, following the first session, Horton recalled the relationship that had prevailed between Protestants and Roman Catholics before the commencement of the Second Vatican Council. An "ecclesiastical iron curtain" had separated the two groups, he reported. Under those circumstances, each side seemed to encounter only "the worst elements"—meaning both persons and ideas—from the other side. Consequently, a Protestant in northern New England was likely to be famil-

---

[30]Tom Stransky, "Secretariat for Promoting Christian Unity," in Lossky et al., eds., *Dictionary of the Ecumenical Movement*, 912.

[31]See Tom Stransky, "Purpose of the Secretariat" (Secretariat for Promoting Christian Unity: Information Sheet Number Three), CDH.

iar with the petty criminals of French Catholic descent who "turn[ed] up with too great frequency in our courts," while not recognizing at all "the names of great Catholic writers of Quebec, the ecclesiastical leaders and reformers, men of the stature of Cardinal Leger of Montreal. . . ." But with the advent of the Second Vatican Council, the "Berlin Wall of the church" was beginning to come down. Horton noted that Protestant leaders and leaders of the Catholic Church were becoming friends. "If this relationship can be multiplied elsewhere," he announced hopefully, "a ground will be laid out of which only good and not evil may grow."[32]

In relating symbols such as the "iron curtain" and the Berlin Wall to the relationships between Catholics and Protestants before the Second Vatican Council, Horton offered a churchly alternative to the inevitable divisions those secular symbols represented. For the Vatican Council involved overcoming divisions among people at the same time that society, both national and international, was separated and segregated. The "Cuban Missile Crisis" was played out during the early weeks of the first session of Vatican II. During the spring of 1963, Martin Luther King Jr. led marches against segregation in Birmingham, Alabama. At the same time, African-American students who participated in "sit-ins" in Greensboro, North Carolina, were violently removed by angry mobs from that city's segregated lunch counters. Horton was not indifferent to this turbulence. In the fragmentation, he saw a call to social action on the part of a united Church. But he also saw in the fragmentation a call for the Church itself to be united.

The Second Vatican Council promised a reordering of relationships among the Christian churches. At Pope John XXIII's insistence, the council would address differences that had divided Christendom since the Great Schism of 1054, and the differences that had divided Western Christianity since the Reformation. Horton perceived in this historic overture an expression of sorrow on the part of the Roman Catholic Church "for any part it might ever have had in initiating or continuing [division]";[33] indeed, for Horton, Vatican II represented the Catholic effort to bring the divisions among Christians to an end.

Horton went to Rome as a representative of the International Congregational Council (ICC). From his earliest years as a minister in Middletown, Connecticut, Horton played a key role in establishing the

[32]Douglas Horton, "The Vatican Council," n.d. (circa 1963), CDH.
[33]Ibid.

ICC as the organization that represented worldwide Congregationalism, eventually serving as its moderator from 1949 to 1953. Although he had not assumed an active leadership role since the mid-1950s, he remained a prominent member of the ICC's advisory board. Thus, when Professor Nathan Micklem of the Hartford Seminary was unable to make the journey to Rome for even a limited period of time, Horton was selected as the man with the stature, the energy, and the sympathy to represent the ICC at Vatican II. A second representative of the ICC, George Caird of Mansfield College in Oxford University, could not be in attendance most of the time owing to his scholarly commitments. Caird's situation opened up the possibility for alternates who would visit for several weeks at a time in Caird's absence. As the person stationed in Rome for the entire first session, Horton helped determine who these alternates would be. During the first session they included Heiko Oberman and George H. Williams from Harvard Divinity School, and Robert Moss, president of Lancaster Theological Seminary and later president of the United Church of Christ. As the years went by, Horton made certain that some of the younger leaders of the United Church of Christ—the church historians Bard Thompson from Lancaster Seminary and John Von Rohr from the Pacific School of Religion, for example—were able to attend the council.[34]

By the general affirmation of the observers, Horton acted as "dean" of the Protestant observers, as *Life* magazine reported in December 1965.[35] This role, too, was unplanned. After the first session ended in 1962, Horton announced his willingness to represent the ICC during the second session of the council, noting that the Secretariat welcomed the continuity he could provide to the observer group.[36] As the second session led to the third and the fourth, Horton had proved himself invaluable to the Secretariat, facilitating communications within the non-Catholic group and between the observers and the Secretariat.[37] As Albert

---

[34]The considerations that led to Horton's selection as an observer are mentioned in a letter from Horton to George H. Williams, 5 September 1962, CGO. Other alternates from the UCC were Elmer Arndt, president of Eden Seminary; Howard Schomer, president of Chicago Theological Seminary; Stuart LeRoy Anderson, president of the Pacific School of Religion; and Ruben Huenemann, president of United Theological Seminary in Saint Paul, Minn.

[35]*Life*, 17 December 1965, 74.

[36]Horton to Ralph Calder, 16 April 1963, CDH.

[37]See the letters of Tom Stransky and Robert McAfee Brown, "I Knew Douglas When He Was an Observer at the II Vatican Council," in "Douglas Horton: A Book of Reminiscences" (1966), RHF.

Outler, an observer delegate from the World Methodist Council, noted: "Doug was the one who led the way toward the full integration of the observers into the conciliar process. . . . If the observers really mattered at Vatican II, Doug Horton deserves more credit for it than any other one man." After the first session, Douglas and Mildred Horton rented an apartment at "The Observatory" on the Piazza Adriana. There they hosted the newcomers and "helped many a neophyte get his bearings." Thus the Horton home served as a base for the transient observers — and, appropriately, as a place of meeting.[38]

When Horton first ventured to Rome, he intended to spend a part of each day translating William Ames's four-volume magnum opus *Bellarminus enervatus*, or *Bellarmine Disarmed* (1628). Ames's book offered a point-by-point refutation of Roman Catholic doctrine as set forth by the Council of Trent (1545–1563) and defended by Cardinal Bellarmine in his three-volume *Disputations Against the Heretics* (1586–93). In *Bellarminus enervatus*, Horton had before him a text that helped codify the differences that had prevailed between Catholics and certain Protestants since the Reformation. But in a letter to his wife, written shortly after the start of the first session of the council, he noted that he was able to spend less time with his William Ames translation than he had anticipated. Instead, he had fallen into a routine of attending sessions in the morning — sessions that were conducted almost exclusively in Latin — and then recording his observations about the proceedings into a dictating machine in the afternoon. At the end of each week, he would send the recorded reels to his colleagues at the International Congregational Council in London. These would be transcribed and distributed to the member churches as an insider's report on the Second Vatican Council.[39]

Initially, in his role as observer and reporter of council proceedings, Horton served only his own confessional community. Soon, however, Pilgrim Press expressed an interest in publishing Horton's diaries for a wider audience. The Secretariat had asked the observers to limit their public reports about the council's activities, lest the Catholic Church find itself misrepresented in print. Horton hesitated to offend his hosts through any breech of implied confidences and was, therefore, reluctant

---

[38]Albert Outler, "I Remember Douglas Horton at the Vatican Council," in ibid., RHF. Earlier Outler had served on several ad hoc committees for faculty appointments during Horton's tenure at Harvard Divinity School.

[39]Horton to Mildred McAfee Horton, 15 October and 29 November 1962, RHF.

to arrange his reports for publication. But after checking with the Secretariat concerning the content of his diaries, and after Robert McAfee Brown, Horton's nephew, published his own diaries covering the second session of the council, Horton was persuaded to publish his own observations. And so Horton's initial Ames translation plan took on a different twist. He ended up "translating" the Latin (most of the speeches, debates, and services of worship during Vatican II were conducted in Latin) and Roman Catholic council proceedings for an English-reading and primarily Protestant audience.[40]

The basic purpose of the Second Vatican Council was to update the doctrine of the Catholic Church: to establish orthodox teachings for the present age and the ages to come. Horton's *Vatican Diary* recorded the drama of doctrine in the making. The observers were granted "the best seats in the house," according to Horton: just a few feet away from the Pope's throne (for special sessions) or the presidents' table (for working sessions) in the center of the rotunda of Saint Peter's Cathedral. Each day after worship, various *schemata* were introduced, debated, amended, redrafted, or voted upon. These proposed statements of doctrine were composed by various commissions of the church in advance of the Vatican Council and rewritten repeatedly to incorporate the insights of the assembled council. When the council, made up of bishops and cardinals, approved a particular document, it was presented to the Pope for final approval.[41]

In addition to witnessing the process of doctrine-making, the observers also participated in it. They met formally once a week with the Secretariat for the Promotion of Christian Unity to offer their insights about the debates in progress. Comments from the observers were taken into consideration by those persons — the *periti*, or expert theologians — who redrafted *schemata* for presentation in the general sessions. Father Stransky noted that the observers' presence at the Second Vatican Council was an *active* presence; inevitably, some of their suggestions ended up in the final documents of the council.[42]

<hr/>

[40]Charles Butts of Pilgrim Press to Horton, n.d. (circa March 1963), CDH; Horton to Bishop Primeau, 16 March 1963, CDH. See chapter 2 for a discussion of Horton's longstanding role as a translator of cultures.

[41]Douglas Horton, *Vatican Diary 1962* (Boston: United Church Press, 1964) 22–23.

[42]Tom Stransky, "Vatican II (1962–1965)," in Lossky et al., eds., *Dictionary of the Ecumenical Movement*, 1054.

As Horton's *Vatican Diary* progresses from one year to the next, the foreign becomes familiar and suspicion turns to respect. When he first arrived in Rome, Horton knew very few leaders of the Roman Catholic Church[43]; by the end of his sojourn, he knew hundreds of them. More importantly, many of these men had become his friends. This move from stranger to friend was of primary significance in all of Horton's ecumenical adventures. It can be traced back at least as far as his days of study and recreation at Tübingen in 1913. Indeed, one way to read the *Vatican Diary* is simply as a record of unfolding friendships.

Horton's friendships with the members of the Secretariat for the Promotion of Christian Unity, in particular, led him to propose a remarkable gathering at Harvard Divinity School. In late November 1962, while the first session of the council was drawing to a close, Horton and Heiko Oberman met with Cardinal Bea and extended a formal invitation for him to speak at Harvard.[44] Bea's acceptance of the invitation led to the Harvard Colloquium on Catholic and Protestant Relations. Held at the end of March 1963, the colloquium marked the first time any such ecumenical event had taken place at the Divinity School. Horton's successor, Dean Samuel Miller, evaluated the event in a letter to Cardinal Bea:

> The public response to your presence was in itself an extraordinary event of great significance. The public lectures in the afternoons and the concern and interest which they elicited in the life of the university were certainly a most signal success. The four colloquies which were conducted in the morning and which involved something like one hundred and sixty scholars, both Protestant and Catholic, were extremely exciting to men who had been working in the field for many years.[45]

After Cardinal Bea's appearance at Harvard Divinity School, long-established fears of the Roman Catholic hierarchy—fears that had played a significant role in the debates surrounding the Stillman Professorship—

---

[43]Early on, Horton identified Cardinals Tisserand and Spellman as "the only [cardinals] I have ever met" (Horton to Mildred McAfee Horton, 13 October 1962, RHF).

[44]Horton, *Vatican Diary 1962*, 161; Horton to Mildred McAfee Horton, 29 November 1962, RHF.

[45]Letter from Samuel Miller, quoted in Stjepan Schmidt, *Augustin Bea: The Cardinal of Unity* (New York: New City Press, 1992) 425.

began to fade away.[46] Horton assessed the colloquium's success in this way: "Many . . . entered the discussions only as friends of the truth, but came out as friends to each other, concerned to know more about each other and each other's position."[47] After the Harvard colloquium, Horton ventured north to his home in Randolph, New Hampshire, with another friend from the Secretariat, Father Gustave Weigel. Later that spring, the two men traveled together to the meeting of the Commission on Faith and Order in Montreal.[48]

Vatican II advanced the cause of friendship among Protestant observers as well. During the first session of the Vatican Council, Horton became acquainted with brothers from the Taizé community in France. Horton described the members of this monastic community as "thoroughly Protestant," insofar as they were practitioners of the priesthood of all believers, and yet "thoroughly Catholic" in the quality of their ordered life together.[49] He looked to them as a bridge between the Catholic and Protestant worlds. Max Thurian, director of the Taizé community, served with Horton as an observer. Through this relationship in particular, Horton invited the Taizé brothers to establish an outpost in the United States. He offered them a retreat center on Pine Mountain, the northeasternmost peak of the Presidential mountain range in New Hampshire, just minutes away from the Horton home in Randolph. For two summers, groups of Taizé brothers lived on Pine Mountain, where they built cabins and conducted ecumenical seminars and retreats for married couples, among other things.[50]

Besides the drama of unfolding friendships, Horton's *Vatican Diary* also recorded a number of ways in which divisions between Catholics and Protestants — and also among Catholics — were being repaired. Horton commented frequently on the role of worship in the daily rou-

[46]See the discussion in chapter 5.

[47]Douglas Horton, "Journey into Ecumenicity," in *Steps to Christian Unity* (ed. John A. O'Brien; Garden City, N.Y.: Doubleday, 1964) 233.

[48]Horton to Bishop Primeau, 16 March 1963, CDH.

[49]Horton, *Vatican Diary 1962*, 35, 133.

[50]John R. Scotford, "Protestant Monks on Pine Mountain," *United Church Herald*, 15 November 1965, 19–21. Horton bought the ninety-one acre Pine Mountain in 1940. A nonprofit corporation was later established to oversee the property's development. It was used from time to time as a retreat center for the Harvard Divinity School. In 1968 it was handed over to the New Hampshire Conference of the United Church of Christ. The camp area is called "Horton Center."

tine of the council. Each morning began with a service that lasted at least an hour, and sometimes two hours or more. These services were conducted by bishops from all over the world and often featured variations introduced by local custom into the context of Catholic tradition. At first Horton found the multiplicity of liturgies confusing and dull. He longed for the simplicity and power of his own Congregational tradition. But as the days, weeks, and years progressed, Horton came to appreciate the diversity and the artistry in the daily Mass. He registered approval, for example, at the discovery that many churches in the Catholic fold used liturgical forms other than the Latin rite. This practice seemed appropriate to him, and it offered a corollary to the diversity of forms in Protestantism. Then too, as the council progressed, modern masses were celebrated: the first fruits of the liturgical reforms that were inaugurated at the earliest sessions of the council.[51]

Ultimately, Horton wrote, "the most important moment at the Vatican Council was the moment of the mass [sic]." He signaled in particular "that moment of silence when all were aware of the presence of Christ in the midst of the company." He noted the advantage of placing the monumental debates of the Vatican Council in the context of the worshiping community: "It is hard to imagine anyone rising from his knees in the eucharist and then when the debate began cavalierly dismissing from his mind all gracious influences that have come from the altar." Although Protestants and Catholics could not yet share the eucharist together, Horton saw the possibility of worshiping together, short of celebrating communion, as a sign of progress in the direction of eventual unity.[52]

Most of the speeches, debates, and services of worship during the council were conducted in Latin. For many of the bishops, Latin was another sign of the Catholic Church's unity. But in the debates about the language question, some church leaders pointed out that Latin created a barrier between clerics and the laity. One quality of Horton's *Vatican Diary* is the sense of immediacy that the entries convey: a result of the fact that Horton needed no translator to interpret his observations. Horton fully understood the language in which the debates were cast, and ow-

---

[51]Horton, *Vatican Diary 1962*, 43, 105–7, 118. Compare, for example, Douglas Horton, *Vatican Diary 1965* (Boston: United Church Press, 1966) 53–54, 156–57.

[52]Douglas Horton, "The Most Important Moment at the Vatican Council," address delivered 24 June 1965, CDH.

ing to the seating arrangements made especially for the observers, he was in a position to hear the speakers clearly.

Despite his Latin abilities, however, Horton felt that the use of the vernacular, especially in worship, would be an appropriate advance for the program of *aggiornamento*, the "principle of the unchanging truth and the adjustable expression of it," as he called it.[53] The language issue had to do not with what the hierarchy understood, but with what the people understood. In fact, after the first century, the church had adopted Latin instead of Greek as its language in order to accommodate the people; progressives at the council argued that this principle ought to prevail in the twentieth century as well. Horton noted somewhat wryly that Latin was perhaps not as universal in the church as some imagined. "The speaker who brought laughter to the lips of all who understood him," Horton wrote, "was the one who exclaimed (in Latin), 'What a joy it would be if we could all understand everything that was said in this council!' "[54]

Inevitably, Horton placed the argument for a multitude of languages in the context of a singular loyalty to Christ and his Church. In a way, the argument for the vernacular was a variation on the desire in the ecumenical movement for unity without an accompanying demand for uniformity. It also resembled the careful balance between freedom and fellowship that had played such a significant role in the debates concerning the creation of the United Church of Christ. Horton found the best expression of "differentiation within unification" in the Roman Catholic orders: the Jesuits, the Dominicans, and the Franciscans, among others. As he recorded in the *Vatican Diary*, Horton visited many of these groups during the days when the council was not in session. He saw the maintenance of orders within the larger church as "a possible design for intrachurch relations involving denominations outside of the Roman Church." He looked to the orders as examples of groups that established "a maximum of . . . individuality within the concept of allegiance to the greater Church." "Diversity in unity," Horton was convinced, was the great hope for a reunited Church.[55]

One portion of humanity, however, was absent from the first two sessions of the Second Vatican Council: women. Small groups of women

[53]Horton, "Journey into Ecumenism," 228.
[54]Horton, *Vatican Diary 1962*, 45.
[55]Horton, "Journey into Ecumenism," 240–41.

religious had been invited from time to time to take communion at the beginning of the day, but they were required to leave the basilica before the plenary sessions began. In a series of remarkable letters, Douglas Horton and Ralph Calder, the ICC executive in London, entertained a proposal to have a woman minister attend the third session of the Vatican Council as an alternate observer. This proposal originated with Viscountess Stansgate, whom Calder described as an "activist in the affairs of the Congregational Union of England and Wales, but who was by no means an aggressive feminist." The viscountess was willing to advance at least £200 (roughly equivalent to $800) for the effort because she felt that a feminine presence "would draw attention to an important feature of Congregational life."[56]

In his replies to the Stansgate proposal, Horton was careful to underscore his commitment to the ministry of women. He had "no theological difficulty" with the idea of a woman being present among the observers. Trouble arose around the matter of propriety, according to Horton. The crucial issue was to avoid sending a message to Rome about Congregationalism. The problem was that "the appearance of a woman [among the observers] . . . would mean the guests were taking an initiative that the hosts were not permitting themselves." Horton felt that such an action, were it to go forward, would rub salt in the wounds of the Catholic women who had been prevented thus far from attending the council. "It would not quite be cricket," Horton suggested to his British counterpart, "to even raise the issue with the Secretariat. The very act would provide tension."[57]

Calder informed Horton that a letter had already been sent to Monsignor Willebrands, raising the possibility of bringing a woman pastor to the 1964 session of the council. For the second (and perhaps last) time during the Vatican II era, Horton felt obliged to reprimand his Protestant colleagues in a matter related to the council. The first time it happened, according to Albert Outler, some of the European observers "decided to boycott the celebration in Saint Peter's on the fourth centenary of Trent" (3 December 1963)—which, Outler continued, "the Romans had gone to great length to make into a gesture of reconciliation." Horton's concern on both occasions centered on the role the "separated

[56]Ralph Calder to Horton, 7 April 1964, CDH.
[57]Horton to Ralph Calder, 10 April 1964, CDH.

brethren" played in relation to the Vatican hosts. "We are observers, not demonstrators," he pointed out to Calder.[58]

Horton wrote a letter to Willebrands apologizing for the breach in etiquette. Then Willebrands wrote a letter to Calder, explaining that women had not been allowed to participate in the proceedings because they did not receive the sacrament of holy orders. "The Councils of our Church, from the very first Council of Nicea," Willebrands continued, "have not had women present in the quality of priest or bishop." Willebrands pointed out that because the council, thus far, had not permitted women to attend the sessions — even as auditors — it would not be possible to offer "Christian non-Catholic brethren a permission which has not been accorded to Catholics."[59]

This tempest in a teapot died down after the first week in July. But it may have had an enduring influence on Monsignor Willebrands and the Secretariat for Promoting Christian Unity. When the council reconvened in the fall of 1964, the wives of the observers were invited to the Secretariat on the opening day of the council. And as the third session progressed, Catholic women were invited to participate as auditors at the working sessions of the council.[60]

Ecumenism after Vatican II

In the years following the Second Vatican Council, two themes characterized Horton's continued care for the Protestant and Catholic relationship. On the one hand, he worked to include his traditional Congregational mentor, William Ames, in the contemporary ecumenical conversation. On the other hand, he returned to the ideal of marriage that had so influenced his understanding of the union between the Evangelical and Reformed Church and the Congregational Christian Churches.

Horton had made very little progress with his translation of William Ames's book *Bellarminus enervatus* between 1962 and 1965. The demands of the Second Vatican Council and the effort to promote ecumenical goodwill during the months between sessions of the council occupied most of his time. Once the council ended, however, Horton

---

[58]Ibid.; Albert Outler, "I Remember Douglas Horton at the Vatican Council," RHF.

[59]Ralph Calder to Horton, 22 June 1964, CDH; Horton to Ralph Calder, 25 June 1964, CDH; Bishop Willebrands to Ralph Calder, 1 July 1964, CDH.

[60]Douglas Horton, *Vatican Diary 1964* (Boston: United Church Press, 1965) 46.

returned to his desk in Randolph and resumed work on the four-volume opus. In *Bellarminus enervatus*, William Ames was responding to the polemical writings of Cardinal Robert Bellarmine, the great defender of Roman Catholic doctrine over against the emerging Protestant position of the late sixteenth and early seventeenth centuries. Ames's work offered a point-by-point response to Bellarmine's critique of Protestantism. It was not a friendly exchange by twentieth-century standards, perhaps; but in their debate both Ames and Bellarmine preferred reasoned and logical argument to mere dogmatic assertion and attacks on the opponent's character. This "cards on the table" approach to theological differences was attractive to Horton in the atmosphere of frank exchange promoted by Vatican II. It also offered a refreshing alternative to the acrimony that characterized the protracted union conversations within the Congregational Christian denomination during Horton's tenure as secretary and minister to the General Council.

Horton completed all but the fourth volume of his Ames translation, called *Bellarmine Disarmed*, and the work was never published. But he did use portions of his preliminary translation in his last published work, *Toward an Undivided Church*. In that book, to which Cardinal Bea contributed an introduction, Horton proposed to return to the sixteenth-century doctrinal debates between Ames and Bellarmine. He considered the passionate exchange an early model of ecumenical dialogue. And he believed that if some of the real differences in the centuries-old conversation could be addressed in an irenic, ecumenical spirit, then the contemporary conversation between Catholics and Protestants would advance. Horton's earlier writings on Protestant ecumenical dialogue had sought to establish common ground between and among denominations by stressing common lines of descent: thus he underlined, for example, the Puritan origins shared by Congregationalists and Unitarians. In his current work on Catholic-Protestant dialogue, Horton likewise encouraged conversation about the prior unity of the churches sundered by enduring disputes, hoping that such conversation would promote unity in the present. Horton thus proposed large-scale conversations about the theological issues that perpetuated separation.

He was equally concerned, however, about very practical obstacles to Protestant and Catholic union. In his capacity as a member of the Roman Catholic–sponsored "Commission for Christian Unity" in the diocese of Manchester, New Hampshire, Horton was engaged in ongoing conversations about the nature of intermarriage. During the latter half of 1967, Horton's local "dialogue group" of ministers and priests discussed the problem from a variety of theological and sociological viewpoints. Finally, at a regular meeting at Horton's home in Randolph, the group composed a letter to the Most Reverend Ernest Primeau, the Bishop of Manchester, who was a friend of Horton and an important advocate of post-Vatican II ecumenism.

According to the dialogue group's assessment of the situation, the existing Catholic practice of barring representatives of the Protestant clergy from participation in the wedding ceremony contradicted the ecumenical spirit of the new era. It seemed especially unfortunate to enforce separation at the precise moment that a couple was making a lifelong commitment to union. Thus the group sought to include a Protestant presence in the ceremony, thereby recognizing the role of both churches in blessing a union that was, according to Catholic theology, a sacrament that the espousing partners actually performed themselves. The letter read, in part:

> Since existing legislation relative to these marriages does not seem to foster Christian unity or provide a harmonious beginning for a Christian family, we would appreciate thought being given to revising the present standards of validity so that a minister might more often be recognized as a competent witness in such marriages.[61]

In his reply, the Bishop remarked that the practice was a matter of canon law, not something he could act on independently. But he promised that he would bring the opinion before the Bishops' Committee on Canon Law.[62] Thus was Protestant counsel introduced into one area of the ongoing deliberations of the Catholic hierarchy.

In the new era that began with Vatican II, Horton shifted his ecumenical approach significantly. Among his Protestant colleagues in the ecumenical movement, Horton always had been quick to assert that the differences dividing Christians from each other were basically nontheological differences. Throughout most of his career, Horton repeated the claim made popular by H. Richard Niebuhr that denominations were essentially enclaves delimited by ethnicity, class, and race.

---

[61]Coos County Koinonia Group to Ernest Primeau, 6 January 1968, CDH.
[62]Bishop Primeau to Coos County Koinonia Group, 19 January 1968, CDH.

The confessional peculiarities to which denominations clung were, by this reasoning, basically irrelevant in light of the urgent call to Christian unity.[63] But the Second Vatican Council itself was structured to take very seriously the prevailing confessional differences among Christians. The Secretariat for Promoting Christian Unity had issued its invitations to observers according to their confessional affiliations. Consequently, there were no delegates at Rome from the various agencies of inter-Protestant cooperation, such as the World Council of Churches, for example, or the National Council of Churches in the Philippines, or the Southern Christian Leadership Conference. Instead, delegates received their invitations through confessionally related organizations such as—in Horton's case—the International Congregational Council, or the World Alliance of Reformed Churches, or the Lutheran World Federation.

In the aftermath of the Second Vatican Council, conversations with Catholics were maintained by Protestant representatives of specific confessional families. Horton's *Toward an Undivided Church* marked a shift, concurrent with a shift in the broader ecumenical movement, from the multilateral ecumenical encounters of an earlier period (such as the Greenwich Plan and the Consultation on Church Union), to the bilateral dialogues that have dominated ecumenical encounters since the mid-1960s—not only between Protestants and Roman Catholics, but also among Protestants themselves.[64]

A second shift in Horton's ecumenism concerned the arena in which the ecumenical relationship was to be played out. From his youth, Horton's ecumenical outlook had been global in scope. By the 1930s, Horton had himself become a national and international leader in the ecumenical movement. He was an active participant in the meetings of ecumenical elites that took place all across the nation and around the world. During the last few years of his life, Horton continued his extensive travels to promote closer ties between Protestants and Catholics. But he emphasized the importance of local—or "grassroots"—action to further the cause of ecumenism in the 1960s. The appropriate place for "responsible experimentation," as he called it, was in the local community. He often cited his own involvement with the ongoing "Roman–non-Roman organization" in the diocese of Manchester as a model for

---

[63]Niebuhr, *The Social Sources of Denominationalism*, 13.

[64]See Harding Meyer, "Bilateral Dialogue," in Lossky et al., eds., *Dictionary of the Ecumenical Movement*, 280–81.

developing the kind of relationships Protestants and Catholics "wished to see regnant in the church of tomorrow."[65]

Horton continued to look to the ecumenical movement as the harbinger of hope in a divided world. For him, the eschatological future of the kingdom of God was coming into being through ecumenism. Some time in the spring of 1968, in the season of the assassination of Martin Luther King Jr., Horton spoke of the world's need for the united Church that was emerging in "a new dawn":

> At long last but inevitably the reordering of relationships within the church will have its effect upon the history of the world, for by it the church will be provided again with one of its most attractive and powerful virtues—a unity to serve as a pattern to nations, races, and classes, themselves desperately needing a unity similar to it.[66]

Throughout his life, Horton believed that church unity would function like a light to the nations, spreading its wholesome rays to all corners of earthly society. Before his death in August 1968, the ecumenical future toward which he had devoted his entire life seemed to lie on the horizon.

---

[65]See, for example, Horton, *Toward an Undivided Church*, 60.

[66]Douglas Horton, "The Church in a New Dawn," n.d. [circa April 1968], CDH, Sermons and Addresses.

The Legacy of Douglas Horton's Ecumenical Career

A professor of theology once remarked approvingly of Douglas Horton: "Congregationalism is his house, but the Church is his home. There is a difference, you know."[1] This difference constitutes the narrative of Horton's ecumenical career. Although he was raised in the house of Congregationalism, he worked passionately to establish a unified Christian home in which all believers could and would dwell under one roof.

The trajectory of Horton's career illustrates the development of twentieth century ecumenism itself. Horton's involvement with what would become the ecumenical movement began among groups that had defined themselves primarily in opposition to Roman Catholicism. By the end of his life, however, he was a friend and advisor to the Secretariat for Promoting Christian Unity at the Second Vatican Council; he was also an important advocate for Protestant-Catholic dialogue in the United States. Similarly, Horton's ministerial career began while the Social Gospel was the reigning theology among liberal Protestants. Early on, Horton preached about the necessity to actualize the biblical ideal of the kingdom of God in society by changing the economic system and advancing the cause of the poor. Horton retained this emphasis on the kingdom of

---

[1] The words were uttered by Joseph Sittler of the Federated Faculty at the University of Chicago Divinity School. Quoted by Donald Ward in his letter to Horton, 14 November 1958, CSM.

God for the rest of his life. But the locus of its enactment in the world shifted for him after World War I. From then on, Horton directed his energies primarily toward establishing the kingdom of God in a united Church, one whose visibility would become a sign of the unity sought by God—as Horton would say—for all of humanity. As the focus of his ecumenical vision, "organic union" was not only the means for bringing about the kingdom of God but also an end in itself. Horton's career thus exemplifies the shift in twentieth-century ecumenism from cooperative work among various denominations drawn together in loose federation to a quest for some kind of visible, organizational "organic union."

Horton's contemporaries and scholars of American religious history alike have wondered about his enduring legacy. In a letter of condolence sent to Mildred McAfee Horton shortly after her husband's death, Nathan Pusey remarked that history would remember Horton for his work in rebuilding the Harvard Divinity School and transforming it into a center of ecumenical learning.[2] Dennis Voskuil's study of the rise of neoorthodoxy in America suggests that his early translation of Karl Barth secured for Horton a significant place in history.[3] The present study locates Horton's legacy in the unique interconfessional union that he helped create by leading the Congregational Christian Churches through a merger with the Evangelical and Reformed Church. While Horton played a key role in the life of the Harvard Divinity School during a period of transition and redefinition, the United Church of Christ stands as the institution most clearly shaped by his ecumenical concerns.

The history of the United Church of Christ is not simply one of success—neither retrospectively nor prospectively. In the first place, while the merger did unite two major denominations in one household of faith, it also led to the establishment of at least two new denominations: the Conservative Congregational Christian Churches and the National Council of Congregational Christian Churches. Schism, in other words, emerged in counterpoint to the theme of union.

Second, Horton and his supporters occasionally changed the rules of the merger game when it suited their purposes to do so. The most pronounced example of this ploy concerned the voting results on the merger referendum in 1949. When fewer than 75 percent of the churches voted for the merger, Horton argued that the General Council had made no

---

[2]Nathan Pusey to Mildred McAfee Horton, 3 September 1968, CDH.
[3]Voskuil, "From Liberalism to Neo-Orthodoxy," 80.

recommendation against proceeding toward union should there be a lower percentage of promerger votes. This kind of deceptive behavior led inevitably to the Cadman case, for if the members of the Cadman Memorial Church could not expect fair treatment from their own denomination (and, ironically, from a son of their own congregation), what recourse was left them? Within the Congregational Christian fold, at least, the United Church of Christ only became possible through political maneuvering and manipulations. Much of the serious self-examination that the prospect of merger demanded—particularly in the realm of ecclesiology, as the report from the Fifield Committee (the Committee on Free Church Polity and Unity) clearly established—was deferred lest it delay actual union.[4]

A third problem that emerged from the merger story has to do with Horton's invention of Congregationalism B. Horton argued that the executive council of the denomination, which he himself chaired, was empowered to act on behalf of the churches because the General Council itself was "like a church" in the traditional Congregational sense—that is, an autonomous body of believers. Whatever else it may have been, Congregationalism B did not accurately reflect the denomination's polity in the present or the past. Thus, although Congregationalism B was written into the constitution of the new United Church of Christ, confusion and misunderstanding about the new church's polity and ecclesiology persist to this day.[5]

In his own lifetime, Horton had every reason to believe that vagaries concerning the United Church of Christ's ecclesiological foundation would be rendered insignificant as the ecumenical impulse guided more churches into union with each other. The United Church of Christ represented merely the first fruits of a much larger movement toward organic union. The Greenwich Plan, which Horton had helped to formulate,

[4]See L. Wendell Fifield et al., *The Report of the Committee on Free Church Polity and Unity* (Boston: Pilgrim, 1954). This important document was accepted by—but never officially recognized by—the General Council of the Congregational Christian Churches.

[5]While *The Report of the Committee on Free Church Polity and Unity* could not come up with a unanimous assessment of what Congregational Christian polity was, the committee was nearly unanimous in its rejection of what Congregational Christian polity was not—namely, Congregationalism B. For a discussion of the ongoing ecclesiological problem in the UCC, see Griffin, "A Movement in Search of a Church," and Schmiechen, "The Church as an Image of Reconciliation."

lurked in the background of the United Church of Christ merger and seemed to promise the union of numerous mainline and African-American Protestant churches in the near future. Parallel to that effort, the United Church of Christ began union conversations with the Disciples of Christ in the late 1950s. In the early 1960s, the Consultation on Church Union advanced a plan for organic union that superseded the Greenwich Plan in size and scope. By the fourth session of the Second Vatican Council, Protestant leaders such as Horton were talking hopefully about reunion with Rome—not, perhaps, in the near future, but eventually and inevitably.

Yet even as partisans of organic union were riding this optimistic wave, strong undercurrents strained beneath the surface and pulled ecumenism in a different direction. If the ecumenical movement had a secular equivalent in the 1960s, it was the civil rights movement. Martin Luther King Jr.'s dream of an integrated society paralleled the ecumenical vision of the kingdom of God. Both integrationists and ecumenists looked toward one world of equals gathered around the table of community and communion. As the 1960s progressed, however, the civil rights movement began to divide into a variety of different groups, each of which demanded separate treatment and what might be called "autonomy in its own sphere." In addition, particularities such as class, gender, ethnicity, and race took on more prominent roles in the larger struggle for social justice.

A similar phenomenon occurred in the ecumenical community, and Horton participated in this change even while he was advancing the cause of organic union. Harvard Divinity School offers an early instance of the embrace of particularities. In his 1955 convocation address to the Divinity School, Horton anchored the school's institutional identity in the common ground of Puritanism shared by Unitarians and Congregationalists. But from the start of his deanship, he also sought to establish an institution in which students and faculty alike stood in their own traditions—their denominational houses, as it were—while engaging in scholarship and training on behalf of the larger and pan-denominational, or ecumenical, Christian home. Loyalties to particular denominations were encouraged and no attempt was made to minimize confessional differences among Protestants or, later, among Protestants and members of the Orthodox Church and the Roman Catholic Church.

In the case of mainline Protestants, at least, this pluralistic point of view may have been the result of the same theological presuppositions that undergirded the union negotiations between the Congregational Christian Churches and the Evangelical and Reformed Church. In other words, the various mainline Protestant denominations were presumed to be already in fundamental agreement on matters of doctrine, and so their seeming differences were not addressed. But the increasing involvement of the Orthodox and Roman Catholic Churches in ecumenical conversations reversed the priorities that had shaped most of Horton's ecumenical career. Instead of proceeding under the motto of "union first, doctrine later," the Protestant-Catholic ecumenical relationship started in bilateral conversations between specific confessional communities. It focused on doctrines while reserving the matter of union for a much later discussion. Horton's call for a return to the debates between Ames and Bellarmine was made in the context of this new ecumenical environment.

In the end, the United Church of Christ was Horton's greatest achievement, but it was also a curious achievement. During Horton's lifetime, it looked as if the United Church of Christ would play the role of prophet in relation to the broader ecumenical movement. Other churches seemed likely to cast off their "sinful" denominational cloaks and follow the UCC into organic union in configurations such as the one proposed by the Consultation on Church Union. But after the 1960s, COCU slowly turned away from the concept of "organic union" and developed a new model of "covenant communion" (somewhat akin to the arrangement advocated by some of Horton's opponents during the merger negotiations in the Fifield Committee's report).[6] By 1984, it was clear to the leaders of COCU that the individual denominations, though they sought closer relations with one another, "resisted . . . any commitment to an eventual merger of church structures."[7] Organic union as Horton had envisioned it and had indeed helped to realize it in the form of the United Church of Christ was no longer workable. Indeed, it was passé.

Despite the decline in commitment to organic union after the 1960s, the passion for closer relationships among denominations did not cease. Horton's ecumenical concerns continued to be advanced by his own

---

[6]See the discussion above and in the previous two notes on *The Report of the Committee on Free Church Polity and Unity.*

[7]Consultation on Church Union, *Churches in Covenant Communion* (Princeton: Consultation on Church Union, 1989) 1.

denomination as well as by other Protestant churches in the United States and abroad during the last quarter of the twentieth century. The dual recognition of ministries and of "unrestricted communion of Pulpit and Lord's Table" were early examples of an ecumenical relationship that offered an alternative to the organic union model. One such relationship was inaugurated between the Congregational Churches of England and the United Evangelical Protestant Churches of the Palatinate in the Upper Rhineland of West Germany. As an American representative of the International Congregational Council, Horton attended the worship celebration of the agreement in April 1957 at the cathedral in Speyer, West Germany. Twenty-four years later, in 1981, the United Church of Christ entered into a similar relationship of *Kirchengemeinschaft* ("full community" and "full communion") with the Evangelical Church of the Union, itself the direct descendant of Philip Schaff's Prussian Union Church, and a church that had parishes in both East and West Germany during the Cold War era.[8]

Other important ecumenical relationships begun in the early 1960s came to fruition during the last years of the twentieth century. In 1970, the member churches of the Consultation on Church Union rejected a Plan of Union that developed out of an organic union model. Instead, they adopted a strategy of "covenanting toward union"—a commitment to live and work together apart from the requirement to merge into one church. In 1997, the General Synod of the United Church of Christ entered into "covenanted communion" with the eight other bodies of the "Church of Christ Uniting": the African Methodist Episcopal Church, the African Methodist Episcopal Zion Church, the Disciples of Christ, the Christian Methodist Episcopal Church, the Episcopal Church, the International Council of Community Churches, the Presbyterian Church, and the United Methodist Church. The agreement avoided any call for an organic union of the member denominations. But it did provide for mutual recognition of the sacraments and ministries of the member churches and the establishment of regional "covenanting councils" to oversee the developing ecumenical relations among participating churches. In the tradition of the Greenwich Plan, COCU continues to draw into relationship the historically European-American and African-

---

[8]See Louis Gunnemann, *United and Uniting: The Meaning of an Ecclesiastical Journey* (New York: United Church Press, 1987) 70–73, 200–1.

American churches. Also in 1997, the United Church of Christ adopted the "Formula of Agreement," a plan for "full communion" with the Evangelical Lutheran Church in America, the Reformed Church in America, and the Presbyterian Church (USA).[9]

In ways that Horton could not foresee, then, but also in ways that he had prepared, the United Church of Christ stands as the institutional embodiment of the ecumenical impulse that gave purpose and passion to Douglas Horton's career.

---

[9]Consultation on Church Union, *Churches in Covenant Communion*, 15; *A Common Calling: The Witness of Our Reformation Churches in North America Today* (ed. Keith Nickle and Timothy F. Lull; Minneapolis: Augsburg, 1993) 65–68.

Chronology

1891	29 July: Douglas Horton born in Brooklyn, N.Y.
1908	Graduates from Brooklyn Boys High School
1910	Horton family travels to Europe: Holland, Germany, Switzerland, London
1912	Earns B.Cl. (classics) degree from Princeton College
1912–1913	Travels and studies at New College, Edinburgh; Mansfield College, Oxford; and University of Tübingen, Germany
1915	Earns B.D. (divinity) degree from Hartford Seminary
1915	15 April: becomes engaged to Carol Scudder Williams
1915–1916	Serves as assistant minister at First Church, Middletown, Conn.
1916	9 May: marries Carol Scudder Williams
1916–1925	Serves as minister at First Church, Middletown, Conn.
1918–1919	Serves as chaplain in the U.S. Navy
1919	Travels to France to see the Front

1920   Horton family travels to Great Britain; tercentenary
                of Pilgrim departure from Plymouth

1925–1931   Serves as minister at Leyden Church, Brookline,
                Mass.

1925   Publication of *Out Into Life*

1926   Publication of *Legend of the Grail*

1928   Publication of Horton's translation of Karl Barth's
                The Word of God and the Word of Man

1930   1–8 July: attends Fifth Council of the International
                Congregational Council at Bournemouth, England

1930–1931   Lectures on practical theology at Newton Theologi-
                cal Institute

1931–1938   Serves as minister at United Church of Hyde Park,
                Chicago, Ill.

1933–1938   Lectures on practical theology, Chicago Theological
                Seminary

1934   Publication of *Taking a City* (sermons)

1935   Publication of *Art of Living Today* (sermons)

1936   National Preaching Mission

1937   Attends Faith and Order and Life and Work meetings
                in Great Britain

1938   Publication of *Basic Formula for Church Union*, ed-
               ited by Horton; travels with wife Carol around the
               world on behalf of the Congregational Christian
               Churches; 12–29 December: attends the International
               Missionary Council in Madras; meets with Ghandi

1938–1955   Serves as minister and secretary of the General Coun-
               cil of the Congregational Christian Churches, New York

1944   Carol Williams Horton dies

1945   10 September: marries Mildred McAfee (commander,
               Navy WAVES; president, Wellesley College, 1936–
               1949); October: serves on government-appointed del-
               egation to Japan; publication of *Christian Vocation*
               (sermons from the CBS radio program "Church of the
               Air")

1948   Attends First Assembly, World Council of Churches
               at Amsterdam, where he chairs the American Com-
               mittee; Mildred McAfee Horton addresses the Gen-
               eral Assembly

1948–1955   Lectures on Congregational polity at Union Theological
               Seminary

1949–1953   Serves as moderator of the International Congrega-
               tional Council

1949   June: attends Sixth Council of the ICC at Wellesley
               College; Mildred McAfee Horton becomes vice presi-
               dent of the Federal Council of Churches; publication
               of *International Congregationalism* (coauthored with
               Albert Peel)

1950   26 January: Cadman decision prohibits the United Church of Christ merger; 26 June: delivers address *Of Equability and Perseverance in Well Doing* in Cleveland

1952   Publication of *Congregationalism: A Study in Church Polity*; 15–28 August: attends Third World Conference on Faith and Order in Lund, Sweden

1953   Attends Seventh Council of the ICC at Saint Andrews, Scotland

1954   Attends Second Assembly, World Council of Churches in Evanston, Ill.

1955–1959   Serves as dean and professor of theology (courses on ecclesiology and ecumenism), Harvard Divinity School

1957–1963   Serves as chair of Faith and Order Commission of the World Council of Churches

1958   Translates John Norton's *Responsio*

1959   Publication of *The Meaning of Worship*

1959–1968   Retires to Randolph, N.H. (age 68); serves as theological consultant to the United Church of Christ Council for Church and Ministry

1960   Accepts position as editor of "Congregational Classics" series for Pilgrim Press; publication of Williston Walker's *Creeds and Platforms of Congregationalism*, with introduction by Horton

1961   Lectures on United Church polity at the Chicago Divinity School

1962   Publication of *United Church of Christ*

1962–1965   Serves as Protestant observer at all sessions of the Second Vatican Council; composes *Vatican Diary 1962–1965*, published 1964–1966

1963   Attends Third Assembly, World Council of Churches at New Delhi; retires from Faith and Order

1964–1965   Invites Taizé community to reside at Pine Mountain, N.H.

1965   Publication of *William Ames*, Horton's translation of theses by Nethenus, Visscher and Reuter

1966   Publication of *Reform and Renewal*

1967   Publication of *Toward an Undivided Church;* labors over translation (begun in 1962, never completed) of William Ames's *Bellarminus enervatus*

1968   22 August: dies in Randolph, N. H.

Select Bibliography

Books Authored, Coauthored, or Edited by Douglas Horton

Horton, Douglas. *Out Into Life*. New York: Abingdon, 1924.

——. *Taking a City*. New York: Harper, 1934.

——. *The Art of Living Today*. Chicago: United Church of Hyde Park, 1935.

——, ed. *The Basic Formula for Church Union*. Chicago: Chicago Theological Seminary, 1938.

——, et al. *The Return to Japan: Report of the Christian Deputation to Japan*. New York: Friendship, 1945.

——. *Congregationalism: A Study in Polity*. London: Independent, 1952.

——. *The Meaning of Worship*. New York: Harper, 1959.

——. *The United Church of Christ: Its Origins, Organization, and Role in the World Today*. New York: Nelson, 1962.

——. *Vatican Diary 1962*. Boston: United Church, 1964.

——. *Vatican Diary 1963*. Boston: United Church, 1964.

——. *Vatican Diary 1964*. Boston: United Church, 1965.

——. *Vatican Diary 1965*. Boston: United Church, 1966.

——, et al. *Reform and Renewal*. Philadelphia: United Church Press, 1966.

——. *Toward an Undivided Church*. New York and Notre Dame: Association and University of Notre Dame, 1967.

Peel, Albert, and Douglas Horton. *International Congregationalism*. London: Independent, 1949

Articles and Pamphlets by Douglas Horton

Horton, Douglas. "The Freudian Theory and Preaching." *Christian Century*, 13 January 1921, 13–15.

———. "To the Gentlemen of the Senate Assembling." *The Christian Work*, 15 December 1923, 718–19.

———. "The Thinking Priest of Paris." *Christian Century*, 15 September 1927, 1072–73.

———. "God Lets Loose Karl Barth." *Christian Century*, 16 February 1928, 204–7.

———. "Karl Barth and the Dreadful Necessity." *The Christian Register*, 24 January 1929, 63.

———. "The Religion of Our Age as Seen by Karl Barth and his Friends." *The Congregationalist*, 7 February 1929, 178–79.

———. "Contemporary Congregational Doctrine." *The Christian Leader*, 15 February 1930, 204–5.

———. "The Place of Congregationalism in the Living Church: Our Distinctive Contribution." Pages 242–51 in *Proceedings of the Fifth International Congregational Council*, ed. Albert Peel. London: Camelot, 1930.

———. "Germany: What Will be the Outcome?" *The Christian Leader*, 11 October 1930, 1286.

———. "A World of Persons." *The City Temple Tidings* 10, no. 117 [circa July 1932], 149–55.

———. "Through Forty Years: A 'Spiritual Autobiography.' " *Advance*, 8 February 1934, 94.

———. "A Veteran's Reaction to the Bonus." *Character*, March–April 1936, 7–8, 31–32.

———. "Prophet or Professor? A Review of Karl Barth's *Credo*." *Christian Century*, 3 February 1937, 146–47.

———. "Toward an Understanding of Congregationalism: A Preface to the Council." Pages 57–70 in *Minutes of the General Council*. New York: Congregational Christian Churches, 1940.

———. *Of Equability and Perseverance in Well Doing*. 1950. Pamphlet.

———. "The Closing Sermon at Lund." Pages 316–17 in *The Third World Conference of Faith and Order Held at Lund, August 15–28, 1952*. Edited by Oliver S. Tomkins. London: SCM, 1953.

Horton, Douglas. "The Desk and the Altar." *Harvard Alumni Bulletin*, 22 October 1955, 116–19.

―――. "Now the United Church of Christ. " *Christian Century*, 12 June 1957, 735–37.

―――. "Let Us Not Forget the Mighty William Ames." *Religion in Life* 30, no. 3 (1960) 434–42.

―――. "Journey into Ecumenicity." Pages 227–41 in *Steps to Christian Unity*. Edited by John A. O'Brien. Garden City, N.Y: Doubleday, 1964.

Works Revised or Translated by Douglas Horton

Ames, William. "An Exhortation to the Students of Theology Delivered at Franeker, 1623." Translated by Douglas Horton. Cambridge: Harvard Divinity School, 1958.

―――. "Bellarmine Disarmed." Translated by Douglas Horton. Cambridge, Mass.: 1969. Microfilm copy of original typescript.

Atkins, Gaius Glenn. *An Adventure in Liberty*. Revised by Douglas Horton. Boston: Pilgrim, 1961.

Barth, Karl. *The Word of God and the Word of Man*. Translated by Douglas Horton. Boston: Pilgrim, 1928.

Bethenus, Matthias, Hugo Visscher, and Karl Reuter. *William Ames*. Translated by Douglas Horton. Cambridge: Harvard Divinity School Library, 1965.

Norton, John. *The Answer to the Whole Set of Questions of the Celebrated Mr. William Apollonius, Pastor of the Church of Middelburg Looking Toward the Resolution of Certain Controversies Concerning Church Government Now Being Agitated in England*. Translated by Douglas Horton. Cambridge: Harvard Divinity School, 1958.

Books

Abbott, Walter M. *The Documents of Vatican II*. New York: American Press, 1966.

Ackroyd, Peter. *T. S. Eliot: A Life*. New York: Simon and Schuster, 1984.

Ames, William. *The Marrow of Theology*. Translated by John Eusden. Boston: Pilgrim, 1968.

Atkins, Gaius Glenn, and Frederick L. Fagley. *History of American Congregationalism*. Boston: Pilgrim, 1942.

Bell, G. K. A., ed. *The Stockholm Conference 1925: The Official Report of the Universal Christian Conference on Life and Work*. London: Oxford University Press, 1926.

Bethge, Eberhard. *Dietrich Bonhoeffer: Theologe, Christ, Zeitgenosse*. Munich: Chr. Kaiser Verlag, 1967.
———. *Dietrich Bonhoeffer: Theologian, Christian, Contemporary*. Translated by Eric Mosbacher. New York: Harper and Row, 1970.

Brown, Robert McAfee. *P. T. Forsyth: Prophet for Today*. Philadelphia: Westminster, 1952.

Burrage, Champlin. *The Early Church Dissenters*. Cambridge, England: Cambridge University Press, 1912.

Burton, Malcolm K. *Disorders in the Kingdom*. New York: Vantage, 1982.

Busch, Eberhard. *Karl Barth: His Life From Letters and Autobiographical Texts*. Philadelphia: Fortress, 1975.

Cadman, S. Parkes. *Answers to Everyday Questions*. New York: Abingdon, 1930.

Cavert, Samuel McCrea. *The American Churches in the Ecumenical Movement, 1900–1968*. New York: Association, 1968.
———, ed. *Twenty Years of Church Federation: Report of the Federal Council of Churches of Christ in America, 1924–1928*. New York: Federal Council of Churches, 1928.

Chrystal, William G., ed. *Young Reinhold Niebuhr*. Saint Louis: Eden, 1977.

The Constitution, Rules of Order and Catalogue of the Pastoral Union and the Charter, Constitution, and Laws of the Hartford Theological Seminary. Hartford: Case, Lockwood, and Brainard, 1886.

Dale, R. W., ed. *The International Congregational Council: Authorised Record of Proceedings*. London: James Clarke, 1891.

Digest of Minutes of Meetings of the General Council of the Congregational Christian Churches of the United States (1931–1965). New York: Executive Committee of the General Council, 1971.

Eliot, T. S. *The Complete Poems and Plays*. New York: Harcourt and Brace, 1971.

Ellwood, Robert S. *The Fifties Spiritual Marketplace: American Religion in a Decade of Conflict*. New Brunswick: Rutgers, 1997.

Fifield, L. Wendell, et al. *The Report of the Committee on Free Church Polity and Unity*. Boston: Pilgrim, 1954.

Fitzgerald, F. Scott. *This Side of Paradise*. New York: Scribners, 1920.

Foote, Henry Wilder, ed. *The Cambridge Platform of 1648*. Boston: Beacon and Pilgrim, 1949.

Gassmann, Günther, ed. *Documentary History of Faith and Order, 1963–1993*. Geneva: WCC, 1993.

Geer, Curtis Manning. *The Hartford Theological Seminary, 1834–1934*. Hartford: Case, Lockwood, and Brainard, 1934.

Goodwin, Thomas, et al. *An Apologetical Narration*. Translated by Robert S. Paul. Boston: United Church Press, 1963.

Gunnemann, Louis H. *The Shaping of the United Church of Christ*. New York: United Church Press, 1977.
————. *United and Uniting: The Meaning of an Ecclesiastical Journey*. New York: United Church Press, 1987.

Halvorson, Peter L., and William M. Newman. *An Atlas of American Religions*. Atlanta: Glenmary, 1994.

Hamlin, Fred. *S. Parkes Cadman: Pioneer Radio Minister*. New York: Harper and Brothers, 1939.

Herberg, Will. *Protestant-Catholic-Jew*. New York: Doubleday, 1955.

Hilke, Elsabeth Slaughter, ed. *Growing Toward Unity*. The Living Theological Heritage of the United Church of Christ 6. Cleveland: Pilgrim Press, 2001.

Horton, Byron Barnes. *The Ancestors and Descendants of Isaac Horton of Liberty, N.Y.* Warren, Penn.: The Mohr Printery, 1946.

Hutchison, William R. *The Modernist Impulse in American Protestantism.* Cambridge: Harvard University Press, 1976.
————, ed. *Between The Times: The Travail of the Protestant Establishment in America, 1900–1960.* New York: Cambridge University Press, 1993.

Jordan, Philip D. *The Evangelical Alliance for the United States of America, 1847-1900: Ecumenism, Identity, and the Religious Republic.* New York: Mellen, 1982.

Keiling, Hanns Peter. *Die Entstehung der "United Church of Christ": Fallstudie einer Kirchenunion unter Berücksichtigung des Problems der Ortsgemeinde.* Berlin: Lettner-Verlag, 1969.

Kierkegaard, Søren. *Concluding Unscientific Postscript.* Translated by David F. Swenson and Walter Lowrie. Princeton: Princeton University Press, 1941.

Kinnamon, Michael, and Brian E. Cope, eds. *The Ecumenical Movement: An Anthology of Key Texts and Voices.* Grand Rapids: Eerdmans, 1997.

Kleiser, Grenville, ed. *The World's Greatest Sermons.* 10 vols. New York: Funk and Wagnalls, 1908.

Leiper, Henry Smith. *S. Parkes Cadman: Great Churchman and Christian.* Boston: Congregational Christian Historical Society, 1967.

Lewis, Sinclair. *Elmer Gantry.* New York: Harcourt and Brace, 1927.

Lossky, Nicholas, et al., eds. *Dictionary of the Ecumenical Movement.* Grand Rapids: Eerdmans, 1991.

Lynch, Frederick, ed. *The Problem of Christian Unity.* New York: Macmillan, 1921.

Mackenzie, W. Douglas. *Christianity and the Progress of Man As Illustrated by Modern Missions.* Chicago: Revell, 1897.
————. *The Final Faith: A Statement of the Nature and Authority of Christianity as the Religion of the World.* New York: Macmillan, 1910.

McNeill, John T. *Unitive Protestantism: The Ecumenical Spirit and Its Persistent Expression*. Philadelphia: John Knox, 1930.

Miller, Perry. *Orthodoxy in Massachusetts*. Cambridge: Harvard University Press, 1933.

Nevin, John W. *The Mystical Presence and Other Writings on the Eucharist*. Lancaster Series on the Mercersburg Theology 4. Edited by Bard Thompson and George H. Bricker. Philadelphia: United Church Press, 1965.

Nichols, James Hastings. *Romanticism in American Theology: Nevin and Schaff at Mercersburg*. Chicago: University of Chicago, 1961.

Niebuhr, H. Richard. *The Social Sources of Denominationalism*. New York: Holt, 1929.
———. *Christ and Culture*. New York: Harper, 1951.

Pauck, Wilhelm. *Karl Barth: Prophet of a New Christianity?* New York: Harper, 1931.

Peel, Albert, ed. *Proceedings of the Fifth International Congregational Council*. London: Camelot, 1930.

Report of Commission V: The Training of Teachers [World Missionary Conference, 1910]. New York: Revell, 1911.

Roof, Wade Clark and William McKinney. *American Mainline Religion*. New Brunswick: Rutgers University Press, 1987.

Rouse, Ruth and Stephen Charles Neill, eds. *A History of the Ecumenical Movement*. 2nd ed. Philadelphia: Westminster, 1968.

Schaff, Philip. *The Principle of Protestantism*. Lancaster Series on the Mercersburg Theology 1. Edited by Bard Thompson and George H. Bricker. Philadelphia: United Church Press, 1964.
———. *The Creeds of Christendom*. 3 vols. New York: Scribners, 1877.

Schenkel, Albert F. *The Rich Man and the Kingdom: John D. Rockefeller and the Protestant Establishment*. Minneapolis: Fortress, 1995.

Scotford, John R. *Church Union, Why Not?* Boston: Pilgrim, 1948.

Spencer, Truman J., ed. *Proceedings of the Fourth International Congregational Council.* New York: National Council of the Congregational Churches, 1921.

Tomkins, Oliver S., ed. *The Third World Conference of Faith and Order Held at Lund (August 15–28, 1952).* London: SCM, 1953.

Von Rohr, John. *The Shaping of American Congregationalism, 1620–1957.* Cleveland: Pilgrim, 1992.

Walker, Williston. *Creeds and Platforms of Congregationalism.* Introduction by Douglas Horton. Boston: Pilgrim, 1960.

Ward, Hiley. *Documents of Dialogue.* Englewood Cliffs, N.J.: Prentice-Hall, 1966.

Warren, Heather A. *Theologians of a New World Order: Reinhold Niebuhr and the Christian Realists (1920–1948).* New York: Oxford University Press, 1997.

Wiley, S. Wirt. *History of Y.M.C.A.–Church Relations in the United States.* New York: Association, 1944.

Williams, George H., ed. *The Harvard Divinity School: Its Place in Harvard University and in American Culture.* Boston: Beacon, 1954.

Wilson, Woodrow. *The Public Papers of Woodrow Wilson.* 6 vols. New York: Harper and Brothers, 1924.

World Missionary Conference, 1910: The History and Records of the Conference. New York: Revell, 1911.

Articles and Pamphlets

Ahlstrom, Sydney E. "Continental Influence on American Christian Thought Since World War I." *Church History* 27 (1958) 256–72.

Bainton, Roland. "Is Congregationalism Sectarian?" *Christian Century*, 24 February 1954, 234–38.

Bartley, William Warren, III. "Religion at Harvard: The Philosopher, the Pundit, the Priest, and the President." *Harvard Crimson*, 28 March 1958, 1, 5.

The Basis of Union with Interpretations. 8th draft. 22 January 1947. Pamphlet.

Bradshaw, Marion, Malcolm Burton, T. M. Shipherd, et al. *Congregationalism B: Replies to the Address 'Of Equability and Perseverance in Well Doing.'* August 1950. Pamphlet.

Bricker, George H. "James E. Wagner Remembers: An Oral History Interview." *Historical Intelligencer* 3 (1985) 6.

Brief Summary of the Basis of Union by a Layman. 1948. Pamphlet.

Brodt, Robert D. "This is Our Opportunity." *The Messenger of the Evangelical and Reformed Church*, 12 January 1954, 16–18.

Burton, Malcolm. *Understanding the Fundamentals of the Merger Trial.* Committee for the Continuation of the Congregational Christian Churches, 9 May 1950. Pamphlet.

Cadman, S. Parkes. "The Nature and Function of the Christian Church." *Advance*, 1 July 1936, 435–37, 461–62.
———. "Can a Divided Church Meet the Challenge of the Present World Crisis?" Pages 1–11 in *The Problem of Christian Unity.* Edited by Frederick Lynch. New York: Macmillan, 1921.

Capen, Edward Warren. *Special Missionary Preparation.* Hartford, 1912. Pamphlet.

Confidential Report of the Commission to Study and Make Recommendations with Respect to the Harvard Divinity School. Cambridge: 1947. Pamphlet.

A Declaration by Members of a Group Gathered at a Round Table During April and May, 1932 at the United Church of Hyde Park Chicago. Pamphlet.

"Disciples, UCC Groups Ask Authority to Draft Union Plan." *The United Church Herald*, 15 December 1963, 25.

Fey, Harold E. "Congregationalism—Plus?" *Christian Century*, 14 July 1954, 845–47.

Fifield, L. Wendell. "An Open Letter." *Advance*, 12 January 1955, 2–4.

Griffin, Benjamin. "A Movement in Search of Church: Some Unfinished Business for the United Church of Christ." *Prism* 7 no. 2 (1992) 52–60.

"Harvard Divinity School Opens with a New Look." *Christian Century*, 16 November 1955, 1344.

Kopf, Carl Heath. "Notes of a Neophyte at Oberlin." *Advance*, 18 November 1934, 579.

Niebuhr, Reinhold. "A Landmark in American Religious History." *The Messenger of the Evangelical and Reformed Church*, 18 June 1957, 11–13.

"An Official Reply to Dr. Fifield's Letter." *Advance*, 12 January 1955, 3–4.

"Peers of the American Pulpit." *Christian Century*, 8 January 1925, 54–55.

Reports of the Visiting Committees of the Board of Overseers of Harvard College for the Academic Year 1943–1944. Cambridge:1944. Pamphlet.

Richards, George H. "With Theologians in Germany and Switzerland." *Bulletin of the Theological Seminary of the Reformed Church in the United States*, October 1931, 6–9.

Schmiechen, Peter. "The Church as an Image of Reconciliation: An Analysis of the Crisis in the United Church of Christ." *Prism* 9 no. 1 (1994) 7–26.

Scotford, John R. "Will the United Church Snowball?" *The Messenger of the Evangelical and Reformed Church*, 19 November 1957, 16–17.

Services at the Inauguration of William Douglas Mackenzie. Hartford Seminary, 1904. Pamphlet.

"Spiritual Value of Church Union Delineated for Synod." *The (Lancaster, Penn.) Intelligencer Journal*, 3 September 1956, 1, 10.

Three Constitutional Proposals: A Study of the Conciliar Tradition Among the Congregational Christian Churches in the United States. New Haven: First Church, 1954. Pamphlet.

Trost, Theodore Louis. "Confessional Identity: An Early Exchange." Pages 108–12 in *In Essentials Unity: Reflections on the Nature and Purpose of the Church.* Edited by M. Douglas Meeks and Robert D. Mutton. Minneapolis: Kirk House, 2001.

Van Dusen, Henry Pitney. "A Blow to Christian Unity." *Christianity and Crisis*, 20 March 1950, 25–26.

"The Veteran and His Bonus." *Christian Century*, 19 February 1936, 286–87.

Wagner, James. "A Communication." *Christian Century*, 2 June 1954, 676.

Wilson, Woodrow. "Speech for Declaration of War Against Germany." Vol. 2, pages 128–32 in *Documents of American History.* 9th ed. 2 vols. Edited by Henry Steele Commager. Englewood Cliffs, N.J.: Prentice-Hall, 1973.

Wright, C. Conrad. "The Growth of Denominational Bureaucracies: A Neglected Aspect of American Church History." *Harvard Theological Review* 77 (1984) 177–94.

Unpublished Manuscripts and Dissertations

Harvey, Charles. "Individualism and Ecumenical Thought: The Merger Controversy in Congregationalism." Ph.D. diss., University of California, Riverside, 1968.

Pangborn, Cyrus Ransom. "Free Churches and Social Change: A Critical Study of the Council for Social Action of the Congregational Christian Churches of the United States of America." Ph.D. diss., Columbia University, 1951.

Peabody, Alan. "A Study of the Controversy in Congregationalism Over Merger." Ph.D. diss., Syracuse University, 1964.

Trost, Theodore Louis. "The Ecumenical Impulse in Twentieth-Century American Protestantism: A Study of Douglas Horton's Illustrative Career (circa 1912–1968)." Ph.D. diss., Harvard University, 1998.

Voskuil, Dennis. "From Liberalism to Neo-Orthodoxy: The History of a Theological Transition, 1925–1935." Ph.D. diss., Harvard University, 1974.

Williams, George H. "Divinings: Religion at Harvard College from its Origins in New England Ecclesiastical History, 1636–1992." Cambridge, 1998. Typescript.

Index

Abbreviations:

CCC   Congregational Christian Churches
DH   Douglas Horton
ERC   Evangelical and Reformed Church
HDS   Harvard Divinity School
UCC   United Church of Christ

Harvard Theological Studies

51. Brock, Ann Graham. *Mary Magdalene, The First Apostle: The Struggle for Authority,* 2002.

50. Trost, Theodore Louis. *Douglas Horton and the Ecumenical Impulse in American Religion,* 2002.

49. Huang, Yong. *Religious Goodness and Political Rightness: Beyond the Liberal-Communitarian Debate,* 2001.

48. Rossing, Barbara R. *The Choice between Two Cities: Whore, Bride, and Empire in the Apocalypse,* 1999.

47. Skedros, James Constantine. *Saint Demetrios of Thessaloniki: Civic Patron and Divine Protector, 4th-7th Centuries C.E.,* 1999.

46. Koester, Helmut, ed. *Pergamon, Citadel of the Gods: Archaeological Record, Literary Description, and Religious Development,* 1998.

45. Kittredge, Cynthia Briggs. *Community and Authority: The Rhetoric of Obedience in the Pauline Tradition,* 1998.

44. Lesses, Rebecca Macy. *Ritual Practices to Gain Power: Angels, Incantations, and Revelation in Early Jewish Mysticism,* 1998.

43. Guenther-Gleason, Patricia E. *On Schleiermacher and Gender Politics,* 1997.

42. White, L. Michael. *The Social Origins of Christian Architecture.* Vol. I and II, 1997.

41. Koester, Helmut, ed. *Ephesos, Metropolis of Asia: An Interdisciplinary Approach to its Archaeology, Religion, and Culture,* 1995.

40. Guider, Margaret Eletta. *Daughters of Rahab: Prostitution and the Church of Liberation in Brazil,* 1995.

39. Schenkel, Albert F. *The Rich Man and the Kingdom: John D. Rockefeller, Jr., and the Protestant Establishment,* 1995.

38. Hutchinson, William R. and Hartmut Lehmann, eds. *Many Are Chosen: Divine Election and Western Nationalism,* 1994.

37. Lubieniecki, Stanislas. *History of the Polish Reformation and Nine Related Documents.* Translated and interpreted by George Huntston Williams, 1995.

 – Davidovich, Adina. *Religion as a Province of Meaning: The Kantian Foundations of Modern Theology,* 1993.

36. Thiemann, Ronald F., ed. *The Legacy of H. Richard Niebuhr,* 1991.

35. Hobbs, Edward C., ed. *Bultmann, Retrospect, and Prospect: The Centenary Symposium at Wellesley,* 1985.

34. Cameron, Ron. *Sayings Traditions in the Apocryphon of James,* 1984.

33. Blackwell, Albert L. *Schleiermacher's Early Philosophy of Life: Determinism, Freedom, and Phantasy,* 1982.

32. Gibson, Elsa. *The "Christians for Christians" Inscriptions of Phrygia: Greek Texts, Translation and Commentary*, 1978.

31. Bynum, Caroline Walker. Docere Verbo et Exemplo: *An Aspect of Twelfth-Century Spirituality*, 1979.

30. Williams, George Huntston, ed. *The Polish Bretheren: Documentation of the History and Thought of Unitarianism in the Polish-Lithuanian Commonwealth and in the Diaspora 1601–1685*, 1980.

29. Attridge, Harold W. *First-Century Cynicism in the Epistles of Heraclitus*, 1976.

28. Williams, George Huntston, Norman Pettit, Winfried Herget, and Sargent Bush, Jr., eds. *Thomas Hooker: Writings in England and Holland, 1626–1633*, 1975.

27. Preus, James Samuel. *Carlstadt's* Ordinaciones *and Luther's Liberty: A Study of the Wittenberg Movement, 1521–22*, 1974.

26. Nickelsburg, George W. E. *Resurrection, Immortality, and Eternal Life in Intertestamental Judaism*, 1972.

25. Worthley, Harold Field. *An Inventory of the Records of the Particular (Congregational) Churches of Massachusetts Gathered 1620–1805*, 1970.

24. Yamauchi, Edwin M. *Gnostic Ethics and Mandaean Origins*, 1970.

23. Yizhar, Michael. *Bibliography of Hebrew Publications on the Dead Sea Scrolls 1948–1964*, 1967.

22. Albright, William Foxwell. *The Proto-Sinaitic Inscriptions and Their Decipherment*, 1966.

21. Dow, Sterling, and Robert F. Healey. *A Sacred Calendar of Eleusis*, 1965.

20. Sundberg, Jr., Albert C. *The Old Testament of the Early Church*, 1964.

19. Cranz, Ferdinand Edward. *An Essay on the Development of Luther's Thought on Justice, Law, and Society*, 1959.

18. Williams, George Huntston, ed. *The Norman Anonymous of 1100 A.D.: Towards the Identification and Evaluation of the So-Called Anonymous of York*, 1951.

17. Lake, Kirsopp, and Silva New, eds. *Six Collations of New Testament Manuscripts*, 1932.

16. Servetus, Michael. *The Two Treatises of Servetus on the Trinity: On the Errors of the Trinity, 7 Books, A.D. 1531. Dialogues on the Trinity, 2 Books. On the Righteousness of Christ's Kingdom, 4 Chapters, A.D. 1532*. Translated by Earl Morse Wilbur, 1932.

15. Casey, Robert Pierce, ed. Serapion of Thmuis's *Against the Manichees*, 1931.

14. Ropes, James Hardy. *The Singular Problem of the Epistles to the Galatians*, 1929.

13. Smith, Preserved. *A Key to the Colloquies of Erasmus*, 1927.

12. Spyridon of the Laura and Sophronios Eustratiades. *Catalogue of the Greek Manuscripts in the Library of the Laura on Mount Athos*, 1925.

11. Sophronios Eustratiades and Arcadios of Vatspedi. *Catalogue of the Greek Manuscripts in the Library of the Monastery of Vatopedi on Mt. Athos*, 1924.

10. Conybeare, Frederick C. *Russian Dissenters*, 1921.

9. Burrage, Champlin, ed. *An Answer to John Robinson of Leyden by a Puritan Friend: Now First Published from a Manuscript of A.D. 1609*, 1920.

8. Emerton, Ephraim. *The* Defensor pacis *of Marsiglio of Padua: A Critical Study*, 1920,

7. Bacon, Benjamin W. *Is Mark a Roman Gospel?* 1919.

6. Cadbury, Henry Joel. 2 vols. *The Style and Literary Method of Luke*, 1920.

5. Marriott, G. L., ed. Macarii Anecdota: *Seven Unpublished Homilies of Macarius*, 1918.

4. Edmunds, Charles Carroll and William Henry Paine Hatch. *The Gospel Manuscripts of the General Theological Seminary*, 1918.

3. Arnold, William Rosenzweig. *Ephod and Ark: A Study in the Records and Religion of the Ancient Hebrews*, 1917.

2. Hatch, William Henry Paine. *The Pauline Idea of Faith in its Relation to Jewish and Hellenistic Religion*, 1917.

1. Torrey, Charles Cutler. *The Composition and Date of Acts*, 1916.

Harvard Dissertations in Religion

In 1993, Harvard Theological Studies absorbed the Harvard Dissertations in Religion series.

31. Baker-Fletcher, Garth. *Somebodyness: Martin Luther King, Jr., and the Theory of Dignity*, 1993.

30. Soneson, Jerome Paul. *Pragmatism and Pluralism: John Dewey's Significance for Theology*, 1993.

29. Crabtree, Harriet. *The Christian Life: The Traditional Metaphors and Contemporary Theologies*, 1991.

28. Schowalter, Daniel N. *The Emperor and the Gods: Images from the Time of Trajan*, 1993.

27. Valantasis, Richard. *Spiritual Guides of the Third Century: A Semiotic Study of the Guide-Disciple Relationship in Christianity, Neoplatonism, Hermetism, and Gnosticism*, 1991.

26. Wills, Lawrence Mitchell. *The Jews in the Court of the Foreign King: Ancient Jewish Court Legends*, 1990.

25. Massa, Mark Stephen. *Charles Augustus Briggs and the Crisis of Historical Criticism*, 1990.

24. Hills, Julian Victor. *Tradition and Composition in the* Epistula apostolorum, 1990.

23. Bowe, Barbara Ellen. *A Church in Crisis: Ecclesiology and Paraenesis in Clement of Rome*, 1988.

22. Bisbee, Gary A. *Pre-Decian Acts of Martyrs and* Commentarii, 1988.

21. Ray, Stephen Alan. *The Modern Soul: Michel Foucault and the Theological Discourse of Gordon Kaufman and David Tracy*, 1987.

20. MacDonald, Dennis Ronald. *There Is No Male and Female: The Fate of a Dominical Saying in Paul and Gnosticism*, 1987.

19. Davaney, Sheila Greeve. *Divine Power: A Study of Karl Barth and Charles Hartshorne*, 1986.

18. LaFargue, J. Michael. *Language and Gnosis: The Opening Scenes of the Acts of Thomas*, 1985.

12. Layton, Bentley, ed. *The Gnostic Treatise on Resurrection from Nag Hammadi*, 1979.

11. Ryan, Patrick J. *Imale: Yoruba Participation in the Muslim Tradition: A Study of Clerical Piety*, 1977.

10. Neevel, Jr., Walter G. *Yamuna's Vedanta and Pancaratra: Integrating the Classical and the Popular*, 1977.

9. Yarbro Collins, Adela. *The Combat Myth in the Book of Revelation*, 1976.

8. Veatch, Robert M. *Value-Freedom in Science and Technology: A Study of the Importance of the Religious, Ethical, and Other Socio-Cultural Factors in Selected Medical Decisions Regarding Birth Control*, 1976.

7. Attridge, Harold W. *The Interpretation of Biblical History in the* Antiquitates judaicae *of Flavius Josephus*, 1976.

6. Trakatellis, Demetrios C. *The Pre-Existence of Christ in the Writings of Justin Martyr*, 1976.

5. Green, Ronald Michael. *Population Growth and Justice: An Examination of Moral Issues Raised by Rapid Population Growth*, 1975.

4. Schrader, Robert W. *The Nature of Theological Argument: A Study of Paul Tillich*, 1976.

3. Christensen, Duane L. *Transformations of the War Oracle in Old Testament Prophecy: Studies in the Oracles Against the Nations*, 1975.

2. Williams, Sam K. *Jesus' Death as Saving Event: The Background and Origin of a Concept*, 1972.

1. Smith, Jane I. *An Historical and Semantic Study of the Term "Islam" as Seen in a Sequence of Qur'an Commentaries*, 1970.